FIGHTING PHARAOHS

In Memory of my Grandfathers:

Philip Gordon Partridge
1889-1948

John Sambells Andrews
1894-1975

By the same author:

Faces of Pharaohs: Royal Mummies and Coffins from Ancient Thebes (1994)
Transport in Ancient Egypt (1996)

O Horrable Murder: the Trial, Execution and Burial of King Charles I (1998)

Published by The Rubicon Press, London.

FIGHTING PHARAOHS

Weapons and Warfare in Ancient Egypt

ROBERT B. PARTRIDGE

PEARTREE PUBLISHING

Published by:

Peartree Publishing,

56 Albert Street,

MANCHESTER M11 3SU

U. K.

© Robert B. Partridge, 2002

British Library Cataloguing-in-Publication Data.

A catalogue record for this book is available from the British Library.

ISBN 0-9543497-3-3 (hardback edition)
0-9543497-2-5 (paperback edition)

Designed by Peartree Publishing

Printed and bound in Great Britain by Biddles Limited of Guildford and King's Lynn

CONTENTS

My long-standing fascination with Ancient Egypt began at an early age and has grown steadily over the years – so much so that having retired from a full time job, it now occupies the majority of my time.

I do, however, somehow find time for a variety of other interests too, which include military and naval history, in particular British history of the Seventeenth and Eighteenth centuries. For over twenty-five years I have been a member of *The Sealed Knot*, a society which re-enacts battles and events from the period of the English Civil Wars. With a membership of several thousand, organised into two separate armies, the society is able to reconstruct and re-enact battles on a large scale. In the time I have been a member, I have undertaken a number of roles, from a humble foot soldier, to a general in command of large units of troops.

My two interests in Egyptology and the English Civil War may appear to be mutually exclusive, but, perhaps surprisingly, there is a connection between the two, especially in the context of the subject matter of this book.

Although *The Sealed Knot* is concerned with battles of a relatively recent date, compared to Ancient Egypt, and despite the fact that many of the events are well documented, when re-enacting battles and manoeuvring troops, members are faced with a variety of problems, the solutions to which have to be re-learnt. In many ways this is real practical archaeology and includes the drill and training of new recruits, communication over large distances and the moving of large units of troops quickly and effectively.

Taking part in re-enactments at this scale gives a real insight into some of the problems that were actually faced by the original participants, although obviously we do not run the same risk of serious injury or death as real soldiers. Training and stage fighting means that our modern battles are safe for all participants.

The practical problems faced by soldiers in the Seventeenth Century were also faced by soldiers from both earlier and later periods of British history. It was, therefore, only a short step to realise that they would have also been familiar to ancient Egyptian soldiers. Once my thoughts developed along these lines, a number of historical parallels became apparent.

I have stood my ground when attacked by a cavalry unit of thirty horses galloping straight towards me, literally making the earth shake beneath my feet. I knew that the horses were scripted to turn away at the last moment, but even so it was very difficult not to give in to the almost overpowering urge to turn and run, which would be potentially dangerous in a real battle. I can well imagine the feelings of soldiers when facing a real attack, be it Napoleonic cavalry or a unit of ancient Egyptian chariots.

It is all too easy for books on historical subjects to be little more than a list of known facts, theories and dates. In this book, I hope to be able to give some flesh to such bare bones and an insight into the feelings and motivation of the soldiers who were in the Egyptian army. I will look also at the type of weapons used and how the soldiers were drilled and trained. It was not just the great military commanders who won or lost battles but the individual and now forgotten soldiers, who, for whatever reason, whether they were conscripted men or volunteers, faced hardship, injury and the likelihood of an early and unpleasant death as part of their military service.

The spelling of Egyptian names always presents a potential headache to authors, as few Egyptologists can agree on the correct spelling of many of the names, or indeed whether the Egyptian or Greek version of the names should be used (e.g. Thutmose or Thutmosis … or even Djehytymose). I have followed the convention of using the most common version of Egyptian names, as used in William Murnane's *The Penguin History of Ancient Egypt*.

Dating of Egyptian events also presents a similar problem, and, as in my previous books, I have used the dates given in *The Penguin History of Ancient Egypt*.

As ever I have to thank a number of people who have helped in a variety of ways in the research, writing and publication of this book.

To Dr. Dorothea Arnold, of the Metropolitan Museum of Art in New York, for permission to use archive images from Winlock's book on the soldiers of Nebhetepre-Mentuhotep. Dr Arnold also discussed information on the bodies, specifically their dating, as did Dr. Carola Vogel of the University of Mainz, who has also commented on the nature of their injuries.

To Miriam Bibby, for sharing her knowledge and research on the history of the horse in Ancient Egypt and in the ancient world.

To The Egypt Exploration Society (and Dr. Patricia Spencer and Chris Naunton in particular) for access to books in the Society Library, for providing photocopies of articles for me and granting permission for the reproduction in this book of archive EES images.

To Dr. Renée Friedman, Director of the Hierakonpolis Expedition for allowing me permission to take photographs at Hierakonpolis and for their use in this book. Renee also kindly provided useful information on her work and findings at this important site and also one photograph taken by the Hierakonpolis Expedition.

To Bill Griffiths, who provided information based on his knowledge and practical experience of the use of ancient weapons.

To Dr. Stephen Harvey, from the University of Memphis for allowing me to use new information following his recent excavations at Abydos of the monuments of Ahmose.

To Robin Page and the Late Anthea Page of The Rubicon Press (publishers of my previous books) for their freely-given encouragement and advice on publishing matters

To Dr. Ian Shaw, from the University of Liverpool for allowing me to use some of his line drawings of forts that appeared in his book *Egyptian Warfare and Weapons*.

To David Soper, for turning my vague idea for a cover design into reality. His artistic skills are considerable and are combined with a unique knowledge of, and feel for, Ancient Egyptian art.

To Michael Tunnicliffe, who proof read and cast a critical eye over the final version of the book (although I must remain fully responsible for any errors that may remain in the text).

To my family, friends and fellow members of the Manchester Ancient Egypt Society, for their continued support and encouragement over the several years it has taken to produce this book.

And finally, but chiefly, to Peter Phillips, for continuing to be a sounding board for my ideas and for helping in so many ways, including the proof reading and checking of the many versions of my manuscript. Peter and I shared the task of setting the book in QUARK Xpress, although, with his greater knowledge, he had to constantly supervise my contribution.
I don't think this book would have seen the light of day were it not for Peter's help, for which I will be forever grateful.

I have dedicated this book to the memory of my Grandfathers, Philip Gordon Partridge and John Sambells Andrews. Both men experienced warfare at first hand during the 1914-18 War.

Philip, at the age of 24 and the Skipper of a Brixham fishing trawler, joined the Royal Naval Reserve and served on board a Minesweeper for the duration of the war. John, at the age of 20, joined the Army before the outbreak of war, serving in the 69th Field Company of the Royal Engineers. He saw action in France for the four years of the war, and was present at all the main battles.

Both men were reluctant to talk about their experiences. Philip died before I was born; but, I understand, spoke rarely about it to his family. John, my Maternal Grandfather would not be drawn into detailed conversation on the subject, even though he knew of my interest. On November 5th each year when we built a bonfire and set off fireworks, he would become very quiet and mention quietly that he had "seen enough fireworks for one lifetime".

Both their lives were changed forever by their experience; they witnessed scenes which most of us can only imagine in our worst nightmares, experiencing the horrors of war, the stress, the fear, the elation and the sorrow. They endured living conditions and food few would tolerate today. Like soldiers before them, and since, they obeyed orders and fought when told to do so. They survived, whereas many did not, and managed to re-build their lives in the new world they found when the war was over, only to find their lives disrupted again by the war of 1939-45.

The history of warfare, often concentrates on the accounts of commanders and politicians, and whilst their role is vital, the importance of the ordinary trooper or sailor is often forgotten.

In the following pages, we will hopefully see the real story of warfare in Ancient Egypt from the point of view of the commanders as well as their soldiers.

Robert Partridge. October 2002.

CHRONOLOGY And Principal Rulers

THE PREHISTORIC OR PREDYNASTIC PERIOD   Before 3150 BC

The Badarian Period   5500-4000 BC
The Amratian (Nagada I) Period 4000-3500 BC
The Gerzean (Nagada II) Period 3500-3150 BC

THE ARCHAIC PERIOD: Dynasties 1 and 2   3150-2686 BC

Dynasty "0"   3150-3050
King Scorpion
Horus Narmer
The First and Second Dynasties   3050-2686
Horus Aha
Horus Djer
Horus Djet
Horus Den
Horus Hotepsekhemwy
Seth Peribsen
Horus and Seth Khasekhemwy

THE OLD KINGDOM: Dynasties 3 to 6   2686-2181 BC

The Third Dynasty   2686-2613
Nebka   2686-2668
Djoser   2668-2649
Sekhemkhet   2649-2643
Kaba   2643-2637
Huni   2637-2613
The Fourth Dynasty   2613-2498
Sneferu   2613-2589
Khufu   2589-2566
Djedefre   2566-2558
Khafra   2558-2532
Menkaure   2532-2504
Shespeskaf   2504-2500
The Fifth Dynasty   2498-2345
Userkaf   2498-2491

Sahure	2491-2477
Neferirkare	2477-2467
Neferefre	2460-2453
Niuserre	2453-2422
Djedkare-Isei	2414-2375
Unas	2375-2345

The Sixth Dynasty — 2345-2181

Teti	2345-2333
Pepi I	2332-2283
Merenre	2283-2278
Pepi II	2278-2184

THE FIRST INTERMEDIATE PERIOD: Dynasties 7 to 10 — 2181-2040 BC

THE MIDDLE KINGDOM: Dynasties 11 and 12 — 2040-1782 BC

The Eleventh Dynasty — 2060-1991

Mentuhotep I	2060-2010
Mentuhotep II	2010-1998
Mentuhotep III	1997-1991

The Twelfth Dynasty — 1991-1782

Amenemhat I	1991-1962
Senuseret I	1971-1928
Amenemhat II	1929-1895
Senuseret II	1897-1878
Senuseret III	1878-1841
Amenemhat III	1842-1797
Amenemhat IV	1798-1786
Queen Sobeknofru	1785-1782

THE SECOND INTERMEDIATE PERIOD: Dynasties 13 to 17 — 1782-1570 BC

The Seventeenth Dynasty — 1637-1570

Sakhenenre-Mentuhotep IV	c1633
Seqenenre-Tao	c1574
Kamose	1573-1570

THE NEW KINGDOM: Dynasties 18 to 20 — 1570-1070 BC

The Eighteenth Dynasty — 1570-1293

Ahmose	1570-1546
Amenhotep I	1551-1524
Thutmose I	1524-1518
Thutmose II	1518-1504
Thutmose III	1504-1450

Hatshepsut	1498-1483	
Amenhotep II	1453-1419	
Thutmose IV	1419-1386	
Amenhotep III	1386-1349	
Amenhotep IV/		
Akhenaten	1350-1334	
Smenkakare	1336-1334	
Tutankhamun	1334-1325	
Ay	1325-1321	
Horemheb	1321-1293	

The Nineteenth Dynasty   1293-1187

Ramesses I	1293-1291	
Seti I	1291-1278	
Ramesses II	1279-1212	
Merenptah	1212-1202	
Amenmesse	1202-1199	
Seti II	1199-1193	
Siptah	1193-1187	
Twosret	1187-1185	

The Twentieth Dynasty   1185-1070

Sethnakht	1185-1182	
Ramesses III	1182-1151	
Ramesses IV	1151-1145	
Ramesses V	1145-1141	
Ramesses VI	1141-1133	
Ramesses IX	1126-1108	
Ramesses XI	1098-1070	
Herihor	1080-1072	

THE THIRD INTERMEDIATE PERIOD: Dynasties 21 to 26   1070-525 BC

The Twenty-First Dynasty   1069-945

Smendes	1069-1063	
Psusennes I	1059-1033	
Amenemope	1033-981	
At Thebes:		
Herihor	1080-1074	
Pinedjem	1074-1070	

The Twenty Second Dynasty   945-712

Shoshenk I	945-924	
Osorkon I	924-889	
Shoshenk II	890	
Osorkon II	874-850	
Takelot II	850-825	
Shoshenk III	825-773	

The Twenty-Fifth Dynasty		712-656	
Piye	753-713		
Shabaka	713-698		
Taharka	690-664		
The Twenty-Sixth Dynasty		664-525	
Psamtik I	664-610		
Necho	610-595		
Psamtik III	526-525		

THE LATE PERIOD: Dynasties 27 to 30   525-332 BC

The Twenty-Seventh Dynasty		525-404	
Cambyses	525-522		
Darius I	521-486		
Xerxes	485-465		
Darius II	423-405		

THE GRAECO-ROMAN PERIOD: 332 BC - AD 323

Alexander the Great	332-323		
Ptolemy I	305-282		
Ptolemy II	285-247/6		
Cleopatra VII	51-30		
Ptolemy Caesarion	36-30		
The Roman Emperors		30BC-AD323	
Octavian (Augustus)	30BC-AD14		
Tiberius	14-37		
Claudius	41-54		
Titus	79-81		
Trajan	98-117		

The spelling of names and all dates are based on those that appear in *The Penguin Guide to Ancient Egypt*, by William J. Murnane.

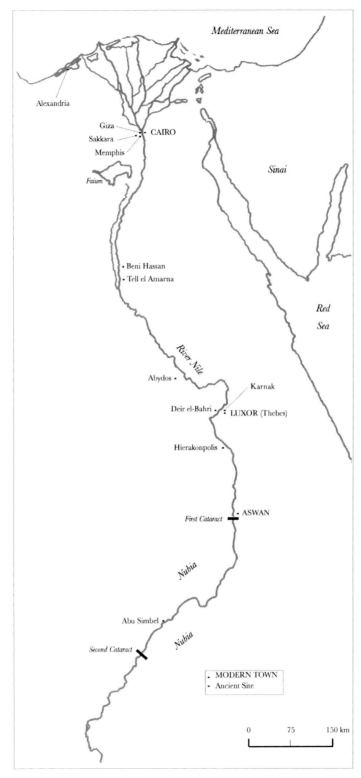

Mediterranean Sea

Alexandria

Giza

Sakkara

Memphis

CAIRO

Faium

Sinai

Beni Hassan

Tell el Amarna

Red
Sea

River Nile

Abydos

Karnak

Deir el-Bahri

LUXOR (Thebes)

Hierakonpolis

First Cataract

ASWAN

Nubia

Abu Simbel

Second Cataract

Nubia

MODERN TOWN
Ancient Site

0   75   150 km

1. Map of Egypt.

INTRODUCTION

Much of the recorded history of the human race is really the history of warfare and conflict, as far back as the time of our primate ancestors, when acts of aggression settled disputes over food, territory and sexual partners.

With the dawning of civilisation our aggressive instinct remained (and still remains today) and disputes could arise over possessions, wealth, food and territory. A new and not insignificant factor also entered the equation: disputes over religious beliefs and practices. Throughout history, religion has been one of the major causes of conflict.

In the early years of Egyptian history, the Nile valley became home to settlers who built their homes on the fertile banks of the river. Each village was probably completely self-sufficient, but eventually, over a period of time, the villages became grouped together in forty "nomes" or districts. Each one of these nomes was essentially a small kingdom, ruled by an Elder or "Nomarch". The reasons for this grouping are varied, but were principally for mutual benefit. By co-operating, the villages could irrigate and cultivate greater areas of land, pooling their resources and sharing the increased harvest. Some of this grouping may have been as a result of force, with one village imposing its will on other, weaker, villages.

By about 3150 BC the forty independent nomes of Egypt had coalesced into the two distinct kingdoms of Upper and Lower Egypt; Lower Egypt being the fertile Delta area and Upper Egypt being all the territories to the south of the Delta. When Narmer, the King of Upper Egypt, assumed control of Lower Egypt, the unification of the *Two Lands* marked the beginning of a civilisation that was to last for over three thousand years.

During this time, the countries around the eastern end of the Mediterranean Sea saw the waxing and waning of a succession of ancient Near-Eastern powers, including those of Sumer, Crete, Assyria, Babylon, Persia, and Greece, which were a potential or real threat to Egyptian security.

From the minimal evidence available, it is presumed that Narmer, King of Upper Egypt, conquered Lower Egypt, possibly after a battle when the king of the north was defeated. Unification was probably only achieved by the shedding of blood. Thus the "enemies" of Egypt were not always foreigners, for the very foundation of the unified Egyptian kingdom arose from power struggles between local chieftains of the late Predynastic Period.

We know that the Egyptians were well able to defend their borders and even to pursue a policy of expansion, which, at its height, saw Egypt ruling a large empire, stretching south into Nubia and around the eastern end of the Mediterranean Sea.

Some of the earliest representations of the pharaoh show him with mace raised, about to smite his enemy. This was to become a recurring image throughout Egyptian history; in dynasty after dynasty, the pharaohs had themselves portrayed as the all-powerful conqueror, in constant battle with the enemies of Egypt. This echoed the mythical conflict between the gods Horus and Set; the continuing battle of good against evil.

2. Narmer, smiting his enemy. Scene from the "Narmer Palette". First Dynasty.

Weapons and equipment changed slowly over the centuries; flint and stone weapons were replaced by copper, bronze and, later, iron. The ambitions and aims of individual pharaohs varied considerably and in order to maintain military supremacy, new foreign innovations, including the horse and chariot, were eagerly adopted and used to great effect.

Before and during the Dynastic Period, most of the military activity probably went unrecorded and much that *may* have been recorded has been lost to us with the passing of time.

Information on aspects of military history is, therefore, sketchy for some periods of Egyptian history. Nevertheless, a wealth of material survives: from scenes on the walls of temples and tombs, correspondence and peace treaties between nations, and actual examples of the weapons and equipment that have been recovered from the ancient sites.

A great deal of this information does, however, have to be treated with caution, for the recorded history we have is selective and biased. We are told what the Egyptians themselves wanted to believe, or what those in authority wanted the population to believe.

Old soldiers may tell you of the battles they fought and their role in them. Truth becomes distorted and often fragmentary. The overall aims and achievements of a particular campaign may be lost, whereas the record of individuals and relatively insignificant actions may assume a much greater importance than they really deserve.

The further away from home the military campaigns occur, the less reliable the information tends to be. Today, with excellent and rapid communication, we can, theoretically, obtain reasonably accurate and fair accounts of events anywhere in the world. Even so, in the many areas of conflict it is still sometimes difficult to understand how and why a dispute started and make sense of propaganda distributed by opposing factions.

Go back in time only a few hundred years and we have to rely completely on the accounts of the officers and soldiers themselves, who may have been the only witnesses to any action. Survival of information depends on how it was recorded. Few people could read and write, so first hand, eyewitness records are rare and third-party accounts can be unreliable. Once recorded, the survival of information for future generations is often down to chance preservation of documents. News of campaigns related or officially released at home had to be taken entirely at face value, as no one would be in a position to dispute the reported "facts".

Throughout history, the selective use of information has meant that doubtful victories have been portrayed as great triumphs. Military commanders have claimed credit for defeating enemies who have, in reality, been overcome by factors other than skill and bravery. We all know, or are told, that the English defeated the Spanish Armada, in 1588 AD; but in fact it was defeated primarily not by force of arms, but by bad weather and poor planning by the Spanish.

The effective use of propaganda is not a new phenomenon and boasting of great victories and of the cruelty and barbarity of the enemy is a regular feature throughout recorded history. We find it for the first time in Egypt.

The real role of the army in ancient times needs to be examined, too. Like today, an army spent very little of its time actually fighting battles. So what did it do for the rest of the time?

The Egyptian army was large, well equipped, well trained and drilled and it performed many of the duties that armies still fulfil around the world today. It could be an extremely effective fighting force when needed, but an army can still be effective without fighting battles. A well trained and disciplined army can be an excellent deterrent, as the Egyptians discovered, and the idea of a "peace-keeping force" is nothing new. Finally, the army could provide a ready supply of organised manpower when needed for specific civil engineering works.

In the following chapters, we will look in more detail at the weapons and equipment used, at the Egyptian army and the life of the soldiers. We will also follow the campaigns and battles fought by the warrior pharaohs, on land and water, from the reigns of the first pharaohs, through to the last, Cleopatra VII.

It has not, however, been possible to include as full an account of some aspects of the subject as the author would have liked and this volume can only really present a broad overview. A full bibliography is, therefore, included for further reading or research.

Unless otherwise stated, all dates mentioned in the text which follows are BC.

The image of a vanquished and prostrate foreigner as a symbol of Egyptian supremacy appears in Egyptian art from the very earliest times. One of the first known representations found came from the famous "Painted Tomb" at Hierakonpolis and dates to around 4000 BC. This image was still being used over four thousand years later by the Roman Emperors, who ruled Egypt as a province of Rome, right at the end of ancient Egyptian history.

3. Drawing from the Painted Tomb at Hierakonpolis.

Captured prisoners may well have been paraded before the successful commander as part of the victory celebrations. Their bound bodies, prostrated before the king, may, quite literally, have been used as a footstool for the victor, who would place his feet upon their necks.

4. The bound enemies of Egypt on the base of a statue of Ramesses III, in his Mortuary Temple at Medinet Habu. The king is represented by his name in a cartouche, with arms holding his enemies captive.

5. Gilded and inlaid wooden footstool from the Tomb of Tutankhamun showing the enemies of Egypt.

6. One of Tutankhamun's sandals showing the enemies of Egypt depicted on its sole.

7. Soles of Graeco-Roman sandals, depicting the enemies of Egypt.

This image, rather than perhaps the actual act, continued throughout the Dynastic Period; and the prostrate and bound enemies of Egypt are often shown carved on the bases of the thrones, and on the footstools of the kings. Splendid examples of royal footstools, which were found in the Tomb of Tutankhamun, have the upper surface decorated with such scenes. When the king sat on his throne and placed his feet upon his footstool, he symbolically trod his enemies underfoot.

Tutankhamun also had the enemies of Egypt portrayed on some of his many walking-sticks.

The idea of treading enemies underfoot was taken a stage further, for they are also portrayed on the soles of the King's sandals. When Tutankhamun was wearing these sandals, wherever he went, he showed his superiority over his enemies and their subjugation to Egyptian domination.

Centuries after the time of King Tutankhamun, at the end of the Dynastic

Period of Egyptian history, this imagery had been adopted for non-royal use and the mummies of wealthy Graeco-Roman Egyptians were buried wearing sandals, the soles of which were similarly decorated.

After a successful campaign, it was usual for the weapons of the enemy (or at least those of their leader) to be destroyed, and the image of a broken bow was used as a symbol of supremacy. The enemies of Egypt were collectively known as the "Nine Bows" and many images survive showing nine bound and captive prisoners, as in figure 8 below, or as nine actual bows (figure 9, over). The reference to nine bows appears in the earliest times, but the exact derivation and meaning of this name is unknown, particularly why, or if, the number nine is significant.

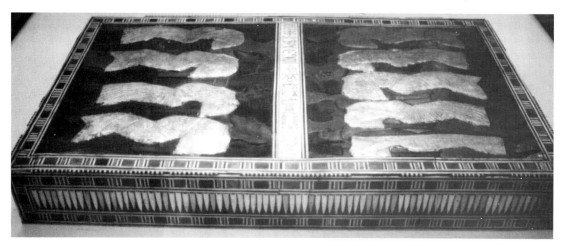

8. A footstool from the Tomb of Tutankhamun, depicting the "Nine Bows": nine images of the enemies of Egypt.

In the Fifth and Sixth Dynasty pyramid complexes at Abusir and Sakkara, limestone and wooden statues of foreign captives have been found. Each complex was probably provided with as many as one hundred of these statues, which, it is believed, lined the causeway connecting the valley temple with the mortuary temple. The king's body was carried along this causeway on its final journey, so that even in death the king was still able to subdue the enemies of Egypt.

The Egyptians had a well-developed sense of national identity and, with their love of symmetry and order, regarded anyone who came from outside the clearly defined natural borders of Egypt as "foreigners" and, therefore, enemies.

Effectively, enemies either came from the coastal area of Libya or Asia in the north, or from Nubia in the south, for there were no organised or clearly identifiable enemy forces to the east and west of Egypt, where lay deserts, inhabited by nomadic tribes. It was the image of a bound Asiatic and a Nubian together which was used whenever reference was made to the enemies of Egypt. Sometimes it is difficult to determine from the references to the ritualistic enemies of Egypt who the *real* enemies were.

This iconography was so established that even for the short period when Egypt was actually ruled by a Nubians in the Twenty-Fifth Dynasty, the image of bound and captive Nubians was *still* used when reference was made to foreigners and the other enemies of Egypt.

Specific names for the enemies of Egypt survive in a series of inscriptions dating from the end of the Old Kingdom to the Middle Kingdom. Known as the "Execration Texts", they list the names of hostile forces which the Egyptians wanted to destroy (including some Egyptian

names too!). The texts were written on small pottery vessels or clay figurines that were ritually smashed and then buried to invoke their magical properties. They have been found at several sites in Egypt including Sakkara and Thebes and also at Mirgissa in Nubia.

The recording of the detailed names of foreign places and people suggests that the Egyptians had a detailed knowledge of people and places in Nubia, Syria and Palestine. This may be because some Egyptians had themselves travelled to these areas, but it is more likely that trade links had been established with these countries at a very early date.

9. The "nine bows" on the base of a statue of a King of the Middle Kingdom, in the Temple of Montu at Medamud.

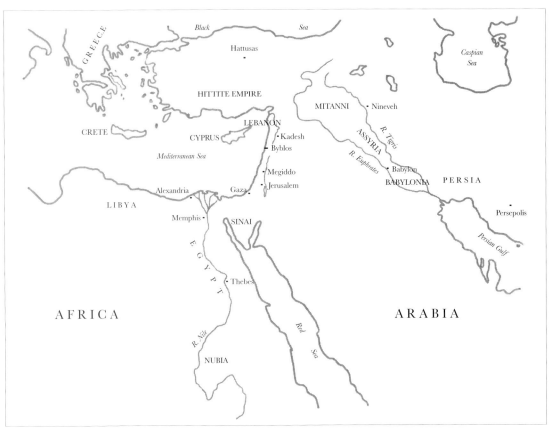

10. Map of the Eastern Mediteranean.

THE NUBIANS

For most of the Dynastic Period, the Nubians (known to the Egyptians as *Nehesyw*) were regarded as the main enemy of Egypt. Constant military campaigns and trading expeditions (often combined) ensured a steady supply of prisoners and cattle and secured the trade route for the many exotic supplies imported into Egypt via Nubia from the centre of Africa. Nubia was vital to Egypt: the most important commodity obtained from Nubia was gold (although some authorities have suggested that ivory, imported through Nubia, was as valuable to the ancient Egyptians as gold). In fact the very name *Nubia* may have derived from the Egyptian word for gold, *nub*. The river Nile, which flowed northwards through Nubia into Egypt was the main artery of trade out of central Africa for the gold and ivory and other items such as ebony, ostrich feathers and ostrich eggs. Any lack of co-operation on the part of the Nubians could easily and effectively cut off this important route.

By the New Kingdom, the conquest of Nubia was so complete that it was regarded as a province of Egypt and was placed under the control of a viceroy. The icon of the captured Nubian as one of the enemies of Egypt remained, however, and still appeared on the inscriptions and monuments of the pharaohs. The physical appearance of the Nubians in such scenes is accurately portrayed, with their distinctive features, hairstyles and clothing.

The Nubians seem to have been an "easy target" for the Egyptians and virtually every pharaoh (especially at the start of their reign) seems to have led a military campaign to subdue the country (whether it was needed or not – it was excellent propaganda). The Nubians themselves are invariably described as "vile" and "wretched".

12. Eighteenth Dynasty wall painting of Nubians presenting tribute.

9

13. *Ramesses III in the act of killing a Libyan. Relief on the southern wall of his Mortuary Temple at Medinet Habu.*

THE LIBYANS

The enemies to the north-west of Egypt, the Libyans, were known as the *Tjehenu*, *Tjemehu*, *Meshwesh* or *Libu*. They lived in the desert to the west of the Delta and were semi-nomadic. The fertile area of the Delta drew the Libyans to Egypt like a magnet, especially in times of drought and poor harvests in their own country. Egypt was always seen by its neighbours as a "land of plenty", which indeed for most of the time it was. Even when harvests were poor in Egypt, the organisation of the country and the practice of storing grain from productive years meant that the Egyptians rarely went hungry. Often there was food to spare.

Many campaigns in the early periods of Egyptian history and the Old Kingdom show the kings in the ritual act of slaying a Libyan foe. Like the images of subdued Nubians, this image also became a fairly "stock scene" and good royal propaganda throughout Egyptian history, regardless of whether any actual campaigns were being waged against the Libyans at the time. The Libyans are generally shown as dark-skinned, with distinctive long dark hair and beards, but occasionally with fair hair and blue eyes (which must record an actual and natural variation in their appearance). Their distinctive costumes are also clearly depicted.

At the end of the New Kingdom, the Libyans allied themselves with other countries from the eastern Mediterranean and attacked Egypt. This may have been prompted by necessity, insofar as there appear to have been climate changes in Libya and a long period of poor harvests.

Merenptah of the Nineteenth Dynasty successfully repulsed one attack and took many Libyan prisoners back to Egypt. This enforced settlement of Libyans in Egypt was followed by a period of gradual and unstoppable infiltration of Libyan refugees into Egypt, mostly through the Delta area. The fact that the refugees settled in Egypt, flourished and became accepted as "Egyptians" led, ironically, to the Libyans' becoming a powerful and organised group within Egypt, eventually ruling Egypt for a while in the Twenty-Second Dynasty.

THE BEDOUIN

It was across the Sinai Peninsula in the countries at the eastern end of the Mediterranean in what is now Syria and Palestine (generally known as the Levant) that the greatest threat to Egypt lay; although major conflict with them did not really develop until the time of the New Kingdom.

14. Asiatics arriving in Egypt. Scene from the Middle Kingdom Tomb of Khnumhotep at Beni Hassan.

15. Image of an Asiatic on a glazed tile from the Mortuary Temple of Ramesses III at Medinet Habu.

The iconography of the bound and subdued Asiatic implies almost constant conflict between Egypt and Asia, but the reality for much of Egyptian history was quite different. From the early Dynastic Periods, complex trade links had been established with this area. The Sinai Peninsula itself was the source of various minerals, including copper and turquoise, and the Levant provided the precious commodity, timber, which Egypt badly lacked. Constant trade through the centuries kept the various states in a reasonably stable and friendly alliance; for it was probably a truly two-way trade, beneficial to all parties concerned. It was only when the various kingdoms in this area were influenced by the rise of strong and ambitious new powers that they began to covet the richness of their Egyptian neighbours and realise the potential benefits of a more aggressive approach.

The area of Sinai was inhabited by Bedouin. Egypt was not alone in distrusting such nomadic neighbours, and battles against them are recorded from the earliest times. Egypt never completely controlled the whole of the Sinai Peninsula, but was able to maintain a "land bridge" from the Delta into the Levant. In the First Intermediate Period, Bedouin invaded parts of the Delta, but were repulsed. Always on the move, the Bedouin were a difficult foe to subdue; and campaigns against them were almost always doomed to failure from the start. Pharaoh after pharaoh led armies into the Sinai, only to find the Bedouin had moved on, for they knew the routes across the desert intimately and were easily able to avoid detection. It was in fact Bedouin guides who were to lead Persian invaders across the Sinai on their way to conquer Egypt in 525 BC.

THE HYKSOS

During the early years of the Middle Kingdom, between 1800 and 1650 BC, Egypt was gradually "invaded" by people known to the Egyptians as the Hyksos. After the end of the Middle Kingdom, it was the Hyksos who ruled Egypt for a while.

Exactly who the Hyksos were is unclear, but they probably originated in the area of Palestine. They settled in the eastern Delta, which was an area not greatly populated by

Egyptians, whose main centres of habitation were on the main branch of the river Nile to the south. As such, the gradual influx of the Hyksos seems to have been unopposed and ignored until it was too late.

Later accounts which imply a more organised "invasion" come from the records of the princes from Thebes who finally drove the Hyksos out of Egypt and should, therefore, be treated with caution as they are undoubtebly propaganda. In practice, the so-called invasion was probably peaceful and a gradual infiltration spread over many years.

The Hyksos became influential in the Delta, where they soon outnumbered native Egyptians. This was at a time when the central power of the late Middle Kingdom monarchs was on the wane. The Hyksos established their capital at Avaris in the Delta and, during the Second Intermediate Period, extended their sphere of influence south to include the city of Memphis.

The names of Hyksos rulers, such as Joam and Jakbaal, indicate their non-Egyptian origins. Finds at their sites have revealed great quantities of Syro-Palestinian material dating from 2000 to 1700 BC. The Hyksos rulers left few monuments, or at least few have survived, but those that do are in the Egyptian style and the Hyksos rulers adopted the same titles as those used by the Egyptian pharaohs.

The Hyksos introduced new weapons to Egypt, including curved bronze swords, known as *kepesh*. Their arrival also coincided with the appearance in Egypt of horses and chariots. These innovations were readily adopted by the Egyptians and later used by them against the Hyksos.

When King Ahmose finally expelled the Hyksos just before the period we know as the New Kingdom, the Egyptians began to pursue a new and vigorous policy of aggressive imperialism. This brought Egypt, for the first time, into direct conflict with the powers beyond the Levant. The rising (and sometimes short-lived) empires of the Mittanians, the Hittites, Babylonians, Assyrians and Persians would all in their turn take up arms against Egypt.

THE MITTANIANS

The state of Mittani developed around 1500 BC in the area of the Tigris and Euphrates rivers. The Mittanians appear to have originated in the region around the Caspian Sea and migrated south into what is now Turkey and Syria.

They became a threat to Egypt during the early Eighteenth Dynasty, but, following the successful campaigns of Thutmose III, their ambitions towards Egypt and neighbouring states were curbed. Mittani became an ally of Egypt, with friendly relations being established that lasted for many years. The kings of Egypt engaged in regular correspondence with their "brother" rulers in Mittani. When Amenhotep III fell ill, a present of a statue of the goddess Ishtar was sent to Egypt from Mittani, in an attempt to effect a cure. Its efficacy or otherwise is not recorded.

Around 1370 BC the state of Mittani was overthrown by the emerging Hittite and Assyrian Empires.

THE HITTITES:

The Hittites, known by the Egyptians as the *Kheta*, were distant neighbours of Egypt who were to prove a formidable and serious threat at the end of the Eighteenth and into the Nineteenth Dynasties. Their origin is not clear, but it is believed they came from Anatolia, having settled there around 3000 BC.

Initially, the Hittite Empire was based in what is now Syria, but when their forces then moved south and conquered the Mittanians between 1450 and 1200 BC, they came into conflict with both the Egyptians and the Assyrians.

Campaigns against the Hittites by the Egyptians in the Nineteenth Dynasty resulted in an uneasy period of peace and a virtual stalemate between the two countries that lasted until the Hittite Empire was overtaken by new powers including that of Assyria in the eighth century BC.

The Hittites knew how to smelt iron and the few examples of iron items in Egypt, which appear from the end of the Eighteenth Dynasty, undoubtedly came from this source. The use of iron gave the Hittites an immense advantage over their enemies, who still used bronze weapons, and they were understandably reluctant to pass the new technology on to others.

THE "SEA PEOPLES"

"Sea Peoples" was the collective name given to a number of different tribes who posed a threat to Egypt in the late New Kingdom. They seem to have been caught up in the substantial mass movements of population, which occurred around the end of the thirteenth century BC, caused by an increasing population (especially in and around Greece) and a period of famine.

Exactly who these people were has been a matter of debate and it was often assumed that, because of their name, they must have been sea-faring people from the main islands in the Mediterranean, including Sicily, Sardinia and Crete. It is now believed that they came from the south west coast of Asia Minor and the Greek islands, and that they slowly moved eastwards and then south along the coast, as they were displaced by famine or pressure from the lands in which they tried to settle. Keeping close to the coast, they managed to maintain their maritime connection and, most importantly, their fleet.

That the "invasion" of the Sea Peoples was more than just a military campaign is evidenced by the fact that the soldiers were accompanied by their wives, families and all their possessions. They clearly planned more than a fleeting visit.

As the Sea Peoples advanced towards Egypt, their ranks grew and Sherden (possibly from the Aegean) and Philistines were included in their numbers.

When in direct conflict with the Egyptians, the Sherden troops fighting on the side of the Sea Peoples will have encountered Sherden mercenaries facing them in the Egyptian army.

The first encounter between the Egyptians and the Sea Peoples occurred during the reign of Merenptah and came to a violent conclusion in the reign of Ramesses III.

THE ASSYRIANS

The Assyrians inhabited the north-eastern part of Mesopotamia and their emerging Empire soon absorbed many of its neighbours in a period from 883 to 612 BC.

In 671 the Assyrians launched a campaign against Egypt, but soon withdrew as their communications and supply lines became stretched. In 669 the Assyrian ruler Ashurbanipal targeted Egypt again and, for the first time, Egypt itself was invaded by a foreign army that the Egyptians were unable to stop. The Assyrians conquered the Delta and headed south towards the city of Thebes. Ashurbanipal appears to have executed several of the rulers of the small Delta states and appointed a vassal king to rule the northern Delta area of Egypt.

Assyria benefited from the riches of Egypt, mainly in the form of gold but also food. Egypt itself, was left to its own devices, and there was a revival at this time in some of the ancient artistic styles and traditions.

16. An Assyrian archer and a spearman. Relief from the palace of Nimrud.

Outside Egypt, however, the emergence of yet more new empires in the east was to prove a further threat to both Egypt and Assyria.

THE BABYLONIANS

The Babylonian Empire first emerged in the southern part of Mesopotamia, based around the city of Babylon, about 1792. The Babylonians expanded their Empire into Syria and Palestine, bringing them into conflict with both the Assyrians and the Egyptians.

Over a thousand years later the Babylonians led a campaign against Egypt entering the Delta, although they were driven back. This resulted in a period of alliance between Egypt and Assyria against Babylon, until Babylon and Egypt were threatened directly by the Persians.

THE PERSIANS

The Persians, who were Indo-Iranians whose heartland was in the area of modern Iran, laid the foundations of their civilisation around 1000 BC. It was to reach its peak around 500 BC.

The rapid and successful expansions of the Persian Empire saw it absorb many other kingdoms and Egypt was regarded as a rich and easy target.

In 525, the Persian Emperor Cambyses led a successful campaign against Egypt, and subjected the country to a period of severe and absolute Persian domination. This period was to last until 332 when the Emperor Darius III was defeated by Alexander the Great.

THE MINOANS

The Minoan civilisation on the island of Crete flourished from around 2400 BC to 1100 BC before coming under Greek control.

The Minoans formed good trade links with Egypt from the earliest times and were probably never really regarded as a threat to Egypt. The main exports of Crete from which Egypt benefited were food items, including olives, oil and wine. Gold and uniquely Egyptian items made of faience were sent to Crete in return.

By the time of the New Kingdom, Minoan pots are depicted in Egyptian tombs and temples and actual examples have been found in Egypt.

It is possible that some Minoans allied with the "Sea Peoples" who proved a threat to Egypt at the end of the Nineteenth Dynasty.

18. *A Minoan bearing tribute. Scene from the Eighteenth Dynasty Tomb of Rekhmire at Thebes.*

THE GREEKS

Close relations with the emerging Greek civilisation were not established until well into the Dynastic Period. The Greeks do not appear to have been considered a *real* threat to Egypt, and the relationship appears to have been mainly one of friendly trade.

By the time of the Saite Period (664-525 BC), Egypt relied on Greek mercenaries in its army and a number of Greeks had settled in Egypt, mainly in the Delta.

Relations between the two countries were good and for a while Egypt was allied with Greece against the threat of the rising Persian Empire. It was around 450 BC that the Greek traveller Herodotus visited Egypt and recorded the sights of the country and many of the seemingly strange customs of the Egyptians he encountered.

Alexander the Great, who was ruler of Macedonia and Greece, defeated the Persian Empire (which included Egypt) in 331 and Egypt then became part of *his* huge Empire. Alexander visited Egypt and seems to have had a genuine interest in the country.

The Oracle of Amun - Ra in Siwa Oasis recognised Alexander as the son of the god and, therefore, the legitimate ruler of Egypt.

Almost immediately on his arrival in Egypt, Alexander sacrificed to the Egyptian gods in the temples of Memphis and, after the severity of the Persian occupation, he appears to have been welcomed as a liberator.

20. The great Temple of Horus at Edfu, built during the reign of the Ptolemies.

Alexander founded a new city, Alexandria, named after him. Built on a virgin site on a branch of the river Nile on the Mediterranean coast, and facing towards Greece, the location was ideal for sea-borne trade. Alexandria soon became one of the most important cities in the ancient world and was regarded as *the* centre of culture and learning.

When Alexander died, following a short illness, in 323, there was no obvious successor to take on his Empire, which his generals divided into more manageable parts. It was one of the most powerful of the generals, Ptolemy, who seized control of the rich country of Egypt. Ptolemy ruled initially jointly with a viceroy, but later became sole ruler and established a new dynasty of Greek rulers, known to us as the Ptolemies. The new rulers seem to have been readily accepted. During this period many more Greeks settled in Egypt.

Greeks and Romans alike seem to have regarded Egypt as a font of ancient wisdom. As such the ancient culture was respected and encouraged and it was even to exert an influence over the Classical world.

THE ROMANS

The emerging Roman Empire was to absorb most of the countries and cultures around the Mediterranean and it was not long before Egypt was targeted, not just because of its wealth, but because of the fertility of its land and its ability to produce substantial crops.

When the Roman general Pompey became more directly involved in the affairs of the Ptolemaic court by being made guardian to the young Cleopatra VII, Rome began to increase its influence.

After Pompey's death (he was killed in Egypt by the Egyptians in 48 BC) Rome and Egypt's fate became intertwined with the relationship between Julius Caesar and Cleopatra. After Caesar's murder, Cleopatra allied herself with Mark Antony, who had become effectively joint ruler of the Roman Empire with Octavian. However, Antony came into direct conflict with Octavian, who wanted to be sole ruler.

Octavian ultimately defeated Antony and Cleopatra at the naval battle of Actium in 31, following which both Antony and Cleopatra committed suicide, rather than be led captive in

21. The fertile fields of Egypt as shown in a harvesting scene from the Tomb of Sennedjem at Deir el Medina.

chains to Rome. Egypt again submitted to foreign rule and the country became a province of Rome and the "bread basket" of the Roman Empire.

Many Romans moved to Egypt, initially into the established Greek cities but also into new towns built to cope with yet another invasion of foreigners into the country. As had happened before, the new settlers soon became "Egyptian", and even adopted and adapted Egyptian beliefs and practices. The Roman Emperors added their names to the ancient temples, repairing and extending them and in some cases, building new temples to the Egyptian gods.

Egypt ceased to be an independent kingdom, and enjoyed a period of peace under the protection of Rome, but its resources were ruthlessly exploited by its new rulers.

22. The Roman Emperor Trajan depicted as an Egyptian Pharaoh on a column from the Temple of Kom Ombo.

2 WEAPONS AND MILITARY EQUIPMENT

Throughout the long Dynastic Period of Egyptian history, weaponry changed slowly, with significant innovations and improvements appearing only in the New Kingdom.

Egyptian weapons and equipment were always very similar, if not virtually identical, to the weapons of neighbouring countries. This suggests that the Egyptian military successes arose from better discipline, training and motivation among its troops, rather than from the possession of superior military technology and weapons.

We know that weapons and military equipment were traded between nations in the ancient Middle East. In the New Kingdom, chariots and horses were exchanged between rulers. Then, as today, there was a flourishing international arms trade.

Almost all of the military weapons used by the ancient Egyptians derived from weapons used for hunting (although this is not unique to Egypt) and identical bows and arrows, spears, maces and axes are shown in both early hunting and battle scenes.

23. Ramesses II in battle, using a bow and arrow.

MATERIALS

The early years of the history of the human race are usually divided into convenient "periods" and given appropriate names which are based on the technological development of tools and weapons. We have, therefore, the "Stone Age", followed by the "Bronze Age" and finally, the "Iron Age".

This simple division of large periods of time is much too simplistic and implies that there was, at a given moment in time, a significant technological improvement, when man lurched from one "age" into the next, simply replacing one outmoded technology.

In practice, the process was extremely slow, and, as we will see in Egypt, the entering of a new "age" did not necessarily coincide with the abandonment of the old technology. Some of the new metal-smelting techniques took hundreds of years to be perfected and introduced on a large scale. The first bronze items may have heralded the start of the Bronze Age, but the new material was difficult to produce and was available to very few people.

24. Copper and flint axe heads, all dating from the Early Dynastic Period.

In Egypt, and probably in other emerging cultures at this time, although the new metal-smelting technologies were both known and used, the country remained, essentially, a Stone Age culture, albeit one far more advanced and "civilised", by our definition of the term, than many others.

Flint

It used to be thought that humans were unique in the animal kingdom, because of their ability to make and use tools. We now know that this is not strictly true, for many animals use "tools", mainly for obtaining food; but it was humans who developed a wide range of specialist tools for a variety of different tasks.

The first tools were made from materials readily available, such as stone, bone and wood, but it was in the use of stone tools, in particular, that early man excelled. Whilst any stone could be useful as a club or a hammer, it was the selection and working of one specific type of stone that was to become particularly important.

This special stone was flint, a material that was widespread (not just in Egypt) and found on riverbanks, in the deserts and in cliffs. We do not known when mankind first discovered that flint could be broken into flakes by striking it with a pebble, known as a hammer-stone. Perhaps someone found flints that had fractured naturally, revealing the special nature of the material.

Flint is a concretion of silica, formed in chalk or limestone rocks. Black or, more usually, a straw yellow in colour, when broken, flint fractures like glass, producing flakes with a fine and *very* sharp edge.

Flint is extremely hard, harder than most other stones; and tools made from it were used to cut skins, meat, wood, and even to carve other, softer stones.

The first tools were simple cutting blades, scrapers, and hand-axes used for hunting. When the techniques of tool-making became more advanced, more complicated shapes and specific tools and weapons were crafted.

Some of the earliest flint tools and weapons from Egypt date from around 4000 BC. There is also evidence from this time that flint blades were being secured to wooden handles, or "hafts" to make them easier to use.

Flint was obtained locally to most of the settlements. Relatively little excavation work has been done at the earliest inhabited sites in Egypt and early Egyptologists often ignored evidence of Predynastic material in their search for Dynastic objects. Much information may have been lost to us.

An additional complication is that many of the early sites are still inhabited today, so material from the first settlements is now buried under centuries of habitation debris. It is only in recent years that archaeologists in Egypt have been looking at some of the few early sites that have survived.

It is not clear, therefore, if each settlement produced its own tools or if the work was concentrated in specific areas, with the finished tools and weapons being traded between communities. There is a huge variety in the shape and size of the early tools and it is likely that there were local variations in techniques and designs, producing differently-shaped tools, which could be used for similar purposes.

The use of flint for making simple tools was extended to weapons, such as blades for fighting knives and spears. Splendid flint-bladed knives survive from the earliest periods, but also from the Middle Kingdom, even though by this time bronze was available. Flint blades have a much sharper and longer-lasting edge than the supposedly superior bronze weapons.

Small pieces of flint could be flaked into arrow-heads or spear-heads, which could then be lashed to wooden shafts.

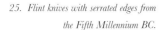
25. Flint knives with serrated edges from the Fifth Millennium BC.

Flint was probably also used as the main tool for carving stone. It is suitable for cutting the hardest of stones, such as granite and diorite, and is even more effective with softer stones such as limestone and sandstone. Very small and fine flint blades and tools could be made, to produce the most delicate carvings and detailed hieroglyphs. Although we know that copper and bronze chisels were used to cut stone, recent practical tests, using reproductions of ancient tools, have indicated that their effectiveness was actually poor and that the more efficient flint tools continued to be used.

Stone

Apart from flint, a variety of other stones were used to make weapons, notably in the early Dynastic Period.

Whilst fine limestone was readily available throughout Egypt, it is easily broken and most of the stone weapons that have survived are made of rare and hard stones. These were often chosen for their colour and appearance and were probably high-status weapons only.

Stones used include breccia (a metamorphic stone made of angular fragments of light stone embedded in a coloured matrix, the colours being mainly red and white) and basalt and diorite, both very hard, dark, igneous rocks.

Alabaster, which is a much softer stone was also used and was popular because of its fine straw colour and delicate veining. Egyptian "alabaster" is actually calcite, a metamorphosed form of limestone.

All these stones were highly polished to bring out the full richness of their colours.

Copper

Copper ore was found in Egypt in large quantities and copper was extracted from it from the Predynastic Period onwards. Small copper objects, such as beads, pins and harpoon heads have been found in tombs from the Badarian Period, even before the first gold objects appear.

By the end of the Predynastic Period, weapons and tools were being made of metal. Axe-heads, chisels, knives, daggers, spearheads and copper vessels have been found at many early sites.

Some of the earliest copper may have been found in its naturally-occurring state, but from the Predynastic Period onwards, it was mainly obtained by the smelting of copper ore, which was found in the eastern desert and in the Sinai. Although there are still deposits in these areas today, they are no longer mined, as copper is now found in more accessible and economic sites elsewhere in the world.

In the Sinai, the copper was found in the same areas as turquoise (a semi-precious stone greatly prized by the ancient Egyptians for use in jewellery from the earliest periods onwards). Many ancient copper mines have been located, along with evidence, obtained by examination of the slagheaps, of the smelting process.

By estimating how much ore would have been needed to produce the amount of slag that survives, it has been possible to calculate the quantity of copper produced from these mines. The indications are that the quantities mined would have been more than sufficient to supply the Egyptian needs until at least the New Kingdom. From this time onwards, copper was also obtained from Asia, usually as part of the tribute from subjugated nations, but also through trade.

Egypt remained a largely agricultural country for all of its history, and as such the need for copper and the demand for it was limited.

The copper ores found include azurite and malachite. Azurite occurs near the surface and is easily found because of its rich blue colour. Malachite is usually found in the same locations, but in larger quantities than the azurite. Both ores, as well as being a source of metallic copper, were used as a vivid and rich blue pigment in paint. Malachite in particular was used to colour faience glazes and glass, and was also used throughout Egyptian history as make-up to decorate the eyelids.

The ores were mainly obtained by surface workings. In later periods, some shafts were dug, but only where particularly rich veins of ore dropped below the ground level and could be mined easily.

Before the ore could be smelted, it had to be crushed and mixed with charcoal in a heap or pit. Copper melts at 1083 degrees centigrade, a temperature that could easily be achieved if the furnaces were placed in a windy location or if bellows were used.

26. *The smelting of copper: metal workers blow air into a fire. An Old Kingdom relief in the Tomb of the "Two Brothers" at Sakkara.*

The copper metal obtained from the smelting process was hammered into the shapes of the objects required, or it was often re-melted into ingots for transportation.

From the Middle Kingdom, we have some of the first evidence of copper being used in pottery moulds, to cast objects. The moulds produced a roughly shaped item, which needed to be finished by hammering. The edges of axes and knives in particular were hammered to form the blade edge and this process also hardened and strengthened the metal.

Most of the copper used in Egypt contains many natural impurities, which include gold and silver in small quantities.

Bronze

Bronze is an alloy made of a mixture of copper and tin (often with other naturally-occurring impurities). Bronze today is normally made with about 10% tin, but the quantity of tin in ancient bronze varies significantly. The range of tin is from 2% (this amount is probably a naturally-occurring quantity) to 16%.

By adding tin to the copper, the metal becomes much stronger and harder. Surprisingly, it also needs a *lower* smelting temperature, from 1015 degrees centigrade for a 5% tin alloy, to 960 degrees, for a 15% alloy. The addition of tin also improves the fluidity of the molten metal and enables better castings to be made.

The use of bronze appears to have originated in Asia and it is found in Ur around 3500 BC. It was some time before bronze appeared widely in Egypt. Examples have been found at many sites and it is presumed that these early bronze items were imported ready-made. Towards the end of the pharaonic period the raw materials were imported separately and smelted and manufactured into items in Egypt.

It is difficult to say exactly when bronze was introduced to Egypt. The matter is complicated because Egyptologists have labelled many objects "copper" or "bronze", and the distinction sometimes is so subtle it can only be made by scientific tests. Relatively few objects have been subjected to such tests, so many objects described as bronze may well be copper, and *vice-versa*.

The first identified *bronze* items (albeit very small) were found by Flinders Petrie in his excavations at the Old Kingdom site of Meidum. Other small objects were found at Sixth Dynasty sites. The number of finds increases at sites of the Eleventh and Twelfth Dynasties and it is usually considered that bronze became generally available from this period onwards.

Copper was still used extensively and of the many metal objects found in the tomb of Tutankhamun, there were far more made of copper than of bronze. By the Late Period of Egyptian history, bronze was being produced in Egypt and was used extensively to produce cast figurines, statues and ritual vessels for the temples. Vast numbers of these objects survive today and can be seen in museum collections around the world.

27. Late Period bronze statue of Osiris.

Iron

The raw materials needed to produce iron are plentiful in Egypt. Hematite was used to make beads and amulets from the earliest times and some compounds of iron were used as artists' pigments, producing a range of colours from a mustard-yellow, to a deep reddish brown.

Few iron objects survive from Egypt. Many argue that this is because iron rusts, especially in damp conditions, leaving virtually no visible trace. Whilst this is the case for the Delta sites in Egypt, very few iron objects have been found in the drier locations to the south.

Small fragments of iron and items made from this metal have been found at Sixth and Eleventh Dynasty sites, but it is possible that this was iron produced by accident when smelting other metals. The only other source for the metal is meteoric iron which can be found, but only in small quantities.

The first real group of datable iron objects comes from the Tomb of Tutankhamun, at the end of the Eighteenth Dynasty. The objects include a splendid iron-bladed dagger, a miniature headrest, an amuletic eye and some blades for model tools. These objects have not been scientifically analysed, so the precise origin of the metal is not known. It is virtually certain, however, that the large-scale, commercial smelting of iron originated in Asia, and that the dagger in particular was probably a gift to Tutankhamun from a foreign ruler. Before Tutankhamun, Amenhotep III had been sent "… a dagger whose blade is of iron", from the king of the Mittani, Tusratta.

The earliest date for iron working within Egypt is the sixth century BC in the Delta city of Naucratis, which was a Greek settlement. Iron smelting needs a very high temperature, 1530 degrees centigrade, and the technical knowledge and experience of how to achieve this was limited. The casting of iron was impossible at this time, and this process was not perfected until relatively recent times.

28. The iron-bladed dagger from the Tomb of Tutankhamun.

Other Metals

The Egyptians were also experts in the mining, extraction and smelting of other metals, especially gold and silver. Silver was considered to be more valuable than gold as it was the rarer of the two metals. Gold was found in large quantities, mainly in Nubia.

Both metals were used to make weapons. Silver is harder than gold and examples survive of silver spearheads and poleaxes. Gold was used mainly for decorative objects and jewellery, but Tutankhamun had one dagger made with a gold blade. The use of precious metals for weapons may have had more to do with status and power than practicality. Certainly the gold blade would be effective if used, but the metal is too soft for it to be considered as a serious weapon.

Leather

From the earliest times animal skins were used for a number of purposes and we know, from examples found in Predynastic tombs, that they were being treated to preserve them. Initially wild animals provided the skins but later skins from domesticated sheep, goats and cattle were used.

The exact method of tanning the leather is not known, but the process was essential to turn a dried skin, from which all the flesh had been removed, into useable, flexible and durable leather. Classical writers describe the use of the seedpods of the acacia tree in the tanning process. The pods contain about thirty per cent of tannin and are still used in the Sudan for preserving leather today, so it is reasonable to assume that this method was used in ancient Egypt too.

29. The gold-bladed dagger found in the Tomb of Tutankhamun.

30. Detail of the chariot of Yuya, showing the leather panels and tyres. In this example the leather has been embossed and coloured red and green.

Once treated, the leather produced was used for a number of military purposes, which included quivers for arrows, archers' wrist guards, sheaths for knives and daggers, floors for chariots and tyres for chariot wheels.

Cut into lengths to make thongs, leather was used to lash items together. It is a particularly good material for this purpose, for if the lashing is done when the leather is wet, when it dries it contracts and produces an extremely tight and strong binding.

The leather could be left in its natural colour, or stained, with red or green being the usual colours. The surface was often embossed with simple designs punched into the surface of the leather (softened first by soaking in water), in a technique still in use around the world today.

Gut

Gut (the cleaned, dried and twisted intestines from animals) produces an extremely strong and durable thread which was used for the stringing of musical instruments, such as harps or lutes, and also for stringing bows.

Many examples of gut have been found from the early periods of Egyptian history. It was a material used throughout the ancient period (and indeed world-wide right into modern times).

Linen

Linen is made from the fibres of the flax plant, grown extensively in Egypt in antiquity. The Egyptians learnt how to use this plant to produce a range of different thicknesses of threads for a variety of uses. Extremely fine threads, when woven into cloth, produced a gauze-like material, whilst thicker threads produced a very coarse sacking or canvas-type fabric for heavier duties.

Linen was the main material used to make clothing for rich and poor alike. Linen thread was used to stitch fabrics and leather together and also to lash items (such as arrow flights to arrow shafts).

31. Women weaving linen into cloth. Model from the Tomb of Meketre.

Rope

Ropes of varying thickness and qualities are known from the earliest periods and a number of examples survive. The fibres used for rope-making included flax, halfa fibre and grass, but the main material was palm fibre, easily obtainable in large quantities from the crown of the trunk of the date palm. The fibres envelop the bases of the new leaves and are easily stripped away and twisted into an extremely strong and durable rope.

32. Example of rope from the Old Kingdom, found with the boat of King Khufu at Giza.

Glue
Strong glue, containing gelatine, was obtained from animal products, such as skin, bone and cartilage. The raw material was boiled and the resultant "soup" concentrated by evaporation. Animal-based glues were used extensively by carpenters and cabinet-makers and were suitable for fixing veneers and inlays into place. These skills were also needed for weapons too, such as composite bows and chariots, which required many of their parts to be firmly and permanently glued together.

Resin from trees was also used as an effective glue and was ideal for fixing arrowheads into place and securing arrow flights.

Bone and Ivory
Bone and ivory are both very strong materials and can be employed in the manufacture of small objects. Bone was easily obtained, probably from cattle, whilst ivory came from hippopotami (still wild in Egypt in the early periods) or from elephants (imported from Nubia).

Sharpened lengths of bone were used for arrowheads, awls, harpoon heads and needles. Ivory, which today is usually considered to be a luxury material, was readily available and used for making weapons too, as well as for decorative inlay on objects.

Wood
For most of the Dynastic Period, Egypt never had a plentiful supply of native timber. Most of it had to be imported, especially when large planks or poles were needed.

A number of different types of wood were obtained from the close neighbours of Egypt. The skilled Egyptian carpenters seem to have identified very early on that the characteristics of certain timbers made them ideal for certain uses. Only a limited amount of research has been done on the various types of wood used in ancient Egypt. Sometimes different species can be identified only by microscopic examination and this is difficult, as in many cases the base wood has been covered with veneers or a variety of inlays.

Ash was imported from the Lebanon. It is tough yet flexible and was particularly suited for the making of chariot wheels and composite bows.

Cedar was also imported from Lebanon, and this wood, above all others, was greatly prized and was one of Egypt's major imports throughout the Dynastic Period. Cedar is easily worked, and, most importantly, the huge cedar trees provide long planks of wood, ideal for boat-building and for domestic use in coffins, shrines and furniture.

33. Huge planks of imported timber, used in a wooden coffin, which dates from the Middle Kingdom, from Deir el-Bersha.

Elm was imported from Asia and is also a very strong wood, used especially for chariot wheels. In fact this particular wood is still used to make wooden wheels around the world today.

Ebony, a very dark and extremely hard wood, was imported from Nubia. It was used most extensively for small items of furniture or for inlay as veneer on larger objects, but it was also used to tip arrows.

The native timbers (which it is believed may have been more plentiful in Predynastic times) included:

acacia, which was used to construct coffins, the hulls and masts of smaller boats and also to make bows,

carob which was initially imported from Ethiopia, but from the New Kingdom onwards grown in Egypt (also used to make bows), and

willow, another strong wood which was particularly suitable for the handles of knives, axes and other tools.

TOOLS

The manufacture of the simplest of weapons required the use of tools. Stones could be cut into shape by other stones and wood cut or shaped using simple stone tools.

The introduction of more complex weapons evolved simultaneously with the introduction of more specialised tools for wood and stone working.

Woodworking skills were developed in the First and Second Dynasties. The carpenters quickly developed effective methods of joining wood together and joints such as mortise and tenon and dovetails are seen for the first time in Egypt. The skills used to produce ornate and detailed furniture were soon adapted to produce weapons of high quality.

Copper and bronze adzes and chisels were used by craftsmen to make better and more sophisticated weapons. Flint and copper saws were used to cut the wood, adzes shaped the

34. Selection of woodworking tools, including drills an adze and a saw.

objects, copper drills cut holes, and rough, flat stone blocks were used to smooth the surface of wooden objects.

WEAPONS
Sticks and Stones

Although the Egyptians, like many other cultures, developed a sophisticated and wide range of weapons, the most obvious and simplest of which and the very first to be used, were probably sticks and stones. Readily available, sticks and stones could easily and quickly be used as weapons and are ideal, for example, if a settlement is attacked and a speedy defence is needed.

Sticks could only be used effectively at close quarters, as clubs. They could of course be thrown at the enemy, but that effectively disarms the thrower and is a distinct disadvantage, unless there is an unlimited supply of missiles available.

Stones could be used as simple hand-axes or clubs and could be particularly effective when thrown at the enemy, especially from battlements or town walls. We do know that the Roman army used hand-thrown stones in training, and some surviving reliefs indicate that they were used in battle, but probably by defenders. Archaeological evidence from Masada in Israel has found piles of stones heaped up by the walls, ready to be thrown down on the attacking Romans. Perhaps some Egyptian towns were similarly provisioned?

The Egyptians do appear to have used such basic weapons and the bodies of some Middle Kingdom soldiers have survived that exhibit wounds consistent with being hit by stones thrown down on them from battlements. Simple weapons like these are perhaps most likely to have been used by civilians, when a weapon was required at short notice.

The development of weapons was rapid, and it was not long before hand-held stones evolved into clubs or maces, and sticks into throwing sticks or spears.

Flails

The flail, or flabellum, is one of the royal insignia, which, along with the crook, is shown on royal statues dating from all dynasties of the Pharaonic Period and well into the Graeco-Roman Period. The origin of both items is unclear. The flail is often described as a whip for the control of livestock, though there is little hard evidence to support this.

A tool with the form of the flail, pieces of wood tied or hinged to a longer handle, was used to thresh grain, and it may well be that the flail had an agricultural origin. However, it was not unusual for tools to be adapted into weapons. Flails appear as weapons in many periods of history, including in Medieval times, and are also used in Eastern martial arts even today.

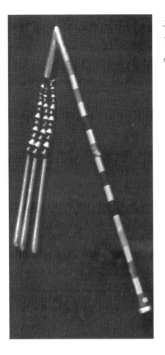

35. A flail from the Tomb of Tutankhamun, made of gold and lapis lazuli.

36. Soldiers shown in a relief from the Mortuary Temple of Queen Hatshepsut, one of whom appears to carry a flail.

One relief of soldiers, in the Mortuary Temple of Queen Hatshepsut at Deir el Bahri, appears to show one soldier carrying something which may well be a flail. Perhaps flails, which would have been easy to make and very effective as a weapon, were used occasionally in warfare.

Maces

The mace is one of the oldest form of weapon found in Egypt (and probably anywhere in the world) and it is also one of the simplest. A mace could be fashioned by lashing a heavy stone to a wooden haft. By the Predynastic period, maces were common but had become a little more sophisticated.

The stone used for the mace-heads was carefully selected, often for colour and veining as well as hardness. Granite and diorite were commonly used, but any hard, coloured and variegated stone could be employed and the surface was often worked to a high polish to show off the colours and texture of the stone. A central hole was drilled through the stone to allow a wooden haft to be fitted securely. The head could simply be wedged into place but may also have been secured by leather thongs. The haft often had a textured surface at the hand end, to allow a secure grip.

37. Drawing of an early mace and haft found in Nubia, but now lost.

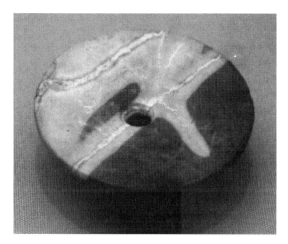
38. A flat, disc-shaped mace head.

39. Pointed mace heads.

The shapes of the actual head varied. The most common was a flat disc shape, but some resemble hammerheads with pointed ends and others are round or conical. Usually the surface was kept smooth, but some were cut with protrusions on the surface. Many examples of mace heads survive, although their shafts have not. Most are relatively small, especially the pear-shaped heads, which are often less than ten centimetres in height. They range in date from 3500 to 3000 BC.

These weapons could be deadly at close quarters. The length of the haft (usually between thirty and forty centimetres) would make a significant difference to the length and power of the swing, and most maces would have been more than capable of breaking bones and crushing skulls. The disc-shaped heads and those with points would also be capable of cutting flesh.

Royal maces seem to have evolved from a simple weapon into a more decorative and ritual object. Surviving examples are much larger than those designed for actual use and the surfaces of these maces are often decorated to commemorate political or religious events.

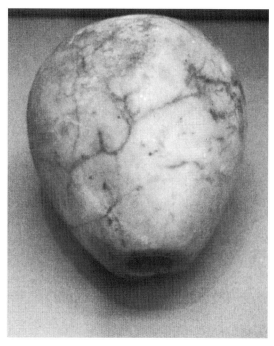
40. A pear-shaped mace head of limestone.

41. *Pear-shaped mace head of red breccia.*

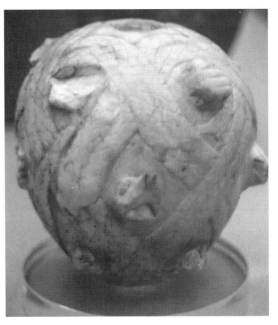

42. *Larger pear-shaped mace head with protrusions and with a simple carved design.*

Interestingly, in other cultures too, the mace evolved from a simple, practical weapon to a symbol of royal or state power. A mace is still used in both Houses of Parliament in the United Kingdom today as a symbol of the authority of the sovereign.

43. *Detail of a gilded-wood life-sized statue of Tutankhamun, found in his tomb in the Valley of the Kings. The boy pharaoh carries a mace in his right hand.*

44. *The large mace head of the "Scorpion King", found in the Pre-Dynastic site of Hierakonpolis. The relief carved on this ceremonial mace head shows the king opening a breach in a dyke to allow flood water to flow into an irrigation basin.*

Slings

Slings and the stones (or "shot") they fired were mainly used for hunting and were a very effective weapon. The sling could be made of woven reeds, leather or linen in the form of a strap, wider at the centre, forming a pouch for the slingshot. Suitable slingshot (ideally round stones or pebbles) was readily available from the banks of the river or from the desert.

With the shot held in the centre of the strap, both ends of the sling were held in one hand and it was whirled around either the head or the side of the body. One end of the strap would then be released to eject the shot.

For hunting and for battle, slings could be used at a distance from the enemy, always a useful technique to adopt. They had the advantage, too, that supplies of shot were almost unlimited and could, if necessary, be picked up from the ground at the hunter or soldier's feet.

The sling was used extensively in antiquity and evidence of its effectiveness as a weapon is available from Classical sources. Modern experiments with slings have shown that they can have an effective range of

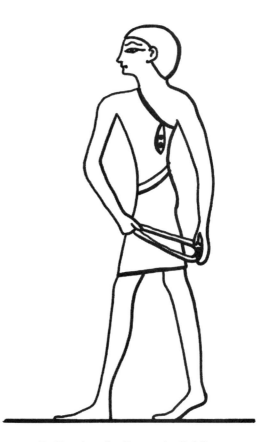

45. *Man using a sling. From a tomb at Beni Hassan.*

around two hundred metres. Classical authors tell us that the range of slingshot could match that of the best archers and we know that Persian archers could fire their arrows about three hundred and fifty metres.

It is clear that people were trained in the use of a sling from an early age and that in skilled hands a great degree of accuracy could be obtained, targeting specific parts of the body or shooting birds in flight.

An example of a sling was found at the Middle Kingdom town of Kahun in Egypt and is now in the Manchester Museum. It was found with a group of objects belonging to a child. Another find, also now in Manchester was of slingshot, again found in a Middle Kingdom child's burial, this time at Abydos, indicating perhaps that the Egyptians taught their children how to use this simple, but very effective, weapon.

Among the many weapons found in the Tomb of Tutankhamun were two fragmentary slings made of finely plaited linen cord, each fitted with a pouch for the missiles and a loop at one end for attachment to the little finger. On the floor of the tomb, Carter found several round pebbles, used as slingshot.

Throwsticks

Throwsticks, often called, erroneously, boomerangs (the Egyptian versions were not designed to return to the thrower), were also a very early weapon. Their primary use was for the hunting of birds. The stick, when thrown, rotated in the air, and when cast into a feeding or even flying flock of birds was capable of injuring, if not killing outright, individual birds. The stick could then be collected for re-use.

46. Hunting in the marshes. A New Kingdom painting from the Tomb of Nebamun.

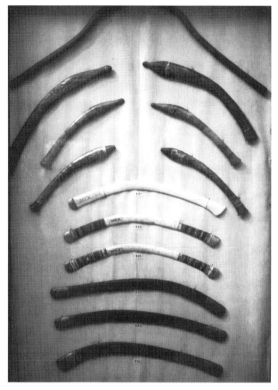

47. Collection of throwsticks found in the Tomb of Tutankhamun.   *48. Hatshepsut's soldiers armed with throw-sticks.*

Many examples of throwsticks survive and a particularly large collection was found buried with Tutankhamun in his tomb in the Valley of the Kings. The sticks are all curved to a greater or lesser degree. Some are simple, most are of plain wood, but many are inlaid with other woods, ivory and ebony. Some are even gilded and inlaid, and clearly important, non-disposable objects.

The effectiveness of a throwstick against a human foe is questionable, although potentially a number thrown together would be able to inflict severe damage. This type of weapon has a disadvantage, for when it is thrown at the enemy, its original owner is rendered defenceless. In fact the original thrower (if his aim was inaccurate) could well have his own weapon thrown back at him!

In the New Kingdom, Hatshepsut's soldiers on the expedition to Punt are shown with throwsticks. Perhaps they were used by the soldiers in hunting for their food, rather than for use in battle.

Spears

A splendid model from the Middle Kingdom Tomb of Mesehti depicts the classic Egyptian foot soldier equipped with a spear and a shield. The wood shaft of each spear (if life-sized which would be around two metres in length) is tipped with a fine, leaf-shaped metal blade.

In the earliest periods, the blades of spears were made of flint, but were then superseded by ones made of copper. In later periods, bronze and then iron were used (although even a simple sharpened pole or reed could be an effective weapon, without any additional blade). Until the end of the Middle Kingdom, the blades were made with a tang that was slotted into the

49. Spearmen; model from the Tomb of Mesehti.

50. Spear head made of silver.

wood of the haft and lashed into place. From the New Kingdom onwards it was more usual for the metal blades to be made with a socket into which the haft was fitted.

Spears were originally intended to be thrown at one's opponent, or prey. Whilst this technique may be fine for the hunting of gazelles, when the weapons could either be picked up from the ground if they had missed their target, or retrieved from the body of the animal, in battles this is not as easy. Under these circumstances, a spear, once thrown, leaves the spearman defenceless.

The primary use of spears in combat was as an extremely effective stabbing weapon. By using the spear as a polearm, the enemy could be kept some distance away and

51. Spear head made of bronze.

the shaft of the spear could also be used as a club, just as such weapons were used in later periods of history.

The shape of the spearhead, with a long, leaf-like blade, sharp point and edges, shows it could be used to slash, cut and inflict deep thrust wounds when used as a stabbing weapon. The width of the blade is important, for a wide blade actually prevents the spearhead from being inserted into the body of a foe too far. From practical experience of stabbing weapons right up to recent times, we know that it can be surprisingly difficult to extract a narrow blade easily and rapidly from a victim. The leaf shape of the blade ensured that a serious wound could be inflicted, but, most importantly, that the spear could be recovered quickly, ready for further use.

All the paintings and models show only one spear per man, which indicates that the spears were *not* thrown like javelins. Spears would probably only be thrown (if they ever were) when there was a real likelihood that they would hit their intended target.

Bows and Arrows

One of the most effective of all weapons, used by both hunters and soldiers throughout the ages, was the bow and arrow, whose use dates from the earliest periods.

The bow and arrow was ideal for hunting, as it could be effective against prey at a distance and the arrow was fast and quiet in flight. For battles, it could be equally effective. A good body of archers could maintain a steady and rapid rate of fire, raining arrows down on their opponents.

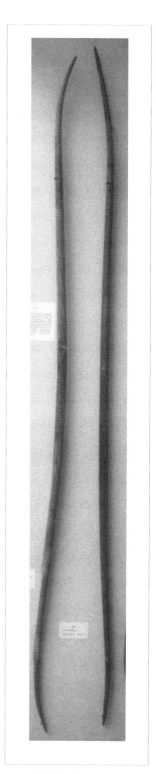

52. Two bows.

53. An archer with his spare arrows in his right hand.

Used at a distance from the enemy, the archers could protect the infantry from attack by the enemy infantry. Fire-arrows could be used, which would have been ideal against towns and cities and especially against enemy shipping.

The most common type of bow was a simple wooden stave, which could vary in length from one to two metres. Native acacia wood was used, and such bows would be capable of firing arrows up to a distance of two hundred metres, although for accuracy and hitting specific targets, a shorter range, probably around sixty metres, would have been the norm. The accuracy of individual archers may not have been too important, for if arrows were fired in a volley, their effect on an enemy could be devastating and, if the enemy were in close formation, many of the arrows would find a target.

The bow stave was tapered towards each end, and notched to allow the fixing of the

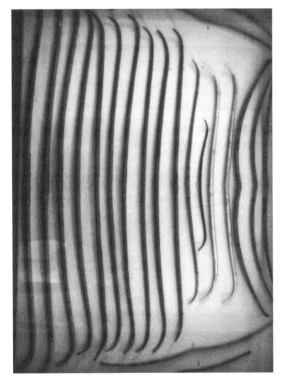

54. Group of bow staves from the Tomb of Tutankhamun.

55. Archers stringing their bows. Scenes from tombs at Beni Hassan and Thebes.

bowstring, which was made of twisted animal gut. Bows were never left permanently strung; they were strung only when they were needed for use.

Sometimes the wood of the bow was strengthened to prevent its splitting, by binding it round tightly with cord.

Double-curved bows, were more complex to make, but had greater power and range.

In the Late Dynastic Period, bows are shown which appear to be made of gazelles' horns joined in the centre by a piece of wood. It is not clear how effective such bows would have been as a certain amount of flexibility is required, although the flexibility in this instance may have been in the bowstring. Such bows would certainly have been decorative if nothing else.

Arrows were usually made of reeds, which were light, grew straight naturally and were easily obtained. Examples found in the Tomb of Tutankhamun, which have been studied were made from a reed that has a hard stem, similar in appearance to bamboo, (*phragmites communis*, var. *isiacus*) but any hard-stemmed reed would do.

The reed shafts were tipped with heads made from a variety of materials, including flint, bone, ebony and ivory, with the earliest copper and bronze arrowheads to survive dating from the Eleventh Dynasty.

56. The tips of a Middle Kingdom bow, with some of the gut bowstring still in place. From the tomb of soldiers of Mentuhotep I at Deir el Bahri.

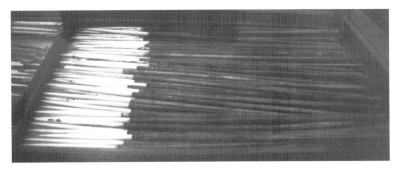

57. Collection of reed arrows tipped with ivory or bone. Early Dynastic Period.

Sometimes it would have been sufficient just to sharpen the end of the reed to a point, which would be effective for hunting small prey, although not perhaps suitable against a larger or human target.

Different shapes of arrowhead were produced depending on the intended target. Barbed heads meant that arrows would not fall out of the victim's body, and indeed would cause more injury when being extracted than when entering the body. Wide heads were designed to cut flesh, and narrow heads were best for penetrating clothing or armour.

The heads were fitted to the shaft by a tang, slotted and glued into the end of the reed or wood shaft, which was tightly bound with fine linen thread to prevent its splitting.

Exactly when (and how) arrow-makers discovered that arrows flew better and straighter by the addition of flights is not known. Some unknown genius had the idea of adding a flight, made from pieces cut from birds' feathers, glued and lashed to the end of the shaft of the arrow. Without a flight an arrow will wobble in flight or even rotate end over end in the air, but with a flight it remains steady, and the arrow always flies headfirst. Arrows with feather flights appear in the earliest representations of bows and arrows. Usually three flights were fitted to each arrow, and in appearance would have been very similar to arrows still made today.

The flight feathers (or fletching) rarely survives, but recent excavations at Hierakonpolis, directed by Renée Friedman, have discovered tombs dating to the Second Intermediate Period, which contain the burials of archers. The burials are of individuals from the "Pan Grave Culture" who are not native Egyptian but possibly Nubian or coming from further south or east. One body was found with the remains of his bow, the bow grip and some arrows with their fletching almost intact. The neatly-trimmed feathers are now incredibly fragile and their preservation is remarkable.

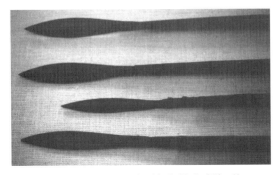

58. Arrows with bronze heads, found in the Tomb of Tutankhamun.

Arrows were carried by the archers in leather or linen quivers slung across their backs. From the New Kingdom, onwards larger quivers were tied to the chariots to ensure a plentiful supply of arrows ready to hand.

In the New Kingdom the Egyptians adopted the use of the composite bow, probably introduced from the Eastern Mediterranean during the period of the Hyksos rule of Egypt. This bow had an even greater strength and range than the simple stave bow. The making of composite bows was

59. Flight feathers from arrows of the Second Intermediate Period, found at Hierakonpolis.

60. An arrow-maker, checking the straightness of an arrow. From an unidentified New Kingdom tomb at Sakkara.

a complex and skilled task, where thin strips of wood, horn and sinew were glued and laminated together. A number of splendid examples of this type of bow (along with the simple stave bow) were found in the Tomb of Tutankhamun.

61. Composite bows from the Tomb of Tutankhamun.

The composite bows had to be treated with care, for they were sensitive to moisture and could easily warp unless protected. Wall paintings and actual examples show that the composite

62. Detail of the decoration on a bow case found in the Tomb of Tutankhamun.

bows were protected in bow cases, carried on the back of soldiers or lashed to the sides of the chariots. Several examples of bow cases, some plain, some elaborately decorated, were found in the Tomb of Tutankhamun.

Composite bows were probably a weapon for the officers and charioteers, where their long range and power would make them effective against any foe protected by body-armour. The composite bow can fire an arrow up to three hundred metres, but its effective range was probably around one hundred and twenty metres (not much different from Seventeenth Century AD muskets!). Most archers in the infantry would have continued to use the simpler wooden stave-bow, which could be produced in larger numbers.

63. Middle Kingdom model from the Tomb of Mesehti at Assuit depicting Nubian archers.

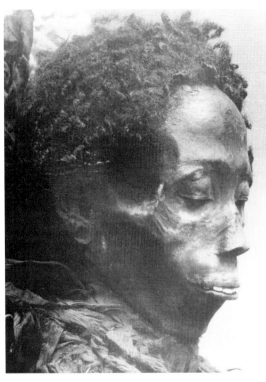

64. The head of the mummy of the Nubian soldier, Maiherpri.

A model, found in the Middle Kingdom Tomb of Mesehti, shows a company of forty archers, armed with small wooden bows. The men carry their bows in their left hands and their arrows loose in their right hands. Usually leather quivers were used to carry arrows and several examples have survived as well as numerous representations on the walls of temples and tombs.

The Nubians seem throughout Egyptian history to have been particularly renowned for their archery skills. Mesehti's model is of Nubians, with their typically dark skin and distinctive hairstyle.

Another useful piece of equipment for the archers, which appears from the Middle Kingdom onwards, is a leather wrist-guard. This protective piece of leather was worn on the left wrist (on the arm which holds the bow) to protect the archer's wrist from the whip of the bowstring after the arrow has been fired.

Early archery equipment, as provided to the ordinary soldier, has been preserved, notably in the tomb of the soldiers of Mentuhotep I, dating to the Middle Kingdom.

65. Arrows and leather quivers from the Tomb of Maiherpri.

The Eighteenth Dynasty Tomb of Maiherpri, a Nubian, was found in the Valley of the Kings with the bulk of its contents still intact. Maiherpri was a soldier, although we do not know which king he served.

His funerary equipment included his weapons: his arrows, leather quivers and decorated leather wrist guards. All the leatherwork was highly decorated with tooled geometric and floral

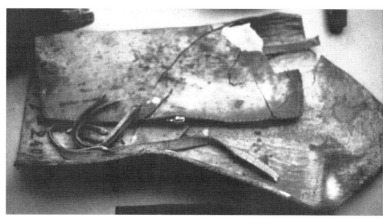

66. The decorated leather wrist-guard of Maiherpri.

45

designs. These were originally a bright red, with details picked out in green; the red has now faded to a deep pink.

The contents of the tomb also included two ornate leather dog collars. Perhaps Maiherpri had dogs of his own or looked after those of the pharaoh, which were used to retrieve prey from the hunt.

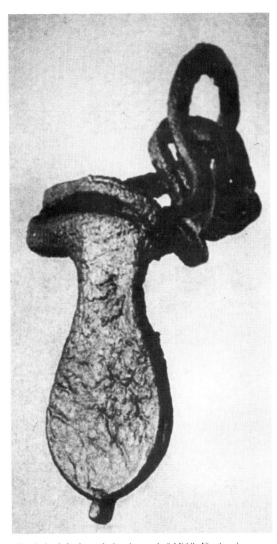

67. A simple leather archer's wrist guard of Middle Kingdom date.

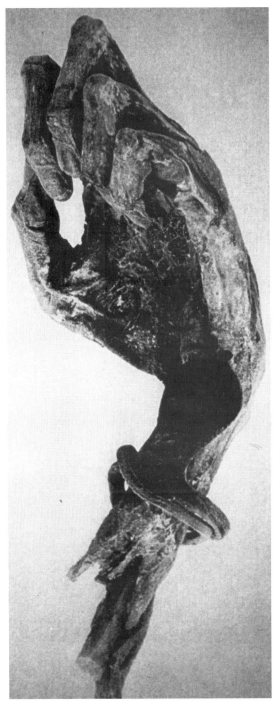

68. The left hand of the body of a Middle Kingdom archer, with his leather wrist guard still in place.

Axes

Stone axes survive from the earliest periods of Egyptian history and by the Old and Middle Kingdoms had been replaced by copper-headed weapons.

The semi-circular metal blades were simply lashed to a wooden handle by cord or leather thongs passing through holes at the base of the blade and around the haft. At this time there was little difference between axes used for woodworking and those used for military purposes.

By the Middle Kingdom, axes were designed specifically for use in battle and the blades had become longer, with concave sides and a curved edge.

In the New Kingdom the blades became even longer, to give them greater penetrative power, especially useful if they were being used against an opponent wearing body armour.

The blades of the axes after the Middle Kingdom were made with projecting lugs near the base, enabling them to be lashed to the wooden handles using leather thongs. This may *seem* to be a flimsy way of securing the axe head, but the use of wet leather thongs, which shrank as they dried, tightening into place, produced an extremely strong fixing. Blades could also easily be removed from damaged or broken hafts which could then be replaced. This would not have required specialist skills and could be undertaken by individual soldiers.

Some of the blades are made with open-work designs, which made the blade lighter, but this development probably reflects the status of the original owner, rather than representing any technological or practical advantage.

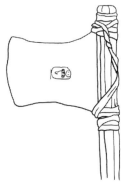

70. Head of a New Kingdom axe, showing how it was secured in place by leather thongs.

47

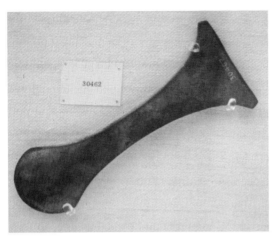

71. Bronze axe blade of the New Kingdom.

Axes would have been used in action very much like the earlier stone maces. Both stone and bronze axes are heavy weapons, and the power and weight behind a swinging axe would be considerable. Such axes could penetrate armour and break bones and skulls. We have real evidence of this, for one pharaoh, Seqenenre-Tao II, died after receiving a number of severe axe wounds to his head.

The wooden hafts of axes varied in shape and could be straight or curved. In the New Kingdom, the shape of the hafts of the battles axes became even more distinctive. They are curved, and the end which is held is wider than the central part of the shaft, almost like the base of an antelope's horn. It is possible, of course, that horn was used for early axe handles and perhaps the shape derives from this. It is more likely, though, that the shape was based on practical considerations, for it makes the axe much easier to grip, especially if the handle becomes wet with sweat. Whilst dropping a carpenter's axe might be of no real consequence, an axe dropped in the heat of battle could prove fatal. The shape also meant it would have been possible to tie a strap around the end of the haft which could be secured around the wrist, ensuring that if the axe were knocked out of the hand it would not be dropped and lost at a critical moment.

Axes are shown being carried by soldiers as their sole weapon, and also by spearmen. When not being carried in the hand, the haft of the axe was tucked into the belt of the soldier's kilt.

Another type of axe blade was scalloped in shape; it was made with three tangs that were

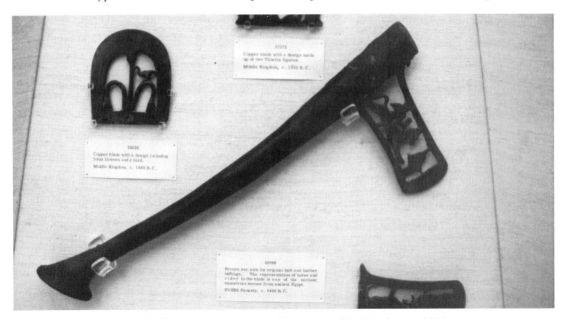

72. A New Kingdom battle axe, showing the distinctive shape of the haft and open-work blades.

48

fitted into a wooden haft. This evolved in the New Kingdom into a type of poleaxe, having a long thin blade and a long cutting edge, fitted close to, and parallel with, the haft.

73. Poleaxe made of silver.

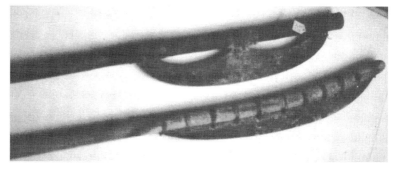

74. Poleaxes made of bronze, with wooden hafts.

Knives and Daggers

For close-quarter combat and despatching one's fallen enemy or prey, the weapon used was a knife or dagger. The weapon used in Egypt throughout the Dynastic Period has too short a blade to warrant being called a sword.

Superb flint knives and daggers were made by the Egyptians and the use of flint continued even after the Egyptians had mastered the smelting of copper and bronze and were making daggers from those metals.

The blades of all these weapons were short and double-edged and were designed primarily for stabbing rather than for slashing. The earliest copper and bronze knives are made from a single sheet of flat metal, whilst later examples are made with a clearly defined mid-ridge to the blade, which gives additional strength. Handles were made of wood, bone or ivory, and

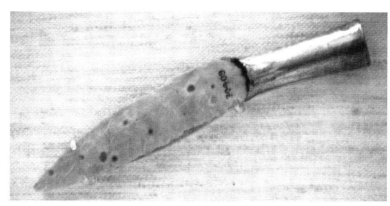

75. Flint-bladed dagger, with a gilded wooden handle. Middle Kingdom.

76. Flint-bladed dagger with a wooden handle and the remains of its leather scabbard.

scabbards of wood or leather were used to protect the blades when not in use. The earliest weapons were small enough to be carried tucked into the waistbands of the soldiers' kilts.

In the New Kingdom, the blades of the daggers and knives became longer and thinner. All these weapons have large pommels on the end of the handles which may appear decorative, but have the practical purpose of helping the user of the weapon keep a secure grip on it and preventing it from slipping from the hand. The addition of the pommel marks the transition from a knife to a dagger. The weight of a pommel, usually cast in one piece with the blade and handle of the dagger, also produced a better-balanced weapon.

Another type of edged weapon, made of bronze, was introduced in the New Kingdom. Adopted from Asia, the Egyptians called it the kepesh; it was a type of scimitar with a long curved blade. The name given to it derives from the word for the foreleg of an animal, the shape of which it resembles.

The kepesh was used as a slashing weapon and, probably because it was exotic and expensive in "smiting of the enemy" scenes, it is the kepesh that is raised above the heads of the fallen foe, rather than the more traditional stone-headed mace.

Another combination mace/kepesh weapon also appears in the hand of kings from the end of the New Kingdom. It appears to be a type of mace, possibly with a stone head as in the earlier examples, but is pear-shaped and has a curved metal blade fitted along one side. The weight of a mace and the cutting power of the kepesh would have made it a formidable weapon indeed.

77. A selection of New Kingdom daggers.

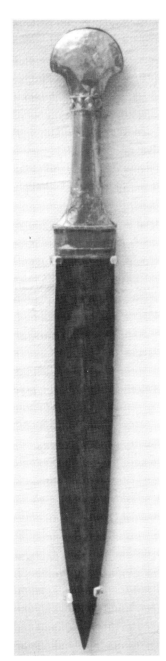

78. New Kingdom bronze-bladed dagger, with a gilded handle.

79. The bronze kepesh or scimitar.

80. Tutankhamun's kepesh, found in his tomb.

Egyptologist Flinders Petrie surmised that the blade of this weapon may have been of the newly-introduced iron and that, to strengthen the blade, an oval of bronze was fitted either side, also giving extra weight to the weapon. No real example of this particular weapon has yet been found.

81. The mace/kepesh as wielded by Ramesses II, from a relief in the Temple of Abu Simbel.

MILITARY EQUIPMENT
Shields

Soldiers of the early periods, the Old Kingdom and Middle Kingdom, wore no body armour at all. Their sole item of clothing and protection for most of the time was a simple white kilt of the sort worn by king and commoner alike.

In battle a shield was used for body protection. Shields were large, usually between one and one and a half metres in height, and must have been quite heavy, as they were made of wood, sometimes solid, sometimes just a frame covered in tough cowhide. A handle was fixed to the rear of the shield and to this could be attached a leather thong to enable it to be slung over the soldier's shoulder when it was not being used.

The solid construction of the shields would have been sufficient to protect the user from arrows and spears. The size of the shields meant that their owners could easily crouch down

82. *A Middle Kingdom tomb model of a hide-covered shield and quiver.*

83. *Painting showing a soldier with a large shield and a poleaxe. From a tomb at Assuit.*

behind them and be completely protected from incoming arrows or other missiles.

The soldiers who used the shields were primarily spearmen, as they only needed one hand (the right) to use their weapon. The other hand could be used to carry their shield. Archers needed both hands free to use their weapons and could not use shields. When necessary, the shields of the spearmen could be used to form a protective barrier to protect both spearmen *and* archers, and the archers could fire their arrows over the heads of their comrades.

Shields are shown in wall paintings and in many Middle Kingdom tomb models. Full sized examples, some purely decorative, others more practical, were found in the Tomb of Tutankhamun. Whilst the common soldier's shield was covered in cowhide, those of the king were covered in the more exotic leopard or cheetah skin. Other shields of the king were made of gilded wood, with an elaborate open-work design, and were probably for ceremonial use, rather than for practical defence.

One of the models from the tomb of the provincial governor Mesehti at Assuit shows a body of forty spearmen, all equipped with large shields. (See fig. 86 over).

84. A leopard-skin covered shield from the Tomb of Tutankhamun.

85. An open-work gilded wood shield, probably for ceremonial use, from the Tomb of Tutankhamun, showing the King as a sphinx, trampling his enemies underfoot.

Each shield has been painted to show the variation in the natural colours and patterns of the cowhide, with patches of black and brown on a white background.

It is possible that from the New Kingdom onwards, some shields were covered in bronze, but no examples have survived.

Scenes of military encampments show surrounding defensive walls made from the shields of the spearmen. The shields form a simple, if light, physical barrier in case of any unexpected

86. *Middle Kingdom model from the Tomb of Mesehti of Egyptian spearmen with cow-hide shields.*

attack. Soldiers rushing to the defence of the camp would find their shields immediately to hand and no doubt their weapons stacked conveniently nearby too. The shield wall could also form a useful fence to enclose and contain any livestock with the troops, such as donkeys, or, from the New Kingdom, horses.

87. *Guards at the entrance to a military camp, showing a protective shield wall.*

Armour

By the time of the New Kingdom, some form of body armour was being introduced, although it was probably only used by the elite units. Scales of bronze or sometimes of hard leather were fixed in an overlapping pattern to either a leather or linen jerkin. The earliest examples of such armour date from the reign of Amenhotep II.

Many examples of bronze scale-armour have been found in Egypt, although dating them is not always easy. This type of armour was most frequently used by the Persians and it is likely that the majority of the scale armour found is not native Egyptian but was used when Egypt was under strong Asiatic influence. The scales vary in size; the smallest pieces were made for the areas which needed to be the most flexible, such as the arms or the fingers of gauntlets.

Such armour would be effective against arrows and spears, certainly at a distance from the enemy. It would also offer significant protection from downward thrusts by knives and daggers,

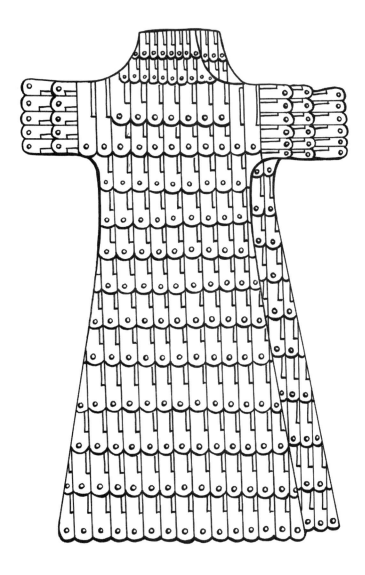

88. Two coats of armour, made of overlapping bronze scales. From a relief in the Mortuary Temple of Ramesses III at Medinet Habu.

89. Pieces of bronze scale armour.

but at close quarters an attacker would try to stab his blade upwards, under and between the overlapping scales and through the backing material of leather or linen.

An example of leather scale armour was found in the Tomb of Tutankhamun. In a delicate and crumpled state it has not been properly studied since the discovery of the tomb. Howard Carter described it as "made of scales of thick tinted leather, worked on to a linen basis or lining, in the form of a bodice without sleeves."

90. Tutankhamun's leather armour as found in a box in his tomb.

The kings are shown wearing armour, usually in the form of the wings of protective deities crossed over their bodies. If these items were made as large pieces of jewellery (made of gold with coloured inlay) they would be both decorative and protective. The only surviving example of such royal armour was found in the Tomb of Tutankhamun and it is known as a corslet. It is

91. The "corslet" or armour of Tutankhamun.

made of gold interlocking and flexible plates, inlaid with semi-precious coloured stones and glass paste, and when worn it would cover and protect the whole of the king's upper torso. Figures of the gods, incorporated into the design, also gave the king magical protection.

The use of armour was, however, limited and large areas of the body still went unprotected. When metal was used as armour, it was only in flexible pieces, rather than in large rigid pieces of plate armour as seen elsewhere in the ancient world and later civilisations.

Helmets appear for soldiers only from the New Kingdom onwards and then they were used primarily for mercenary units. The Sherden mercenaries who fought in the army of Ramesses II, are always shown wearing distinctive round helmets. We do not know if these were made of metal or of leather. The helmets were surmounted by distinctive horns and a central disc.

One rare bronze helmet was found in the area of Thebes and is now in the Manchester Museum. It is non-Egyptian in design and may have belonged to a mercenary or have been taken as plunder. Petrie dated the helmet to the Assyrian period and their invasion of Egypt in the seventh century BC.

Whilst the Egyptians had the technology to manufacture metal helmets and plate armour, perhaps their almost complete absence can be explained by the fact that under the Egyptian sun, any metal helmet or any form of body armour, would become extremely hot and uncomfortable to wear, perhaps unbearably so, and be more of a handicap than a help.

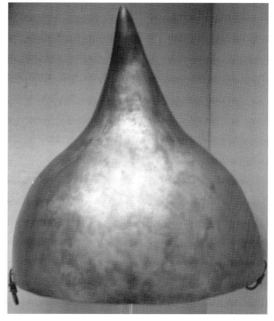

92. Bronze helmet from Thebes.

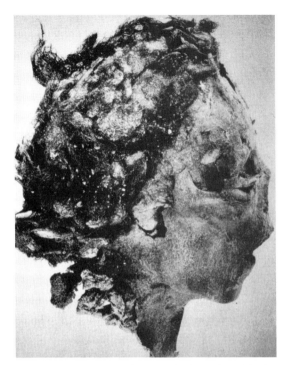

93. The head of a Middle Kingdom soldier, showing his curled and greased hair.

It would appear that for most Egyptian soldiers, the only head protection was a good covering of hair. The hair on the heads of some bodies of Middle Kingdom soldiers was dressed in tight small curls covered with grease to hold it in place. Exactly how much protection this would offer against blows is debatable, but perhaps the grease had another function too? Long hair could be a handicap and even dangerous, for in close combat, it could be grabbed by one's enemy. Possibly the grease would make a secure hand-hold on the hair difficult.

The pharaohs appear to have adopted a special form of headgear for military use. It appears only from the New Kingdom onwards and is known as the Blue Crown, as it is always shown in this colour. It is also known, although possibly erroneously, as the "battle crown" as it appears in many of the military reliefs of the time, although kings are shown wearing it on non-military occasions too.

No examples of *any* royal crowns have survived and it is not clear from what the Blue Crown was made. It is usually presumed that it was made of leather, possibly covered with small round metal discs, but it could have been made of a white metal, probably silver. This crown certainly does resemble a helmet, rather than any of the usual head-dresses worn by the pharaohs, but its exact origin remains unknown. The shape of the crown is complex and because of this, metal as the material seems to make more practical sense than leather.

Gloves/Gauntlets

Egypt, with its hot dry climate, is not a country where one would expect to find anyone wearing gloves, certainly not to keep warm, yet there are several depictions of gloves shown in reliefs, and examples of gloves and mittens were found in the Tomb of Tutankhamun.

94. The Blue Crown, as worn by Tutankhamun, from a relief in the Temple of Luxor.

Gloves or gauntlets *were* used, possibly exclusively by chariot drivers, especially those of a high status. The fabric of the gloves, either leather or stiff linen, would enable a tight grip to be maintained on the reigns and protect the hands from rubbing.

Mounted soldiers throughout history have always ensured that their vulnerable hands were protected and gloves would also provide a measure of protection in close action. In some instances their thickness might be enough to turn an edged blade.

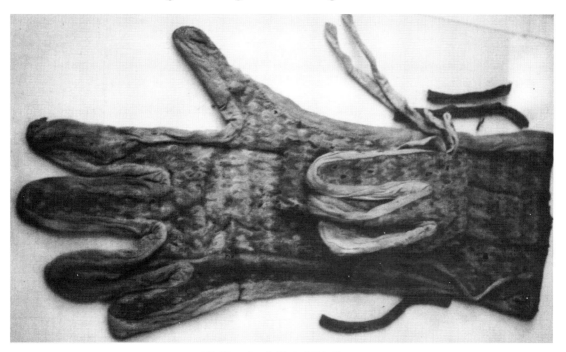

95. Gloves from the Tomb of Tutankhamun.

There is, however, evidence that gloves were used *before* the New Kingdom, which rules out the theory that they were used exclusively by charioteers, so perhaps they were simply status symbols amongst the wealthy (or possibly some Egyptians just felt the cold in the winter and the cool evenings).

Certainly in the New Kingdom, gloves were considered a status symbol and were presented by the king to favoured courtiers.

A relief from the Tomb of Ay dating to the reign of Akhenaten, shows the courtier returning home, proudly showing off the red gloves he has just been given by the king.

96. Ay showing off his new gloves and his gold collars.

Horses and Chariots

Horses and chariots appear to have been introduced to the whole of the ancient Near East from the beginning of the seventeenth century BC. Around 1600, the so-called Hyksos peoples moved into Egypt and began the period of Hyksos rule. It was at this time that horses first appeared in Egypt, relatively late in Egyptian history. Although the Hyksos are credited with this introduction there is no real evidence to connect the arrival of horses in Egypt to any invasion by foreigners.

The Egyptians adopted the Semitic names for both the horse and chariot, *susim* and *merkabot*, but for the horse, a new Egyptian name was also used, which perhaps sums up the Egyptians' thoughts on encountering the horse for the first time: translated, it means "the beautiful".

97. A horse. After a painting from the Tomb of Thanuny at Thebes.

The horse arrived too late in Egyptian history to be included in the pantheon of gods. One can but wonder what role the horse would have had, if it had been a native Egyptian animal. At the time of the New Kingdom, Egypt became influenced by the religions of other countries and horses were associated with the Canaanite goddess, Astarte, who was called the "Mistress of Mares".

Horses were small by modern standards and appear Arab-like in appearance, although the presence of skewbald horses (with brown and white dappled markings) indicates that there may not be an Arab connection, for this is not seen in the modern breed of the horse. Using the yoke measurements of the surviving chariots, an average height of about 1·35 metres (thirteen and a half hands) has been calculated.

The horse was introduced in conjunction with the chariot and it was this partnership that impacted greatly on the early New Kingdom and the expansion of the Egyptian Empire.

No training manuals survive for the horse owners, but it is assumed that the nobility would be schooled from an early age in the use of the chariot for hunting and warfare and in the care and training of the valuable animals. Experienced charioteers would teach others and we know that there was a royal appointment of "Master of the Chariots". Recruits into what was probably seen as an elite part of the army would have come from the homes of the upper classes.

Horses were clearly much loved and prized possessions. Amenhotep II, whilst still a prince, is said to have adored his horses and was "conversant with their training, having close acquaintance with their disposition." Ramesses III is recorded "inspecting the horses which his own hands have trained." A later ruler, Piye, having captured a city after a long siege, was concerned over the welfare of the horses and was distressed to find that they had not been fed properly during the hostilities.

The royal horses, which pulled the king's chariot, were given grandiose names. Those which pulled Ramesses II at the battle of Kadesh in 1275, were called "Victories in Thebes" and "May Mut be Satisfied".

Surveys near the vast site of the palace of Amenhotep III at Malkata, situated on the west bank of the river Nile opposite the city of Thebes, have revealed a straight stretch of desert from which all large stones and boulders have been removed. Four kilometres long and one hundred and twenty metres wide, this area may have been used as a training ground for the charioteers and horses. Other military ceremonies and events of state may also have been held here, such as the great *Heb-Sed* Jubilee festivals of the king which were celebrated in his regnal years thirty, thirty-four and thirty-seven.

Unlike ancient Rome, as far as we know, the Egyptians held no formalised sporting competitions such as chariot races, but it is more than likely that horse breeders and owners would be keen to show that they possessed the fastest horses and could drive their chariots better than anyone else. Locations such as Malkata would have been ideal for such events.

Horses adapted well to the climate of Egypt and they were raised in the fertile Delta area. Stud farms flourished and the stock was often improved by gifts to pharaoh of new horses from the Asiatic kings. Stable blocks were attached to most of the great palaces and estates and the horses were well cared for. The great Eighteenth Dynasty tomb of the Vizier Ramose, who served under two kings, Amenhotep III and Akhenaten, shows a horse in the hieroglyph inscriptions detailing his duties. Ramose was "Overseer of the Cattle" and these duties probably also included supervising the care of horses too.

Burials of horses are rare, but Senenmut, an important courtier from the time of Queen Hatshepsut (1498-1483) may have had his own horse buried near his tomb at Deir el Bahri,

99. *Hieroglyph of a horse in the titles of Ramose. Relief from his tomb at Thebes.*

although there is no archaeological evidence that the horse found there was indeed his. It must be presumed that this horse died a natural death, for there is no evidence or implication that the horse was killed to be included as part of the burial of Senenmut.

"Senenmut's horse" was about 1·5 metres in height (fifteen hands). The body was not mummified, but was simply wrapped in layers of linen, before being placed in a large, rough coffin. The horse was a mare and chestnut in colouring.

Apart from the figure presumed to be the goddess Astarte, mentioned above, representations of the riding of horses are rare. Certainly we know that the Asiatic nobility thought it undignified to ride the horse and preferred to be pulled in a chariot, and this seems to be the idea adopted by the Egyptians, at least in the early years of the Eighteenth Dynasty.

A scene from the Tomb of Horemheb at Sakkara shows a mounted rider, seated not on the horse's back, but directly above the animal's rear hips – the usual position for riding a donkey.

100. *Relief from the New Kingdom Tomb of Horemheb at Sakkara, showing a man, possibly a messenger, astride a horse in the so-called "donkey-*

Scenes from the battle reliefs of Ramesses II on the exterior walls of the first court of the Temple of Luxor also show horses with their riders in this position. However, the style of this depiction may have arisen because the artist was familiar with riders on donkeys rather than horses, and the scene may not portray the way horses were actually ridden. Later representations show the riders in the more conventional position although the artists sometimes incorrectly showed both legs of the rider on one side of the horse. The horses are equipped with a bridle and reins, but have no saddles or stirrups. Cloths are sometimes shown on the horses' backs for the riders to sit upon. The use of cloths was probably common, but the hard evidence has been lost to us. Such detail was often painted onto carved scenes, and the paint has been worn away over the centuries.

Surviving scenes on the walls of the Temple of Luxor, dating to the reign of Ramesses II, and also in the Mortuary Temple of Ramesses III at Medinet Habu show mounted men. These are usually identified as messengers, but the fact that they are holding weapons (as does the mounted figure mentioned above from the Tomb of Horemheb, who appears to hold a bow, whilst the Ramesses II relief scene shows a quiver) indicates that horses *were* used in battle. It is likely that, at least in the early years of the Eighteenth Dynasty, horses would have been considered too precious to risk in direct combat. Once, however, the "Egyptian" stock of horses had increased, the taking of risks with some animals might have been considered acceptable. A sustained and controlled breeding programme could dramatically increase the stock of horses within a relatively short period of time.

101. Man on a horse, from the battle reliefs of Ramesses II in the Temple of Luxor.

Towards the end of the Dynastic Period, the riding of horses must have been common because of the influence of the Greeks and Romans, although there is no direct evidence of this from Egyptian sources.

Both the horse and the chariot arrived relatively late in Egyptian history. The Egyptians soon adapted the original Canaanite chariot design, applying their own considerable carpentry skills to make lighter and faster vehicles. It is possible that, when first adopted by the Egyptians, the chariot was only used for hunting and as a means of transport for the aristocracy when visiting their estates. Akhenaten mounted his "great chariot of fine electrum" when he marked out the boundaries of his new city for the god Aten at Akhetaten.

It was in battle, however, that the chariot really made its mark. The New Kingdom pharaohs and their army commanders were quick to realise the full potential of this method of transport. Thutmose III (1504-1450) the pharaoh who pushed Egypt's boundaries further than any pharaoh before or after him, rode in his chariot at the battle of Megiddo and was described as setting out "on a chariot of fine gold".

Whole battalions of chariots were raised and Ramesses II is shown in many reliefs leading his chariots into action. The basic construction of all the chariots would have been the same, but those of the senior officers, and of the king in particular, were finely and richly decorated.

The practical use of chariots in battle is limited, as their use and the use of the horse as a weapon has never throughout history proved effective against well-entrenched and disciplined enemy infantry. Even Napoleon discovered this at the battle of Waterloo in 1815 AD, when the British infantry, who had formed up in defensive squares, could not be broken.

However, a division of chariots, galloping in close formation directly towards an enemy would have been extremely intimidating. Only the sturdiest and best-disciplined troops would have been able to stand their ground. In tight formation, the appearance of the attack would have seemed to have been like a moving wall rapidly, and noisily approaching through a cloud of dust and often literally making the ground shake. In a tight formation and with sufficient speed and momentum, the horse's natural inclination to veer away would have been overridden and the chariots would have been able to plough straight into any infantry.

Chariots were used as a swift-moving firing platform, from which arrows could be poured into the enemy. They were especially effective when attacking a disorganised enemy or one fleeing the field of battle. The use of chariots also greatly improved the means of communication during the confusion of battle. They enabled the king to keep in touch with his commanders and the divisions of his army and also to keep the commanders visible to their troops.

Horses, chariots and their occupants would have presented a large target for enemy archers, but if they were approaching at speed, and possibly partially hidden in clouds of dust, they would have been more difficult to hit. There may have also been some reluctance to shoot

102. Userhet, an officer from the reign of Amenhotep II, in his chariot. Painting from his tomb at Thebes.

the horses, since it may well have been seen as preferable to defeat the enemy and capture their valuable animals.

Many scenes showing chariots survive and are very detailed. The king is often shown in his chariot with his enemies trampled under the hooves of his horses. The conventions of the artists only show the chariots in profile, but from these representations alone we have a clear idea how they were made and used. In Egypt, however, we are fortunate in having actual examples of the chariots, which have been found in the funeral equipment buried with their owners. Sealed in tombs for thousands of years, they are in almost pristine condition.

The vehicles are two-wheeled, light carriages, designed to be drawn by two horses. Based on modern, accurate, reconstructions of ancient Egyptian chariots, we know that they weighed about thirty-four kilograms. This is light enough for them to have been manoeuvrable, and they could even be lifted by one person, if necessary.

By selecting woods best suited to the task and, no doubt, learning much from the first chariots to arrive in Egypt, the chariot-builders created vehicles whose main strength was their lightweight and flexible construction.

Ancient Egyptian woodworking skills are well known and evidenced by many superb examples of furniture, but perhaps this skill can best be seen in the construction of the chariot wheels, which are a triumph of both woodworking and engineering. The wheels needed to be light, but also very strong and the ancient craftsmen achieved success in meeting this difficult combination of requirements.

The surviving examples of chariot wheels are all just under one metre (about three feet) in diameter. Slight details vary. The earlier examples from the Eighteenth Dynasty, up to the reign of Thutmose IV, have only four spokes, whereas the later versions have six. Some reliefs show eight-spoked wheels, although no actual examples of these have been found and the six-spoked wheel seems to have been the norm.

It is likely that the chariot, as introduced to the Egyptians, had wheels with just four spokes, but that these were not found to be strong enough when used over rough ground. To be safe, the

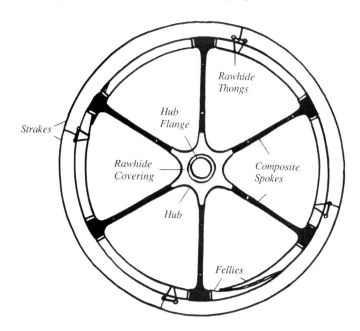

103. Diagram showing the component
parts of a chariot wheel.

Egyptians initially made their wheels with eight spokes, but then, presumably as the result of practical experience and testing in the field, found that six spokes produced a strong enough wheel. It is possible, therefore, to date scenes showing chariots by the number of spokes shown.

The spokes have a complicated, composite construction, with each spoke made from two pieces of wood. U-shaped elements of wood are used, the legs of two adjacent elements being glued back-to-back to form a single spoke. The bottom of the U was either joined to the wheel hub or formed the hub.

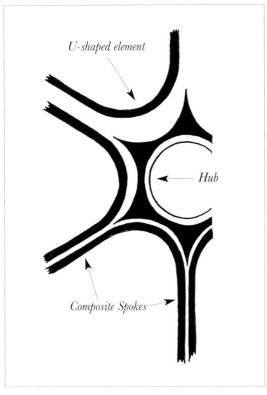

104. Diagram showing the construction of the spokes of a chariot wheel.

The rim of the wheel was usually made of two pieces of wood, known as "fellies", scarf-jointed together and secured by "felly bands". The outer rim of the wheel was made of bent pieces of timber known as strakes.

The wheelwrights stretched a green rawhide strip over the outer edge of the wheel, which served two purposes: firstly it provided a tyre and secondly, the rawhide shrank and tightened up all the elements of the wheel to consolidate the pieces. The leather tyres could easily be replaced when worn. This is exactly the same way as modern cartwheels are made, except that metal now replaces leather tyres.

The bodies of the chariots are small, with just room enough to enable two adults to stand side by side. The majority of scenes of chariots in use show a single occupant only, usually the king, and the reins are tied around his waist, leaving his hands free to use his weapons, usually a bow and arrow. Whilst this potentially dangerous technique *may* have been possible when hunting over known or prepared ground, it is doubtful if the king actually drove in his chariot alone. Ramesses II is shown alone in his chariot in the many reliefs of his famous battle of Kadesh, but the accompanying text always mentions his charioteer, who drove the chariot for him.

The floor plan of the chariot body is D-shaped. The rear of the body, the straight side of the "D", is formed of a solid bar of timber set directly over the axle. The framework of the sides and front of the body is made of bent wood with the spaces filled with leather or thin wooden panels. The floor was made from thongs of leather, often fitted with animal skins or other matting. This flexible construction of the floor was light and also acted as a shock absorber when the chariot was driven over rough ground.

The chariots intended for use in war had more solid sides made from either wood or laminated linen or leather, often given a plaster and gilt decoration. The hunting and sporting models had open sides. The chariot of Yuya has open sides, which could be filled by special leather hangings. The side and front rails also provided a ready handhold. It must have been

105. Chariot and horses. Painting from the Tomb of Nebamun.

essential under many driving conditions for the driver and other occupant of the chariot to have a secure hold. The back of the body was generally left open.

The wide wheel base, the positioning of the weight of the chariot body and of its occupants directly above the axle, and the lightness and flexibility of construction made the chariots fast and extremely manoeuvrable.

Additional equipment found with the chariots and shown in scenes on the walls of temples and tombs included bow cases, quivers for arrows, spear cases and a pouch for supplies. This

106. Ramesses II's horses, equipped with coloured cloths and ostrich feathers. A painted cast of a scene from the Temple of Beit el Wali in Nubia.

pouch may have contained items such as spare thonging for emergency repairs, or perhaps food and water for the charioteer.

The complex harnessing used for the horses is clearly detailed in reliefs and paintings, and has been confirmed by surviving examples (albeit fragmentary in most cases, for the leather has rarely survived). It is thus possible to see how the horses were used with the chariot. The chariot driver and his pair of horses would have needed to train together closely over a long period to be able to work effectively as a team and for the horses to recognise and obey the driver's commands.

The horses themselves were equipped with brightly coloured cloths to cover their backs and their bridles were adorned with ostrich feathers. In their brightly painted and gilded chariots and wearing their best clothes and jewellery, the chariot owners can have had no better way of proclaiming their wealth and status in society. The Egyptian chariot was the "Rolls Royce" of the ancient world and was used to impress the native Egyptians and to instil fear in their enemies.

The number of chariots in use in the Egyptian army at any one time must have been considerable, with a correspondingly large number of skilled workers needed to keep them in working order and repair any damage or wear and tear.

At the battle of Megiddo, Thutmose III captured nine hundred and twenty-four chariots and two thousand and forty-one horses, which then entered the Egyptian army. His son Amenhotep II, in successive campaigns, added nearly two thousand more chariots to the Egyptian army.

We also know that chariots were traded between nations. Records preserved from the time of Akhenaten record the fact that chariots were sent as gifts to Egypt from the rulers of Babylon and Assyria. Correspondence from Babylon to Egypt is also preserved, where the Babylonians ask for chariots and horses, so clearly the trade was a two-way affair.

The chariots of the enemies of Egypt appear to have been of similar construction, but much heavier and larger. In the Ramesses II Kadesh reliefs, the Hittite chariots are shown with three occupants. The extra weight must have made them less manoeuvrable and slower than the Egyptian chariots with just two occupants. We also know that their axles were in the middle of the chariot body, not at the rear of it as in the Egyptian chariots, which would also have severely affected manoeuvrability and stability. (In many reliefs, however, the Egyptian artists, being more familiar with the Egyptian version, have depicted the Hittite chariots inaccurately).

Thutmose IV's Chariot

When the Tomb of Thutmose IV in the Valley of the Kings was discovered in 1903 by Theodore Davis and Howard Carter, only fragments of what had been splendid pieces of funerary equipment were found. One of the largest surviving objects from the tomb was the badly damaged body of a chariot. This chariot body only hinted at the splendour of the chariots which Carter was to discover nineteen years later in the Tomb of Tutankhamun.

107. Detail of the decoration on the chariot body of Thutmose IV showing captured Asiatic prisoners.

Made of a wooden framework and panelling, the body of Thutmose's chariot is covered with fine linen and canvas overlaid with a layer of stucco plaster, into which elaborate scenes and ornamentation have been modelled in low relief. All the surfaces were originally covered in gold or possibly silver, but all the metal has been stripped away by robbers. The details of the decoration are, however, still clear from the plaster layer.

108. Drawing by Howard Carter of the decoration of the exterior of the right side of the body of the chariot of Thutmose IV.
The King is shown in the protective embrace of Montu.

The pictorial scenes are on four panels, two inside and two outside the body; they are divided by non-pictorial decorative panels. Howard Carter made detailed drawings of the scenes: the two exterior panels show the king mounted in his chariot and wielding a bow in one scene and an axe in another, confronting his enemies and causing havoc and destruction.

The two interior scenes, which are almost identical, show the king as a sphinx, trampling over his northern and southern enemies, with the hawk-headed god Montu standing behind him.

The survival of the coat of plaster and decoration of the chariot body has prevented a detailed examination of the method of its construction and the materials used, but it appears to be very solid and this chariot may well have been designed for use in battle.

If the details of the scenes shown on the side of the chariot body are accurate, the missing wheels of the chariot would have been made with eight spokes, which would have made them very strong, but still light, quite suitable for riding over unprepared ground.

109. Drawing by Howard Carter of the decoration of the interior of the left side of the body of the chariot of Thutmose IV.

Yuya's Chariot

Yuya was the father of Queen Tiye, Great Wife of Amenhotep III. He was originally a priest in the temple of the god Min at Akhmim. After the marriage of his daughter to the king, Yuya and his wife Thuya were elevated in status and given favours by the king. Yuya was appointed to the important position of Commander of the Chariots.

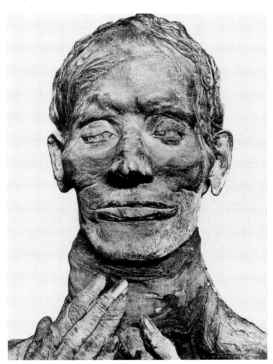

110. The mummy of Yuya.

When Yuya and Thuya died around 1365, they were given the rare honour of a tomb in the Valley of the Kings. Theodore Davis discovered the tomb in 1905 AD. Although it had been robbed in antiquity, a large proportion of the funerary equipment survived intact. It was fitting that a chariot was included in the grave goods of the Commander of Chariots. It was found at one end of the small burial chamber on top of a layer of pots. The pole of the chariot had been broken off, either by robbers, or at the time of burial, when those responsible for stacking all the objects in the small chamber may have found it easier to manoeuvre the chariot without its pole.

In many respects, this chariot is similar to the examples found in the Tomb of Tutankhamun, but it is at least fifty years earlier in date.

The body of the chariot is made of wood overlaid with canvas which has been plastered

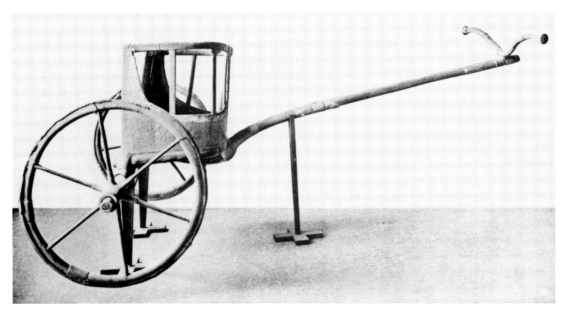

111. Chariot found in the Tomb of Yuya and Thuya.

and gilded. The floor of the body is made from woven leather straps, over which was placed a piece of red leather. This piece of leather was very brittle and little of it remains today.

The open spaces of the chariot body were originally filled in with pieces of red leather. Only one piece still remains in place at the rear of the chariot and it is edged with a strip of green appliqué leather.

The inside of the chariot body is painted green and the outside is covered by gilt decoration, applied over a layer of plaster. The entire surface is decorated in relief, although the outlines appear indistinct, as if they were carved whilst the plaster was still moist. The main decorations are floral and geometric designs, but at the front of the body there is shown a large floral bouquet with an antelope on either side of it (perhaps some allusion to the use of the chariot for hunting).

The rear of the chariot body is partly enclosed, unlike all the other surviving examples, which have open backs.

The chariot is small in size and it could not have been pulled by the usual full-sized horses. It is possible that this chariot may have been made especially for funerary use and could be considered as a large-scale "tomb model". It is equally possible that smaller-scale chariots were made. It is tempting to think that, as Master of the Chariots, Yuya would have been responsible for teaching the skills of a charioteer to the princes of Amenhotep III, including Amenhotep IV (Akhenaten), and that this reduced-scale chariot was used for this purpose. It could also have been used by the young princess Sitamun, the eldest daughter (and later wife) of Amenhotep III. Chairs belonging to the princess were found amongst the other funerary items from the Tomb of Yuya and Thuya. This might explain the partly-enclosed chariot body, which would make the vehicle much safer for novice riders. When Yuya died, this chariot may no longer have been needed, or may have been nearing the end of its working life and been available for use in the afterlife, when its size may not have been considered important.

When new, the chariot would have presented a colourful appearance, with its gilt

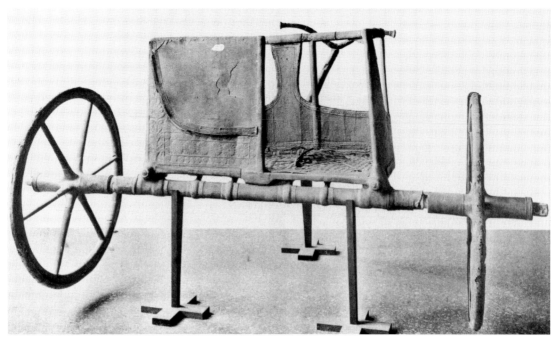

112. Rear view of the chariot found in the Tomb of Yuya and Thuya.

decoration and red and green leather. Even today, with the red now faded to a deep pink, the chariot, now in the Egyptian Museum, Cairo, is a spectacular object. It is evident from the apparent lack of wear that the chariot was in good condition when it was buried. Perhaps it was given a last refurbishment in readiness for the final journey. It would appear to have been carried to its final resting place, judging by the complete absence of any wear marks on the leather tyres.

Tutankhamun's Chariots

Other surviving complete examples of chariots came from the Tomb of Tutankhamun, in the Valley of the Kings, which was discovered by Howard Carter and Lord Carnarvon in 1922 AD.

Although plundered by robbers on at least two occasions, the tomb still contained a vast amount of funerary equipment and objects, which the young king had used during his lifetime. Tutankhamun remains the only pharaoh to have been found undisturbed in the tomb in which he was laid to rest around 1325.

Included in the jumbled heaps of furniture and funerary objects were six chariots. Four were found in the Antechamber of the tomb and the other two in the room known as the Treasury.

All the chariots had been dismantled in order to get them into the tomb. This "dismantling" included the sawing through of the axles and the removal of the wheels. The component parts of the chariots were all stacked together, but no attempt had been made to re-assemble them in the tomb. The Tomb of Tutankhamun is exceptionally small, when compared with other royal tombs in the Valley of the Kings. In the larger tombs, there would have been sufficient space to accommodate complete chariots.

As with most of the objects in the tomb, the chariots were well preserved, although most of the leather had decayed. This has made it impossible to reconstruct the exact form of the

113. One of Tutankhamun's state chariots.

harnesses, which would have been included in the equipment. The horses were controlled by either bitted bridles, or by a noseband, placed low on the head of the horse to exert pressure on the sensitive part of the nose. Four long reins, two to each horse, were attached to the ends of the mouthpiece of the bits.

The tomb also contained many elements of related equipment, the exact uses of some of which remain obscure. These items include whips, fly whisks, and blinkers for the horses, all heavily decorated with gold and inlay. Various purely decorative elements were also found, such as gilded figures of hawks, with solar discs on their heads. These may have been fitted to the poles of the chariots.

Two of the chariots were instantly recognised by Carter as "State Chariots" because of their splendid decoration. Gold and coloured inlay was lavishly used over a

114. Detail of the decoration of the body of one of Tutankhamun's state chariots, showing the god Bes.

backing of plaster. These are the chariots Tutankhamun would have used for parade and ceremonial occasions.

Both these state chariots were found dismantled in the southeast corner of the Antechamber of the tomb. Only fragments of the flooring, which was of leather, remain.

Two other dismantled chariots were found in the jumble of the Antechamber. One was only slightly less ornate than the state chariots, and was still covered in gold. The other is heavier in design and undecorated, and may have been a practical travelling chariot or a war chariot.

The remaining two examples were both found in the Treasury of the tomb. Both are much lighter in construction than the other four examples from the tomb and are gilded only in places. They were probably used for hunting. It is known that the king was a keen hunter, as there are many scenes on objects in the tomb that show him hunting lions, gazelles and ostriches. On these occasions, and on the battle scenes on his painted chest, the king is accompanied by his courtiers and personal bodyguard in their own chariots.

115. Tutankhamun's courtiers in their chariots. Detail from the painted chest of Tutankhamun.

Some damage was caused to the chariots by the robberies in the tomb and many of the fittings, which were probably heavily gilded and portable, were stolen. Humidity in the tomb had caused great damage to the leather, which effectively melted. From the surviving fragments it is possible to determine that the leather was probably coloured (as with the surviving examples from the Tomb of Yuya and Thuya) and in many cases was covered with gold.

All the chariots found in the Tomb of Tutankhamun were real vehicles, which the king used in his lifetime and which he took with him in death. It must be supposed that all the other later royal tombs had their full compliment of chariots buried with their owners, but apart from the examples mentioned here, no others have, as yet, been found. Numerous detailed reliefs do survive, however, showing the great warrior pharaohs, Seti I and Ramesses II riding in chariots, identical to those of Tutankhamun. Once the design and manufacture of these vehicles had been perfected, it remained unchanged.

3 THE GODS OF WAR

The mythology and religion of ancient Egypt is complex and beyond the scope of this book. However, in times of conflict, successive pharaohs invoked the assistance of various gods. If they were successful on campaign, the victorious pharaohs gave full credit to the gods, whose temples received their share of any plunder.

We also know that the names of some gods were given to divisions of the army and that images of the gods were paraded before the troops. Presumably priests of those particular gods accompanied the army on campaign.

Unlike other cultures, the gods of Egypt do not sit in little compartments, neatly labelled "god of this" or "god of that". To complicate matters still further, over the three thousand year span of history the attributes of some gods became associated with other gods, and their individual popularity waxed and waned.

We will look here briefly at the principal gods who are mentioned in this book in connection with military matters.

AMUN

The name of Amun means "The Hidden One" and he is sometimes described as the god of the wind. His principal temple was at Karnak which is today the largest known religious complex in the world.

Amun is shown as a man, wearing a crown with two tall plumes attached. He was initially a local god of Thebes, but from the Middle Kingdom onwards, and particularly in the New Kingdom, the kings, who came from Thebes, raised Amun to a position of eminence nationally.

116. The god Amun. Relief from the Mortuary Temple of Ramesses III at Medinet Habu.

117. The god Amun presenting Ramesses II with weapons. Scene from the Temple of Ramesses II at Abu Simbel.

ANHUR

Anhur was associated with war, but mainly in the later periods of Egyptian history. He was later identified by the Greeks with their god of war Ares. Anhur is shown as a bearded man carrying a spear or rope and wearing a crown topped by four plumes.

BES

Bes was a dwarf god, shown with fearsome features, a long beard and the ears and mane of a lion. Despite his ferocious appearance, he was primarily a protector of the family and a household deity, particularly connected with childbirth and sexuality. His image appears on a number of domestic objects, including chairs and beds throughout the Dynastic Period.

This protection extended to the king too and it is interesting to see that the image of Bes appears on one of the chariots of Tutankhamun. His ferocious nature seems to have been promoted in the Roman Period, when the god is shown carrying a round shield and a sword.

118. The god Anhur.

119. Bes as a war god, shown carrying a sword and shield.

120. The traditional appearance of Bes as a dwarf.

MONTU

Montu was another local god of Thebes and Armant; he is the personification of the aggressive aspects of the king.

Depicted with the head of a falcon, he was associated with war and had a major temple at Karnak. His name was included in the names of the Middle Kingdom pharaohs who re-unified the country and made Thebes one of the principal cities and cult centres. The early Middle Kingdom rulers called themselves Mentuhotep; however, later rulers of the period took the name Amenemhat when they favoured the other main Theban god, Amun.

121. The falcon-headed god Montu from the Temple of Tod.

PTAH

Ptah is represented as a mummiform human figure, whose hands protrude from the wrappings to hold his sceptre, made up from an *ankh* symbol, a *djed* pillar and a *was* sceptre. He is shown wearing a tightly-fitting skullcap.

Ptah was an important god throughout Egyptian history. He was the creator god of Memphis.

The importance of Ptah is often overshadowed by other gods, mainly because of the monumental remains of the Temple of Amun at Karnak. Ptah's own temple in Memphis would have been just as large, if not larger, and as splendid, but only the foundations and a few very badly damaged portions remain today. The close proximity of modern Cairo has meant that the site has been used for centuries as a convenient quarry, with the stone going to build much of the medieval city.

122. Gilded wooden figure of the god Ptah, from the Tomb of Tutankhamun.

123. *The sun god Ra, as Ra-Horakhty, from the Temple of Ramesses II at Abu Simbel.*

124. *The sun god, the Aten, spreading his rays on Akhenaten and Nefertiti.*

RA AND THE ATEN

Ra was the great falcon-headed sun god, whose cult centre was at Heliopolis, just north of modern Cairo. He became especially important from the Fourth Dynasty, when his worship was at its peak and the pharaohs included the name of the god as part of theirs.

Over the centuries, Ra became associated with other gods, notably Horus as Ra-Horakhty and Amun as Amun-Ra. He was perhaps the most visible of the gods of Egypt for his disk could be seen in the sky each day.

It was an aspect of the sun god that was worshipped by Akhenaten in the Eighteenth Dynasty, when the god Aten briefly gained prominence over the other principal gods of Egypt.

The Aten is shown as a solar disk whose rays give the breath of life to Akhenaten and Nefertiti. After the reign of Akhenaten and his immediate successors, the worship of the Aten was abandoned and the cult of Amun restored. Images of the Aten (and of the kings who worshipped him) were erased from the monuments.

The principal temple to the Aten was at Akhenaten's new city of Akhetaten (now known as Tell el Amarna) in Middle Egypt.

SEKHMET

Sekhmet was the consort of Ptah and was the lioness-headed goddess of war, the personification of the aggressive aspects of female deities. Her name means "She who is Powerful".

In the New Kingdom, Sekhmet was seen as the aggressive aspect of the goddess Mut, consort to Amun. Hundreds of statues of her as a lioness-headed woman were erected in the temple of Mut at Karnak by Amenhotep III, and fine examples can be seen in many museum collections today.

125. Statue of the goddess Sekhmet, originally from the Temple of Mut at Karnak.

SET

Set was seen as the god of chaos, of storms and of confusion. He is shown with the body of a man but with the head of a strange dog-like animal, with long, square-tipped ears.

It was Set who killed his brother Osiris and who engaged in a long and bloody struggle with Horus, son of Osiris. Horus gained the throne, but the conflict between Horus and Set continued, symbolising the constant battle between good and evil.

126. The god Set, detail from a statue of the god with Ramesses III and Horus.

Whilst the pharaoh and his appointed priests could talk directly to the gods and invoke their help, it is not known how Egyptian soldiers approached religion when on campaign. Perhaps they had their own favoured gods, maybe the local gods of their hometowns, or perhaps they were content to leave such matters to the pharaoh and the priests.

4 THE ARMY: A SOLDIER'S LOT

The following text, preserved on the "Papyrus Anastasi 3", was written during the reign of Seti II around 1210, but the text probably dates to a much earlier period. The hardships of being a soldier are pointed out by a scribe to a potential recruit to the army, one Inena.

> "What is it that you say they relate, that the soldier's is more pleasant than the scribe's (profession)? Come let me tell you the condition of the soldier, that much castigated one. He is brought while a child to be confined in the camp. A searing beating is given to his body, an open wound inflicted on his eyebrows. His head is split open with a wound. He is laid down and beaten like papyrus. He is struck with torments.
> Come; let me relate to you his journey to Khor and his marching upon the hills. His rations and water are upon his shoulder like the load of an ass, while his neck has been made a backbone like that of an ass. The vertebrae of his back are broken, while he drinks of foul water. He stops work only to keep watch. He reaches the battle and he is like a plucked fowl. He proceeds to return to Egypt, and he is like a stick which the worm has devoured. He is sick, prostration overtakes him. He is brought back upon an ass, his clothes taken away by theft, his henchmen fled. ... turn back from the saying that the soldier's is more pleasant than the scribe's profession."

We know Inena heeded this advice, as he became a scribe, *not* a soldier.

The amazing thing about this passage is that, although it was written well over three thousand years ago, the sentiments expressed would have been familiar to soldiers through the ages; as much to those who fought with the English King Henry V at the battle of Agincourt (AD 1415) as to those who fought at the Somme (AD 1915).

A soldier's lot has never been a happy one and this brief passage gives us a vivid insight into the *real* life of a soldier, not just in Dynastic Egypt, but in more recent times and in different lands.

The first "armies" were probably seen in Predynastic Egypt: any able-bodied man who was able to use a weapon would be available to defend his village from the attacks of man or beast. The ability to use some type of weapon would have been common in a world where hunting wild animals was necessary to provide food.

The effective use of a weapon is important to a soldier, but *motivation* is essential. The defence of one's home and family has always been one of the strongest incentives to violence. If motivation is sufficiently strong, then bare hands can prove as effective as clubs or spears. If this personal motivation is *lacking*, then strong discipline and training can also produce an effective warrior, who will do exactly as he is told without question.

The unification of Egypt was probably achieved by military activity and it is likely that by 3150 there were a number of formal trained armies, or local militia groups, fighting for superiority. There must have been, at some time before this, a critical period, when the transition was made from a group of men who could and would fight *if* specific circumstances dictated it, to a more organised, permanent and disciplined fighting force, who would fight simply when *ordered* to do so.

THE NEW RECRUIT

It is likely that recruits were taken into the army at an early age. Most Egyptian families would have been large, even with a high infant mortality rate, and feeding such large families may at times have been difficult. Families may have been encouraged, or perhaps even compelled, to send one or more sons into the army: – a form of conscription. In Egypt today, conscription is compulsory for virtually all adult males, but, interestingly, if there is only one son in a family, then he is exempt. This may have been the case in Ancient Egypt too, where sons took on the professions and skills of their fathers and needed to remain at home to help the family. If a family had only one son, it would fall to him to take on the skills and occupation of his father to ensure the family was supported.

The prospects for employment in Ancient Egypt were limited and for most people were restricted to agricultural work or semi-skilled manual work. The more skilled professions tended to remain within specific families, with the skills passed from father to son. This continuity was important to both the family and the country.

Military service began at the age of twenty, although this was lower in later periods. We do not know how long a soldier had to serve in the army – possibly a year – before being allowed to return to his village, but he would have been liable to be called to arms at any time for military operations or campaigns. In later periods it is clear that many soldiers served in the army for longer periods as a career.

A military life has always had a certain appeal and glamour, even if the reality is actually quite different. The modern idea of joining the army and seeing the world would have been just as valid in ancient Egypt. Travelling to new and exciting places might be one incentive, but one additional factor, common to all periods of history, was the prospect of booty and plunder. Virtually every victorious army in history has returned home with plunder. Whilst the officers invariably commandeered the best and most valuable items, the common soldiers rarely returned empty-handed.

127. Scene from the New Kingdom Tomb of Nebamun, showing a man herding cattle.

Plunder in ancient times would have included not just precious objects, but also women, cattle (always a valuable commodity), and even ordinary domestic items looted from enemy encampments or captured towns and villages.

These benefits were often enough to override the obvious drawback to a military life: the possibility of injury or death. Soldiers throughout history have either faced voluntarily, or have been forced to face, this major military "fact of life". Most seem to be able to put it to the very back of their minds and work on the often mistaken belief that "it won't happen to me".

During most of the Old Kingdom, there was probably no need for a permanent standing army (other than a small unit as a royal bodyguard). If an army were needed, young men were recruited or, as is more likely, conscripted for specific purposes, be it a military campaign or some civil engineering work. We know that Pepi I raised such an army for a campaign in Palestine and that many soldiers were recruited or conscripted for him by the provincial governors of Egypt. An inscription dating to around 2300 describes a military campaign into Palestine, with "... tens of thousands of conscripts".

During the First Intermediate Period, the provincial governors, who at this time had assumed more power as a result of the weakening central command of the pharaoh, were raising small armies for their own use and protection. At the start of the Middle Kingdom, Amenemhat I, like Pepi I before him, had also to rely on his provincial governors to raise a force to fight in Nubia, but by the end of this period, Senuseret III had exerted his control and was able to raise an army himself. At this time there was a need for more full-time soldiers to man the many garrisons on Egypt's frontiers and particularly in Nubia.

Turning a new, raw recruit into a soldier has never been an easy task and the process, once developed, probably changed little over the centuries. Techniques first recorded in ancient Egypt would be clearly recognisable to recruits into any army today, and were probably just as effective, if slightly more brutal than modern sensibilities allow.

128. New recruits as shown in the Tomb of Userhet at Thebes.

A scene from the Theban tomb of the scribe Userhet, dating to the reign of Amenhotep II, shows new recruits being registered by scribes. Another scene shows them receiving their obligatory new military haircut, the ancient equivalent of the "short back and sides" given to recruits into the army today and an essential part of the process of removing any individuality.

129. New recruits receiving their military haircut, Scene from the Tomb of Userhet at Thebes.

Training in the use of weapons is, of course, a vital part of the "militarisation" process, but the *most* important part of the process is the turning of a free-thinking individual into a soldier. A well-trained and disciplined soldier will do *exactly* what he is told to do, even if his natural instincts tell him otherwise, to the extent of killing when told to do so.

In most societies (and Egypt was no exception) the killing of a fellow human was taboo and punishable. The militarisation process had to break this taboo and turn new recruits into killers.

It is possible that new recruits were subject to some form of "initiation ritual", of the type common in military life throughout the centuries and in all cultures, although any direct proof of this is lacking. In armies today, and historically, it is usual for there to be a formal swearing of an "oath of allegiance" to the sovereign or ruler, but again there is no evidence that this happened in Egypt. Knowing, however, how the Egyptians worked, some form of oath seems likely.

The initial process appears to have involved a certain brutalisation and de-humanising of the new recruit – the "searing beating" mentioned in Papyrus Anastasi.

The ancient Egyptian equivalent of sergeant majors would set to work to break the recruit's spirit, using a harsh combination of physical work and exercise together with physical and verbal abuse. The men would be subjected to a vigorous fitness regime and scenes survive showing men undertaking what we know as "weight training" to build up their strength, using weights made of bags filled with sand.

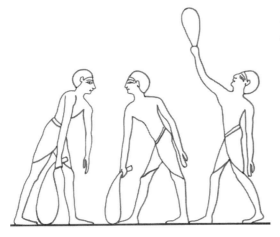

130. Men exercising using bags of sand as weights. From a tomb at Beni Hassan.

Wrestling also seems to have been a part of this training and to have been a popular activity throughout the Dynastic Period, as was a form of boxing.

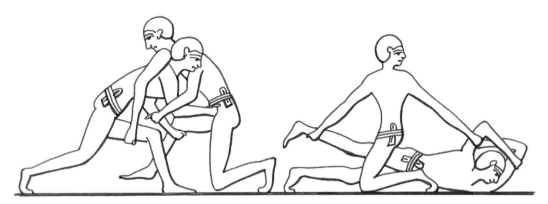

131 Men wrestling; Middle Kingdom scene from a tomb at Beni Hassan.

132. Men wrestling; New Kingdom drawing on an ostracon.

The recruit would be driven up to and past the pain barrier and on to absolute breaking point, to the stage where he gave in to the pressure and relinquished completely his free will and the ability to think for himself. Once this point was reached the recruit would do *anything* he was told, without question. This was the ancient equivalent of getting modern recruits to do seemingly meaningless and senseless tasks, like painting stones or cleaning floors with a toothbrush! This was the first and critical stage and, for any new recruit, probably the most unpleasant.

The "sergeant-majors" would then set about moulding the new recruit into a soldier, giving him back some of his self-esteem and instilling in him a team spirit. Drill and the training in the use of weapons would continue, along with more physical activities. Weapon training was an essential and an on-going process, which would continue right through any soldier's military career.

Knives were thrown at wooden targets and sword skills were perfected in a form of stick fighting, where wooden sticks replaced edged weapons. In this activity the left arm was protected by an arm guard, which could also be used to parry any blows. (A form of stick fighting still survives in Egypt today and although the moves are now more stylised, the origins probably lie in a military past). The new recruits might drill and play hard, but it was important not to incur *too* many injuries whilst training.

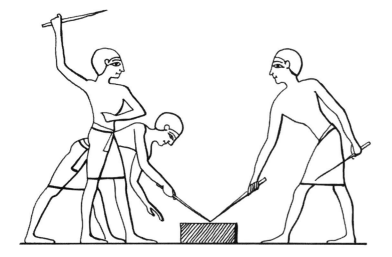

133. Men throwing knives at a wooden target. From a tomb at Beni Hassan.

134. Men fighting with sticks and arm guards. From a tomb at Thebes.

Many scenes of such activities are preserved on the walls of tombs from all periods of Egyptian history. These competitive activities encouraged teamwork and also individual skills and prowess.

At the end of the period of training, the recruit would be much fitter (certainly physically and most probably mentally too) than before and a real member of a team, where group solidarity was all-important.

It would seem that the soldiers were issued with their weapons when they were specifically needed and the event was made a formal occasion. We know that Ramesses III supervised such an issuing of weapons in person. From a platform in front of the army he issued the order "Bring forth the weapons, bring them out into the open so that the courage of my father Amun may humble the rebellious lands which know not Egypt!"

The weapons were stacked in piles, swords in one pile, bows and arrows in another and so on. The soldiers, wearing nothing but their simple kilts, advanced in single file and collected their weapons. A large number of scribes were present to record the number of weapons issued. (No doubt they would also check them all back into store after use, too.)

Discipline in the Egyptian army, like any other army in history, must have been strict, although there is little hard evidence to go on. We know that farmers were punished for failing to pay their annual taxes and the severity of the punishment imposed reflected the severity of the crime. For a minor offence it seems to have been a simple beating across the back by one man. If the misdemeanour was greater, then the guilty party was stripped, tied to a post and beaten by *two* men. Such punishments were probably applied to any offences in the army too.

In a rare, but sadly fragmentary, document from the reign of Horemheb, there are lists of practical legislation intended to deal with the abuses of tax collectors and anyone who stole from the population. One specific section deals with soldiers who steal cattle and appears to be based on an actual case.

Tax collectors went to collect the taxes from the population and were told that goods intended to pay taxes had just been stolen by some soldiers. The king decreed that the people should not be punished for non-payment of taxes if they had been the victims of crime. The penalty for soldiers caught effectively looting in their own country, was "… a beating of one hundred blows, opening five wounds and taking from him by force all the hides he took".

The most serious offences would have probably warranted even more severe punishment, ranging from the severing of ears and noses, to capital punishment for offences such as treason or cowardice.

135. A hieroglyphic determinative, showing a man being impaled on a stake.

In any army, stepping out of line by an individual needs to be swiftly and publicly dealt with, in order to maintain discipline and obedience. This is still the case today and we can easily imagine ancient Egyptian "courts martial" taking place as and when required. Once a clear code of conduct had been established, it needed to be maintained and this applied to civilian as well as military life. Each individual knew the rules and his own place and role in society and transgressed at his peril.

After their period of initial training was complete, the new recruits would be absorbed into existing units of the army, each of which had its own identity. We know that the army of Ramesses II at the Battle of Kadesh had four major divisions, each with a separate identity and a recognisable standard, and that these units were sub-divided into smaller units. This produced rivalry both within and between units, which encouraged the soldiers to perform better. By scattering new recruits amongst existing established units, the experience and training of veteran soldiers could be passed on. Training would continue as the new entrants drilled and exercised with the more experienced men of their new unit.

Once soldiers had seen action and the taboo of killing had been overcome, then killing again invariably became easier as they became battle-hardened. The hard-earned experience of the veterans and mercenaries would be passed on to the new soldiers, who would probably be treated fairly harshly in their new unit. Once again, some form of initiation into a regiment may well have been the norm in a process that would further help to strengthen the group solidarity of the unit.

THE STRUCTURE OF THE ARMY

By the New Kingdom, there was a need for a *permanent* standing army, ready and able to go on campaign at short notice.

The army had a clearly defined hierarchy and structure, with a recognised chain of command, which is essential for any efficient fighting force. With full-time soldiers in a permanent army, there was the potential for men to rise through the ranks, through merit, skill or experience.

The bulk of the army was comprised of infantry (foot soldiers) and was organised into divisions; each with about five thousand men. Each division bore the name of a god, perhaps the principal god of the region where the division had been raised. The name of the god was followed by an epithet, such as "Amun – Rich in Bows". A division of the army was commanded by a general known as the "Great Overseer of the Division", who would usually have been a son of the king. Age appears not to have been a major concern or a handicap to such an appointment, although it is likely that such generals did not exercise direct command, this work being done, at least whilst the princes were still minors, by senior army officers.

In the New Kingdom, we know that in the reign of Horemheb the army had two divisions which corresponded to the north and south of the country, and this may well have been the case in earlier times too. As the Egyptian Empire grew, a larger army was needed; by the time of Seti I, there were three divisions and by the reign of Ramesses II, the number had increased to four.

The basic unit of the army was the platoon, which was made up of fifty men, commanded by a "Chief of Fifty". Five platoons made up a company and twelve companies made up a division. The platoon itself was made up of squads, each of ten men.

The Structure of the Army in the New Kingdom

Division:	5,000	men
Host:	500	men (at least 2 Companies)
Company:	250	men (5 Platoons)
Platoon:	50	men (5 Squads)
Squad:	10	men

The divisions of the infantry were supported by smaller companies of elite troops, made up of experienced or specially trained soldiers. In the New Kingdom, the cavalry (essentially the chariots) made up a separate specialist unit, which was used to support the infantry.

In addition to the regular Egyptian soldiers, the Egyptian army also often included mercenaries, soldiers who volunteered and were paid for their services. Medjay troops, mercenaries from the eastern deserts in Nubia, were used in the Early Dynastic period. The Medjay were employed as scouts and as light infantry troops.

By the time of Amenhotep III in the New Kingdom, the army included in its ranks Syrians, Libyans, Sherden and even some Hittites. These soldiers were usually defeated enemy who had been given their freedom (and their lives) on the proviso that they changed their allegiance and fought for Egyptian army.

Libyan mercenaries are shown wearing distinctive feathers in their hair and seem to have been experts in the use of spears and kepesh daggers. The Sherden appear mainly in the time of Ramesses II in his campaigns against the Hittites.

136. Sherden mercenaries. Relief from the Temple of Ramesses II at Abydos.

137. A Syrian mercenary drinking beer. Relief found at Tell el Amarna.

The Sherden also fought with a spear and dagger and are shown wearing helmets surmounted by horns and a disc.

Surviving evidence shows that some of these mercenaries enjoyed a good life style. Many settled in Egypt when they retired from active service and married Egyptian wives.

Officers were probably also recruited into the army at an early age. Most will have come from the families of the nobility, although there were some field-promotions of men from the ranks. In the New Kingdom there appear to have been special schools for the sons of wealthy families, military academies almost, where new officers were trained in the use of weapons, especially in the use of chariots. They also presumably learnt military tactics and the skills needed to command units of the army.

When the Egyptian (or any army) was on campaign, it was in effect a small city on the move, and like any community it needed a large number of non-military skills to keep it functioning and to support the combat troops.

Many of the Egyptian soldiers were probably multi-skilled, insofar as they could turn their hands to a number of different tasks, and undertake duties they had performed in their civilian lives. These might include the roles of barbers, cooks and armourers. Other specific skills needed included those of quartermasters, adjutants and scribes.

Scribes were an essential part of the administration of the army. They were needed to record the events in any campaign, sometimes in bloody detail, for it seems to have been the scribes who were employed to count and officially record the severed body parts of slain enemy troops.

138. Scribes at work, from the Memphite Tomb of Horemheb.

Whilst on campaign, there must have been a great deal of correspondence between the absent court and the Egyptian administration at home. Dispatches came from the ends of the empire and needed to be read, recorded and replied to. Good field communications were vital, as they still are today.

The titles of scribes recorded at some Nubian forts include "army scribe" and "master of the secrets of the king". The latter duty is probably of great importance. In an age where literacy levels were low, reports and orders could be passed in writing and only be accessible to those senior officials who could read (or who themselves had access to their own scribes).

Correspondence survives dealing with the close surveillance of the area around the fortresses and the submission of regular reports to the military commanders. Even over three thousand years ago paper-work occupied much time and effort. Some things never change!

Surviving evidence shows the efficiency and organisation of the army. In the fortress of Uronaroti, wooden tokens were found that, it would appear, were issued to soldiers which could be exchanged for bread.

The following chart shows the structure of the army and chain of command in the New Kingdom, including the non-combatant arm.

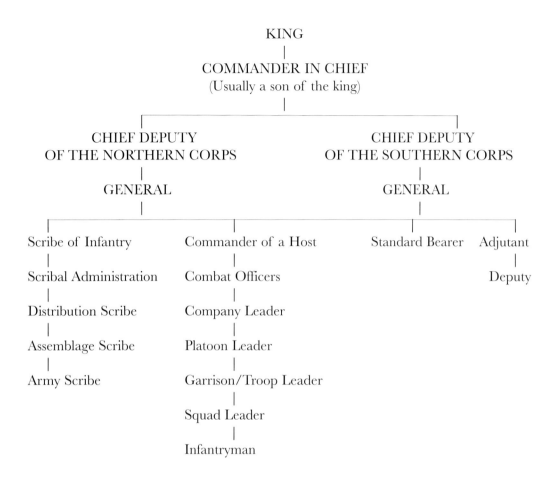

MILITARY STANDARDS

An important position in the army was that of standard bearer and the standard carried was a vital piece of military equipment.

Throughout history, a military standard, be it a Roman Eagle or a large brightly coloured piece of material, has been part of military life. A standard was needed for a purely practical purpose: to enable members of individual troops or companies to recognise that unit's location. In the confusion of a hand-to-hand battle it is all too easy to become disorientated and separated from one's colleagues and some way of locating them could be a matter of life or death.

A standard, raised on a tall pole, could be clearly seen by the soldiers and would be used as a rallying point. Standards were also seen as an embodiment of a regiment's identity, and the thing which made it different from other regiments. Recognition of the standard by the individual members of its company was vital, which is why, even today in ceremonies like the "Trooping of the Colour", standards are paraded before the troops, so they can see and remember its distinctive design.

140. Examples of Egyptian military standards.

141. Military standards being carried by soldiers of Hatshepsut. Relief from the Mortuary Temple of Queen Hatshepsut at Deir el Bahri.

139. A nome standard on a statue of Menkaura of the Old Kingdom.

Standards were also useful to the commander of the army, who could see the progress across the battlefield of individual units. Without such identifiable "markers" the battles would simply appear to be a seething mass of men and dust.

The form of the standard in Egypt varied. Most were simply a tall pole supporting a small platform, on which was a three-dimensional figure or effigy. It could be the image of a particular god, or perhaps the emblem of one of the nomes of Egypt. In its simplest form it could just be tall ostrich feathers, sometimes with coloured streamers attached.

Standards are seen today as the embodiment of the "spirit" of a regiment. Great care has always been taken to ensure that a unit's pride is not damaged by standards' being captured by the enemy, and it may be that the Egyptians regarded their standards in the same way.

142. Gilded figure of a hawk on a pole, similar to military or nome standards. From the Tomb of Tutankhamun.

MILITARY DRESS

Part of the de-personalisation process, which also helped a recruit with his new group identity, was the use of a uniform dress. For the Egyptians, during most of the historical period, the standard male dress, for both the military and civilians, was a simple white linen kilt or loincloth, although over the centuries the design, length and cut of the kilt changed.

A standard uniform does much to take away the individuality of each soldier, making him both look and feel part of the group. Small differences, such as a coloured collar or belt could be used to identify individual units if this were needed.

Kilts were made from a simple triangle of linen. The base of the triangle was placed around the back of the wearer and the two corners tied in front of the body. The third corner was pulled between the legs and under the other tied corners and then allowed to hang down in front of the body. Some of the kilts shown in reliefs appear to have the front padded or stiffened, to provide some additional (if limited) protection to this particularly vulnerable part of the body. Exactly how effective these kilts would be must be a matter of conjecture as no example of the padded or stiffened kilts has survived. The only evidence we have for many of these is from reliefs, paintings or sculpture which does not give us any idea how they were actually constructed.

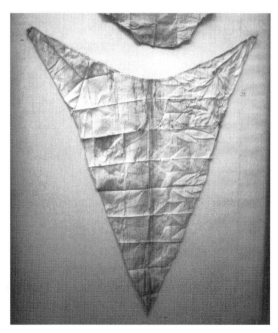

143. Loincloth from the Tomb of Tutankhamun.

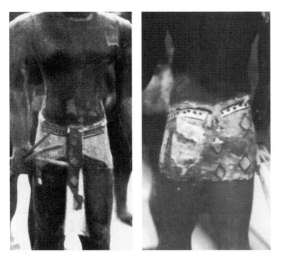

Surviving articles of clothing from the Tomb of Tutankhamun, include loincloths, which were effectively underwear for the King, worn beneath the larger and more elaborate kilts. Such loincloths may, however, have been the sole article of clothing for the poorer classes and soldiers.

One notably different style of kilt is seen in the well-known Middle Kingdom tomb-model of Mesehti at Assuit. It shows Nubian archers who wear elaborate green and red loincloths, which were probably made of leather. Leather was much easier to obtain in Nubia than linen. Some of the men wear predominantly white kilts, with bright red decoration, whilst others wear red kilts with white decoration. The seemingly random

144. Leather (?) kilts worn by Nubian archers. Middle Kingdom tomb-model.

distribution of the different kilts between the men implies that they were not used to differentiate between a rank or file of men, although there is no reason why different coloured kilts could not have been used for different companies of men. The soldiers in this model all wear a green collar or necklace and similarly coloured anklets.

145. Nubian Mercenaries, wearing distinctive leather skins over their kilts and carrying a military standard depicting wrestling men.

146. Example of a gazelle-skin leather kilt.

Another distinctive piece of clothing, seen in the New Kingdom, is a leather skin worn over the kilt. A whole gazelle skin was used to make this unusual garment. The hide was slashed with very fine cuts using a sharp implement, so that it resembles a net, although a square area was left intact at the seat. The slashing made the skin more flexible.

Exactly why such a strange piece of clothing was used is not known, but it is believed to have originated in Nubia. Any protection that such an item might give is probably minimal, but perhaps it simply stopped the linen kilt from wearing out too rapidly. For a soldier on campaign who would have to sit on the ground when resting, a relatively light and cool kilt cover might be very practical.

The few examples that have survived are of extremely fine workmanship, but these may have been used for ceremonial parades, whereas a heavier and tougher version may have been used on campaign. In the early periods of Egyptian history, these leather kilts seem to have been worn by a variety of manual workers, almost as some kind of protective apron. By the time of the New Kingdom, they are seen being worn mainly by soldiers

On a purely practical level, the soldiers, and indeed most Egyptians, probably wore more and heavier clothes than those shown on the temple and tomb walls. At night, and certainly in winter, the temperatures within Egypt can be quite cool and most people would have worn longer, heavier kilts and also long over-garments or multiple layers of clothing to keep warm. The reliefs and paintings show people in their "Sunday best", not in the day-to-day clothing they usually wore. Tutankhamun was buried with many items of clothing, which included not just the standard kilts, but also many heavier and longer robes. These were the *real* day-to-day garments, sometimes depicted in the noble's tombs, but rarely in any of the numerous reliefs and paintings of the lower classes and soldiers.

Soldiers on campaigns, particularly in countries to the north-east of Egypt, would have had to endure lower temperatures than they had ever experienced in Egypt, and they would have encountered rain, and even snow, in some areas. Keeping warm and dry must have been a real problem and the actual appearance of an army on campaign must have been very different from the reliefs and surviving paintings. People used to living in a hot climate have a very low tolerance of cold, at least until some period of acclimatisation has taken place. Thick linen cloaks and robes, probably not too dissimilar to the modern Egyptian galabieh, may well have been the norm, probably in multiple layers to keep the cold out and conserve body heat.

When actually fighting, too many clothes would restrict the movements of the soldiers, so it is likely that the troops reverted to the simple kilts no matter what the temperature. Battles are a time of great activity and physical movement. Fear and the consequent surge of adrenaline would ensure that the cold was the last thing any soldier would worry about.

Too much clothing can also present other problems to soldiers: in close combat, loose clothing can be a real disadvantage as it gives an enemy something to hold on to, which could prove fatal. Another problem is being cut or wounded through clothing, for, should this happen, fragments of material could be driven into the wound causing infection that could be more dangerous than the wound itself. The Greeks realised this, which is why their soldiers fought with

147. Ranks of soldiers: scene from Hatshepsut's Mortuary Temple at Deir el Bahri.

no clothes at all. It would be surprising if the Egyptian physicians were not aware of this potential risk.

Despite these risks, a uniform, or at least an easily recognisable and distinctive form of clothing, has always been essential in battle in particular, to enable rapid recognition of friend or foe. The Egyptian army, from the earliest time, adopted a simple and recognisable uniform, which differed only slightly through the dynasties.

THE WORK OF A SOLDIER

The amount of time a soldier would actually spend in performing the principal task for which he had been trained, i.e. *fighting*, was often minimal (and still is, even today). Many soldiers would have served their time during peaceful periods of Egyptian history without seeing any "action" at all. Training and drill would have taken up a lot of their time, certainly initially, but the bulk of their time would have been spent on other duties. It is fairly certain that soldiers, in ancient times as now, would have been kept *busy* for all their waking hours. Idleness and boredom can cause unrest, which has always been a potential danger for any army.

The army was used to garrison the series of forts and border-crossings on the boundaries of Egypt, and possibly on internal borders within Egypt itself, protecting the trade routes and restricting unauthorised movements of the population. Soldiers also provided guards for anyone of sufficient status, or on particular places, such as the Valley of the Kings.

High above the Valley, the burial place of the kings of the New Kingdom, and overlooking the tomb entrances, is the so-called "Way Station", where it is believed the workmen lived when they were working a shift to construct the royal tombs. This site is on one main path into the Valley and it is likely that a small garrison would have been maintained there and probably at other vantage points around the Valley too. The bases of the walls of a number of small houses survive.

At other sites, sometimes quite remote, the remains of simple huts have been found, and graffiti on the rocks nearby appear to mark off the number of days. It would appear that a twenty-day tour of guard duty was not unusual and was duly recorded by the bored soldiers, waiting to return to their base camp.

Military units accompanied trading expeditions and the trained and disciplined manpower of the army was used for civil engineering activities where large numbers of men were needed. We know soldiers were used on occasion to help with the transportation of large blocks of stone for the sarcophagi of kings and to move colossal statues. They may have also been used in

148. The so-called "Way-Station" above the Valley of the Kings, showing the remains of the walls of the buildings.

transporting ships across the desert for trade expeditions to places such as Punt. The method of construction of the ships, with the parts of the hull lashed together with ropes, meant they could easily be dismantled and re-assembled, but it would have needed a large, fit and disciplined body of men to do this.

It would also appear that soldiers helped each year with the vital job of bringing in the harvest. In the New Kingdom Tomb of Menna at Thebes, men wearing the distinctive soldiers' gazelle skin kilt are shown in the harvesting scenes. It is possible that at this critical time of year, soldiers were drafted to help with the harvest. Perhaps they were allowed to return to their own towns and villages to help, or were simply sent to allocated areas. Throughout history, few campaigns have tended to be mounted when it was time to harvest the crops, which was a very labour-intensive task, and an absolutely vital part of the economy and welfare of the country.

149. *Harvesting scene from the Tomb of Menna at Thebes*

Troops could also be used to fulfil the role of a police force. Certainly we know that, at the end of Ancient Egyptian history, troops were used to control the problem of local bandits and Mafia-type groups who controlled some parts of the country. Also at this time, with Egypt under a succession of foreign rulers and suffering from political instability, there were many riots especially in the Delta area. These would have been put down by troops fulfilling a policing role.

In a recently translated papyrus, a Greek tax collector, one Timcyenes, asked his superior to send soldiers to help him extract the tax from a recalcitrant villager. He writes, "I have collected the taxes from the residents of the village, all except for Johannes … he refuses to pay his account … please send two soldiers to the village where he is being held, because in that way we may be able to get the money that is owed." Sadly we do not know if the tax was successfully extracted, but it shows clearly the police-type role the army undertook at this time, and it is reasonable to assume that this also occurred in earlier periods.

Movement of the army within Egypt was mainly by river. With the river Nile running through the country, transportation by boat was both fast and effective.

The Nile was the main "highway" within Egypt and boats capable of carrying large bodies of men and their equipment would be available (or could be easily pressed into service) when necessary. The river flows northwards through the length of the country and the prevailing

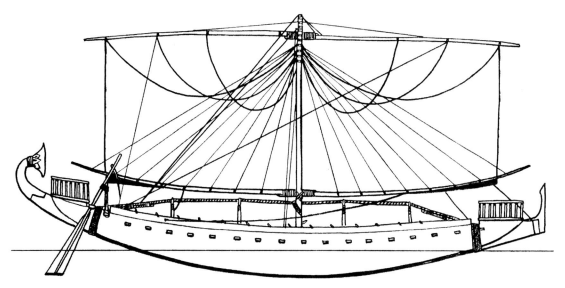

150. A New Kingdom boat, of the type used for the transportation of goods and passengers on the river.

wind, for the most of the time, blows from the north. This means that boats could travel downstream with the current and upstream harnessing the power of the wind, supplemented by the use of oars when necessary.

The journey from Memphis in the north, to Thebes (modern Cairo to Luxor) took around thirteen days to complete, assuming all the travelling was done in the hours of daylight and the wind was sufficient to fill the large sails of the boats for the journey. Travelling at night would shorten the journey, but some parts of the river have dangerous sand and mud banks and night journeys could be particularly hazardous, if these obstacles were not visible. During the daytime, lookouts were always placed at the bows of the ships, to look out for other craft on the river, for sandbanks and even for herds of hippopotami which could be a serious danger to shipping.

Travelling northwards from Thebes to Memphis relied mainly on the speed of flow of the river and this could vary dramatically at different times of the year. Strong winds which blow in

151. A Boat with a sail; Middle Kingdom tomb model.

152. A Boat with oars. Middle Kingdom tomb model.

the spring and autumn could also cause delays to navigation. Various accounts from antiquity and more modern times indicate a journey length of around twenty days, with perhaps a minimum time of twelve days.

In addition to troop movements, almost all communication would be by river, and these travelling times are important, as there could be a significant time delay in the relaying of information. For major events, be it the death of a pharaoh or unrest on the borders, almost a month could pass between the reporting of the incident and the receipt of a response. Used as we are to instant communications today, it is easy to overlook or not appreciate this factor which must have caused administrative nightmares, frustration and great concern at times when rapid responses were needed.

In times of unrest in Egypt, travel by river could be dangerous and any boats on the river could easily be attacked from the riverbanks. It is interesting to note that the flotilla of model boats buried in the Middle Kingdom Tomb of Meketre at Thebes included several that carried soldiers. Their shields, made of cowhide, are shown hung on the outside of the cabins, as a clear sign to anyone watching that there was an armed escort on board.

Although the river Nile is wide, at many points along its course it is hemmed in by high cliffs, and good vantage-points meant that any river traffic could be seen for many miles. During periods when central control broke down, it was even possible for some regions effectively to put a strangle-hold on the country by restricting or even stopping the flow of river traffic both northwards and southwards. Even as recently as the early

153. Shields on the cabin of one of Meketre's boats.

Nineteenth Century AD, "pirates" in the area of Beni Hassan in Middle Egypt were doing just that and it took severe action from the Egyptian government to ensure that boats could travel in the area without being attacked. The town was demolished and its inhabitants were forced to leave the area – though they soon moved back, building a new town.

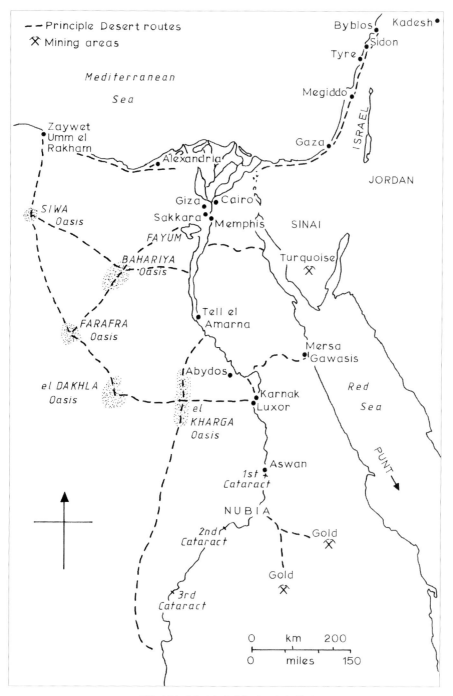

154. Map of the principal desert routes in Egypt.

For more distant campaigns, although the army might have been transported by sea-going boats from the river Nile to ports on the eastern Mediterranean, it would have had no alternative but to travel on foot. Well-established desert routes linked the oases with the Nile valley, and other routes led to the mining areas and to the east and west of the Delta.

So how fast could the army actually move? The time taken to move troops and supplies both within Egypt and beyond was critical to the success of any campaign.

The pace any army could travel depended upon the exact circumstances and the terrain of the particular campaign. There are no reliable records from Egypt which supply this information, but it does survive in Classical writings for the armies of Greece and Rome, which often operated under similar conditions. Even this information has to be carefully interpreted, for armies may have been trained and drilled to move at a particular speed, only to find the realities of campaigns to be very different.

We know the Roman army could cover about eighteen miles a day over a period of five hours (roughly three and a half miles an hour). Forced marches of forty miles a day are recorded, but few troops would be able to maintain this pace over a long period.

Alexander the Great's army covered around thirteen miles a day on average. This has been calculated over long campaigns and is based on the troops' being able to rest every five or seven days. On shorter campaigns a distance of fifteen miles would seem to be reasonable. As this sort of pace seems to be fairly universal for marching on foot for armies of all periods in history up to relatively modern times, it is not unreasonable to assume that the Egyptian army was capable of the same standard of performance. Even so, some period of rest must have been required before the troops engaged in any action.

It was not just the troops who had to be moved around the country, but their equipment and supplies as well. Donkeys were used as beasts of burden for the army and these would need to be moved with the troops, or, more likely, pressed into service from the local towns and villages.

In the New Kingdom campaigns of Ramesses II, oxen appear to have been used to draw two-wheeled carts, probably containing fodder for the horses. Whilst fodder could easily be obtained in friendly territory, on a long distance campaign it had to be gathered and stored whenever available, because of the uncertainty of future supplies.

Most of the time, though, the soldiers would have needed to carry the bulk of their food with

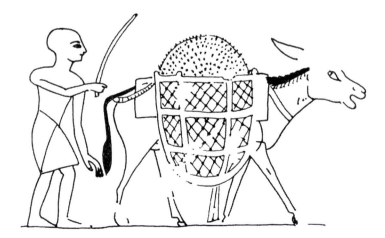

155. A donkey and driver. Scene from the
Tomb of Panehsy at Thebes.

156. Ox and baggage carts, from the
Battle of Kadesh scenes of Ramesses II.

them, along with all their equipment. This
would include their principal weapons: spears
and shields, bows, quivers of arrows etc.. Like
soldiers today, they would have been carrying
substantial loads over long distances. Physical
fitness was, therefore, of great importance, for
it would have been a disaster if the soldiers
arrived at the site of a battle too exhausted to
actually fight. No wonder that papyrus Anastasi
compares the foot soldier to an ass – little more
than a beast of burden.

The rations needed could be substantial.
Based on estimates for the army of Alexander
the Great, it is believed that an army of
10,000 men and 2,000 horses would have had
a daily consumption of fourteen tons of grain,
eighteen tons of fodder and over 90,000 litres
of water. From Middle Kingdom sources we
know the ordinary worker or soldier received
ten loaves a day, although when on campaign
the issue was probably often lower.

Supplies were carried in bags or baskets.
In a rare tomb model, dating to the Old
Kingdom, a man is shown carrying a basket
on his back, secured by two shoulder straps,
very much like a modern rucksack. For fit and
well-nourished soldiers fairly heavy loads
could be carried this way with relative ease (as
soldiers continue to do, right up until today).

A well-established series of forts around
the borders of Egypt meant that supplies and

157. Old Kingdom wooden model of a porter, from the Tomb of
Niankh-Pepi at Meir.

158. The Egyptian army in camp. Scene from the battle reliefs of Ramesses II.

food could be stored there. The army would have also made full use of any towns or villages it passed through to obtain food and water. Within Egypt, local communities were probably obliged to help to feed a passing army and troops may have been billeted with local inhabitants. This is most likely to have been the case with the officers, who may have expected, or even demanded, some degree of material comfort as befitted their status. For the common soldier, in a mild climate, no cover is needed at night for most of the year and they probably slept in the open.

In hostile country, the local inhabitants may well have had some warning of the approach of an enemy army and, if they had any sense, would have fled with as many of their possessions and stored food as possible. In these circumstances, the army would have been forced to travel further afield for food, possibly sending out small raiding parties. Depending on the time of the year and the area, the soldiers would harvest any local crops or raid food stores in nearby towns and villages. Food had to be found not just for the men, but for the donkeys and horses too.

When on a major campaign, it is likely that the officers at least had tents transported with the army, to provide some privacy and comfort. Exactly how many "home comforts" such as furniture and personal belongings were also taken along is not known, but in the case of the king, it was probably a substantial amount of equipment.

No examples of military tents have survived and depictions of them are rare and lacking in detail. We do know of one portable canopy that dates to the Old Kingdom, made for Queen Hetepheres, mother of Khufu. It was found in her tomb at Giza. Made of wood overlaid with gold, it was intended to be hung with curtains. Such a structure, perhaps less ornate, could have been transported on campaign.

A leather canopy or tent of Queen Istemkheb of the Twenty-First Dynasty survives, although this was made to cover her coffins in her tomb.

Other canopies are shown in some paintings and reliefs, which are really sunshades erected to protect the king when he was attending open-air functions. One such portable canopy does

159. *The canopy and furniture of Queen Hetepheres.*

survive, from the Tomb of Tutankhamun. When hung with fine linen, it would have provided ideal cover from the heat of the sun. This particular canopy is strange in that it does not come with a base, which was presumably lost in antiquity. It could perhaps have been fixed to a portable throne or even have been fitted to the royal chariots. The latter use would be particularly useful when on parade or inspecting the troops. A canopy such as this could also have been stood on the ground, if necessary, with the bases of the upright poles buried or held upright by ropes or even servants.

Simple tents would have been easy to carry, for a tent can be improvised from little more than a piece of material, supported by wood scavenged from the countryside, or even by the shafts of spears. This would provide some protection if needed. Egyptians were well used, however, to sleeping in the open, especially within Egypt in the summer months, and on campaign probably had little choice but to do the same, finding whatever cover they needed from trees, palm leaves, logs and rocky outcrops. If more substantial protection from adverse weather was needed, and if suitable local buildings could not be

160. *The portable canopy from the Tomb of Tutankhamun.*

commandeered, then the soldiers would have been able to produce fairly quickly some temporary structures, using whatever materials were readily to hand.

TIME TO FIGHT

Training an army is one achievement; getting it to the location where any military action is likely is another; there then remains the problem of actually getting the soldiers to *fight*.

Motivation of the soldiers was, therefore, important. If the individuals of the army felt they were under personal attack, with their homes, possessions or families in danger, then sufficient motivation to fight in their defence was generally not a problem. To take offensive action well away from the soldier's home and family is more difficult.

The reasons for any military action might not have been clear to most soldiers, and whilst it could be argued that perhaps the common soldier did not *need* to know the reasons, there may have been times when some selective information would have produced a more motivated army.

Effective leadership and guidance from the army officers was essential and it would have helped the soldiers if the overall commander of the army himself took firm control of the situation. The chain of command and the communication system within the army needed to be effective to ensure that the soldiers were given just enough information/propaganda to provide sufficient motivation.

Every army in history has probably considered its actions to be justified. Even extending the boundaries of one country at the expense of another could be justified if it could be argued that it was really self-defence. To attack an enemy who might be preparing to attack you, *before* he actually attacked could be argued as being perfectly reasonable. Another argument might have been that the territory under dispute did not belong to the enemy because of some historical claim and that, therefore, it was simply a question of seeking to regain that which was yours in the first place.

The reason *any* army finds itself with the prospect of a fight is almost always because of the will or actions of one powerful individual, usually the army commander, who will be acting on behalf of (or who may actually be) the ruler of the country.

Sometimes the ruler invoked the gods: Thutmose III in his Annals tells how his own attack on Syria was actually instigated by Amun and how it was the god himself who granted victory to the King. This is the "God is with us" syndrome, adopted by almost every army in history, from Thutmose III to recent conflicts. Thutmose III actually paraded the image of Amun before his troops prior to battle.

Motivation could be also increased if the soldiers believed that any enemy action should be regarded as open rebellion against the king, the gods of Egypt and the rule of Maat (the Egyptian concept of truth, justice, and the natural pre-ordained order of things). Battles and conflicts with religion at their heart are nothing new.

Practical experience of battle was vital for soldiers and ideally this would be in smaller actions rather than in a full-scale battle for the first "blooding". Whilst drill and mock battles help to perfect the techniques, the first real "kill" was important. Success bred success and a victorious army could all too easily think that it was invincible. Any losses the army may have suffered before could be forgotten by the individual soldiers in the euphoria of being a survivor and victor. Conversely, a series of defeats could seriously demoralise an army, to the extent that it completely lost the will to fight: go into a battle *expecting* to lose, and the outcome is almost a foregone conclusion. This is the time when the long years of hardship, drill and discipline on the part of the soldiers pay off and when the need for a strong and respected commanding officer is vital.

Fear of injury or death is an ever-present concern amongst soldiers. The use of battle-hardened mercenaries in the Egyptian army during the New Kingdom was important, as soldiers who knew what to expect on active service could steady the nerves of new recruits. This mix of experienced and new troops ensured continuity and a high level of practical experience, which would have greatly helped the introduction and assimilation of any new recruits into the unit.

The understandable worries about the outcome of any military action could be alleviated to some extent if it was thought that the enemy was ill-equipped, badly trained and lacking in motivation. The propaganda machine could work extensively in this area and soldiers could be made to believe the stories and be motivated by them. If the propaganda proved to be wrong … by then it would be too late to matter.

The troops needed to feel both empathy and respect for their officers, from the lowest to the highest ranks and especially for their commander. The fact that the commander might have been the king himself would not necessarily have been enough to inspire the confidence needed. If, however, the king led his army in person and shared some of the hardships of his soldiers, then he could have been a commander they would have been prepared to die for. Thutmose III, Ramesses II and other later pharaohs all personally led their troops into battle and placed themselves at risk in so doing. Many earlier kings must have done the same although not all left as detailed accounts of their exploits and personal bravery as Thutmose and Ramesses.

Thutmose III gained the respect of his officers by listening to their views and acting on their advice before the battle of Megiddo. He was an expert at man-management: the final decision was his alone, and it may have been one he intended all along, but by getting his officers involved, he knew they would be behind him and that they, in turn, would motivate the soldiers under their direct command. Thutmose III led his army from the *front*, confident of the support of his soldiers. We know this about Thutmose III and Ramesses II, but doubtless other pharaohs were equally adept at man-management and motivational skills.

A pre-battle pep talk by the king was probably the norm. This was a tradition followed by later commanders in different countries and centuries, such as Henry V before the battle of Agincourt, although few of the soldiers would probably have *heard* their leader's words. The commander would praise his own army and belittle the enemy, hopefully encouraging the men to fight to prove their own valour. The troops nearest the commander might cheer with enthusiasm and this would no doubt be picked up by those further away. Those who did not actually hear the words would soon do so as they were passed to the rest of the army by the soldiers who had heard them, and who may have been suitably inspired and motivated by them.

If all else failed, men could be coerced into fighting, shamed into it by the pointing out of past mistakes and the opportunity to "redeem themselves" by brave action on the field of battle.

Martial music can help to encourage the troops. We know that trumpets were used, but possibly only for communication and the passing of signals, as the surviving examples, when played by professional musicians, were found to have only a relatively limited range of notes. Two splendid examples were found in the Tomb of Tutankhamun, one being made of bronze and one of silver. The silver trumpet was blown in the 1930's and recorded. The sound was very piercing and, perhaps as expected, loud. It would have been heard easily above the din of battle and, most importantly, over large distances.

The bell of the silver trumpet is decorated with incised relief, which shows Tutankhamun

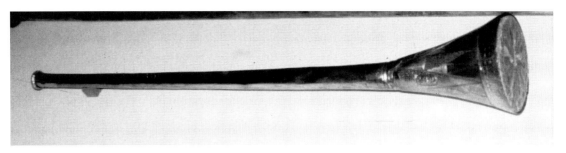

161. One of the trumpets from the Tomb of Tutankhamun.

162. Detail of the decoration on the bell of the silver trumpet of Tutankhamun.

with Ptah, Amun and Ra, three gods we know to have been associated with the divisions of the army.

The passing of signals to an army in the field has always been difficult and the use of pre-arranged trumpet calls could enable complicated manoeuvres and advances or retreats to be co-ordinated. Superior drill and a standardised signalling system could give one army a significant advantage over a less disciplined and organised enemy.

Drums were used throughout Egyptian history and can be seen in many reliefs and surviving paintings. Actual examples have survived, although rarely. The drum's main use was probably when the army was on the march, to keep the soldiers in step. The use of drums to maintain a beat makes it much easier for soldiers to keep a steady pace. Evidence that armies at any period in history actually marched in step is almost non-existent, but the use of drums naturally makes people fall into the same step and into the same rhythm, rather like the effect of a strong beat in dance music. The actual act of marching can become almost automatic and the soldier does not have to think about what he is doing, just concentrate on keeping moving. This enables greater distances to be travelled with fewer complaints and less unrest.

Contemporary reliefs and models of soldiers do show them all in step, usually with the left leg forward. This, however, may have simply been the artistic convention for showing groups of men.

The drums were simply made from an open-ended cylinder, usually of wood or metal, capped at each end with a skin of leather tensioned by leather thongs or fine rope laced tightly between the skins. The drum could be played with one or both hands, with or without a drumstick.

163. A drummer and a trumpeter. Relief from Thebes.

164. An Egyptian drum.

Before or during battles, a corps of drums beating together can produce an almost hypnotic and euphoric effect amongst men who may, in reality, be terrified. Drums can also be used to signal specific manoeuvres although this is only possible within a well-trained army. The beat of drums can also be very intimidating to an enemy. Drumbeats can signal the approach of an army and be heard even before the army is actually in sight of the opposing force. The hope would be that the enemy would decide *not* to fight, but to seek the safer option and flee.

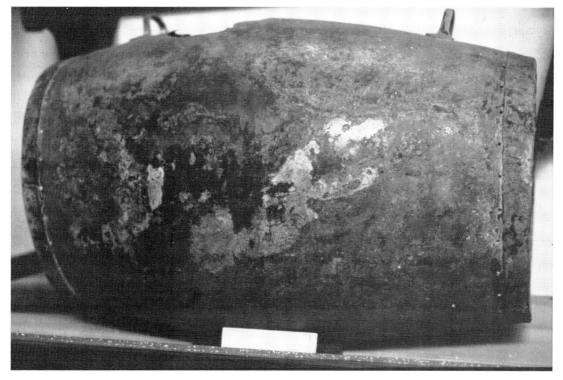

165. A copper or bronze drum, possibly dating to the Eighteenth Dynasty.

It is more than likely that the soldiers sang whilst marching. We have evidence that they did so when performing other tasks like the harvesting of crops (another activity where rhythmic and co-ordinated movement makes the task easier). The workers are shown accompanied by musicians.

The first "military bands" are seen in Egypt and are pictured in temple processions, such as the Festival of Opet held at Thebes, when the image of the god Amun in his shrine was paraded. Trumpets, drums, sistrums (percussion instruments, which produce a rattle sound), clapper sticks of ivory or bone, stringed lutes, reed flutes and pipes must have made a splendid sound (or racket depending on one's taste in music).

166. Military musicians at the Festival of Opet. Relief in the Temple of Luxor.

The use of war cries was probably important too, either at unit level or for the whole army. The use of a war cry can have a unifying effect on the whole army and can be really intimidating to an enemy. Soldiers were probably trained to shout or yell when making an attack on an enemy. We should not forget that this was hand-to-hand fighting, when each soldier would have needed to get close to his enemy, and would have been able to see the expressions on his face and to smell his fear. A suitable blood-curdling yell when making an attack can have a dramatic effect on the success of any attack; sound as if you mean business, and the enemy may be convinced too! Even in the Twentieth Century, soldiers at bayonet practice were taught to yell as they attacked their enemy.

Before fighting actually commenced, the army invariably engaged in the final bluff: by parading before the enemy, by forming up in his sight, by manoeuvring, by beating drums and by shouting war cries. The enemy would have had plenty of opportunity to gauge the strength and determination of the opposing force.

There may well have been a set "code of conduct" for battles, although no formal document or version of any rules has survived. A hint that there was such a set conventions for

for the fighting of battles survives from the reign of Piye. When leading his army north through Egypt he issued an order:

> "Let neither side attack by night, but in full view, in obedience to the rules of the contest: give your adversary notice of the conflict from afar. If he says that his infantry or the cavalry from some other town are behind their time, then wait until the whole of his army has assembled and fight only when he gives the word. If his allies happen to be in some other town, wait for them."

This order was, however, preserved in stone *after* a successful campaign and with the benefit of hindsight. Piye may simply have wanted to make his victory appear fair and justified. There certainly seems to have been a convention where adversaries were expected to meet on equal terms, almost like a game of chess, and that the outcome of any battle would be decided by the courage of the troops and the support of the gods. The mention of not fighting battles by night is practical, for to control and co-ordinate a successful major attack in the dark would be difficult.

The reality of warfare may well have been very different from any "idealised" set of rules, for few generals in history would have actually waited for the enemy to reinforce its lines.

Unless an army was taken completely by surprise (which sometimes happened) then there was generally plenty of time to prepare for battle. This would involve making sure all the men and animals were fed and watered. We know the Egyptians drank wine and beer, but exactly how much may have been consumed immediately before a battle is not known. Throughout history armies and navies (with the tot of rum) have sent men into battle with at least a modest amount of alcohol in their blood. Officers would have the wine, the soldiers the beer. Some alcohol could have had a positive effect, increasing the confidence of the soldiers and helping to calm their nerves, both of which factors could give one army a significant advantage over another.

Once the army was ready for action and assembled, most commanders would have tried, wherever possible, to choose the place for action, thus possibly gaining an advantage over the enemy by forcing him to make the next move.

The way any army formed up in line of battle very much depended on the individual commander. The ideal position was on higher ground than the enemy, for it is harder to fight uphill, and being above the enemy, even by a small amount, gave the archers an advantage as they could fire down on the enemy troops. Any local topographical features would also have been used to the greatest advantage, especially those that provided some cover, such as ditches, vegetation or rocky outcrops.

It would have been usual for the archers to be placed, at least initially, in the front ranks of the army to protect the infantry behind them. In the New Kingdom, when divisions of chariots were added to the army, they were usually divided and placed on the flanks of the army.

Before committing both armies to action, there always remained the possibility of a tactical withdrawal or surrender by one side, before the first arrows flew, the ranks of soldiers surged forward and battle commenced. Many commanders were, perhaps understandably, reluctant to commit their armies to combat unless they were reasonably certain of success or had no alternative.

To begin any action, one or both of the armies would advance until the archers were within range; this would be around three hundred metres. The army might advance a division at a time. Commanders would not have committed all the troops to action at once and one unit, possibly quite small, could be advanced to test the strength of the enemy. In more modern battles, this unit was called the "Forlorn Hope", the name implying that their chances of survival could sometimes be slim! A division of fast moving chariots was often considered ideal for this purpose for they could advance rapidly, were very intimidating, were a hard target to hit and could get out of any trouble quickly. A closer view of the enemy would have confirmed any earlier estimates of numbers, equipment used and troop deployment.

The chariots often made the first move on the enemy, charging from both flanks of the army in a "horned" attack, harassing the enemy infantry or meeting their chariots in combat.

As the main armies advanced towards each other, the archers would have keet up a steady rate of fire, which would become more intense as the distance between the armies decreased and the archers were surer of finding a target. At this range the arrows would not have needed to be aimed at specific individual targets: fired in volleys, arrows fired up and above the enemy were sufficient, as enough of them would have found targets as they fell to the ground. Even if the arrows missed any target, they would (terrain permitting) have stuck into the ground when they landed, and would have hindered the movements of troops as they moved through them.

The main stage of the battle was the all-out attack, made when the armies were very close. This final thrust would have needed to be at speed and the soldiers would have surged forward to meet the enemy. There is a general impression, perhaps created by Hollywood films, that both armies rushed towards each other over some distance, to meet with a great clash of arms. In reality, this probably rarely happened, for in such an attack units moved at different speeds and any tight formation and military advantage was lost. Soldiers would have arrived in disorder, and, more seriously, out of breath and not capable of serious or prolonged fighting.

There was a distinct advantage in standing ground and letting the enemy attack, as *their* soldiers would have arrived out of breath and having lost any formation and grouping. On the other hand, being confronted by an attack of weapon-wielding soldiers, running and yelling, could be very intimidating and, unless units were well trained and disciplined, they could break and flee. The decision on which tactic to adopt will have been made by the commander, given the nature of the terrain and the condition of his own and the enemy forces.

167. Pharaoh in battle. Seti I in his chariot ploughs through his enemy. Relief from the north wall of the Hypostyle Hall at Karnak.

Battles at close quarters did not last long, as men rapidly became tired. Whilst some accounts of battles do indicate a longer period, invariably the battle itself was only a short part of the time, whilst the "mopping up" of any pockets of resistance might take longer. Most battles were probably over not long after the first onslaught, when one side or the other would have quickly gained the advantage.

The reality of close combat was very unpleasant and this is where the years of training and discipline could win or loose the day. Soldiers fighting hand to hand needed to get *very* close to the enemy, and this resulted in one to one combat. Every soldier would have had to watch his side and back in the heat of the action. Telling friend from foe could be difficult, and if weapons hit their mark, then all combatants were probably covered in their enemies' blood as well as their own. To stand and fight when friends and colleagues are being butchered all around would have taken a lot of courage and discipline.

Even to battle-hardened soldiers, this reality and the brutality of close combat would have been difficult to cope with. Weapons would have become difficult to hold as they became covered in sweat and blood. The sights, smells and sounds of battle would have been all around them: men suffering injuries most of us can only imagine in our worst nightmares, severe cuts, disembowelments, men screaming in their agony.

Movement on the battlefield would have been difficult and there was always a danger of tripping over the fallen bodies, particularly likely if an enemy was pushing soldiers back and they were unable to see where they were going. Fall over on a battlefield, and the enemy immediately has the advantage. For the new recruits this must have been a real baptism of fire; far, far different from the drills and mock battles they may have taken part in before. Many of the surviving troops would have been severely mentally traumatised by the battle. Often this manifested itself after the event, but soldiers caught up in the heat of the battle could also be affected. Soldiers needed to work together, to look out for their colleagues, in the knowledge that they would do the same for them. Anyone lost, disorientated, or in shock, needed to be shouted at and pushed or pulled in the right direction. This utter reliance on colleagues made the loss of any one of them in battle very personal and must have added greatly to the mental strain. Today after combat soldiers often receive counselling, whereas historically they would have had to deal with the problems themselves and the veterans would no doubt have played an important part in the process, looking after the newest recruits.

The commander would usually have made sure he was in a position to see the overall battle, so he could advance fresh troops and manoeuvre units as necessary. However, once armies have engaged, moving troops from one part of the battlefield to another can be very difficult, and although the commander might see problem areas, by the time he could move units to help, it could be too late. Messages and orders were passed between units by runners and in later periods by chariots or possibly messengers on horseback, but they all ran the risk of being intercepted en-route and of their message never being delivered.

Some pharaohs, as we shall see, adopted the "leading from the front" policy. Whilst this could be particularly good for morale, it could be very dangerous for the pharaoh concerned. It is likely that, after the initial deployment of troops and the main attack, he would need to have got to a position where he could see what was happening and control, as far as possible, the battle. Battles had a momentum of their own, and the success of an army depended on a number of factors such as morale, motivation, drill and discipline, not necessarily on how the units were deployed.

168. The chaos of battle. Dead and wounded enemy as shown in a battle relief of Ramesses II from his temple at Abydos.

As the battle progressed, with each side pressing hard and seeking out the strengths and weaknesses of the enemy, invariably one side would begin to gain the advantage, although there might have been different outcomes on different parts of the battlefield. It is known that in many battles, one flank of an army might appear to be winning, whilst the other might be soundly defeated. As enemy units faltered it was the ideal time to move in the chariots, who were particularly effective when attacking broken units, especially those who were withdrawing from action.

Deciding who actually won a particular battle was, perhaps surprisingly, not always as easy as might be expected. Some battles may well have had a decisive conclusion with the enemy being killed, surrendering or fleeing the field, but in the majority of cases the outcome was less than clear. There are many such battles in history, not just in ancient Egypt, where *both* sides claimed to have been the victor.

Battles could stop of their own accord as both sides became exhausted, or units suffered heavy casualties or the fighting lines drifted apart almost of their own free will. Both armies could disengage and withdraw with no clear victor. Unless battle was continued, the armies could withdraw still further apart, possibly even leaving the immediate battle area. This would enable units to draw their breath, to re-group and perhaps parley with the enemy to try to persuade them to end hostilities. On some occasions the armies might well have rallied sufficiently to return to the battle area and re-engage. In many instances, though, a stalemate would ensue, with neither army being willing or able to fight on to a definite conclusion.

For troops in any army that was facing possible defeat, advance knowledge of the enemy's attitude to prisoners could make a dramatic difference. If it were known that captured soldiers were fairly treated and not harmed, then surrender might appear to be a preferable option. If, however, the enemy were known (either based on sound knowledge or perhaps just the word of their officers, and, therefore, good propaganda) to be vicious in victory, with captives being tortured or slaughtered, then the prospect of surrender could be worse than continuing to fight.

169. Captured prisoners paraded by Ramesses III before Amun. Relief from his Mortuary Temple at Medinet Habu.

Soldiers thus motivated could turn a potential defeat into a victory. Perhaps it made sense for the officers always to make sure their troops believed that the enemy was cruel and barbaric; what better motivation could there be to succeed and win the day.

Both sides could invariably, with justification, claim that they had achieved some measure of a victory, often with both armies surviving relatively intact to fight again another time. When two armies were evenly matched, in any battle resulting in a "stalemate", neither side would have actually conceded defeat and their respective propaganda machines would have ensured that the official records told of a resounding victory.

The reward of victory was plunder and the victorious troops would strip the bodies of their slain enemies, taking their clothes and weapons. There was even the chance of gold and other valuable booty if the enemy camp was captured or if a siege was successful (not to mention the prospect of women – always a strong motivational force for any army away from home).

The lure of plunder could even turn the course and outcome of a battle. Thutmose III succeeded on one occasion in getting his enemy on the run, but failed to pursue them as his troops fell to plundering the empty enemy camp. Prince Rupert, a successful general during the English Civil Wars would have done well to have learnt from history. He too failed to follow up on his military successes in a number of battles, when the prospect of plunder became irresistible. All too often individual soldiers or units who had been fighting for a while and had achieved some measure of success, adopted the attitude "we have done our bit now" and looked for some respite from the action and also for some material benefits from their efforts. Only strong discipline and command can prevent this, but the world's most successful armies have found this a particularly difficult problem.

In addition to such "spoils of war" officers and individual soldiers were sometimes singled out for their individual exploits and could be rewarded by their senior officers or even personally by the king. The Egyptian army seems, in the New Kingdom, to have initiated a formal system of awards, or medals. Known as flies, these were gold pendants in the form of the common fly, awarded for bravery.

The symbol of the fly may seem a little odd, but think of a fly's persistence and determination in getting to its food and of the difficulty in driving it away and the connection with soldiers makes sense. Several examples of such awards survive and one set of three flies was found on the body of Queen Ahotep of the Seventeenth Dynasty. Their inclusion in the burial equipment of a queen is unusual, but this was a time when the Egyptians were driving out the Hyksos from the Delta, and perhaps Ahotep played a more important and active part in this process than we know.

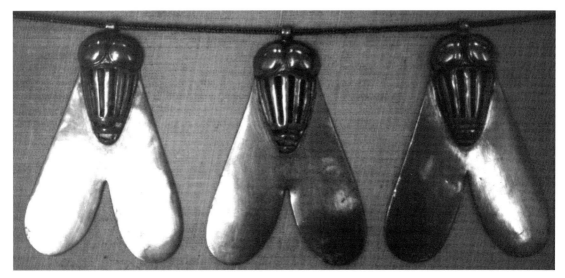

170. The gold flies of valour of Queen Ahotep.

171. Horemheb being presented with gold collars. Relief from his tomb at Sakkara

The burial equipment of Djehuty, a general under Thutmose III, contained many gold flies. Some we know to have been a direct gift from the king to honour his exploits. Gold was also awarded to the generals and officers, in the form of heavy collars made of solid disks of the metal. General Horemheb of the Eighteenth Dynasty is shown receiving such collars from the king as a reward for his services after a presumably successful campaign.

Known as *shebyu collars*, some splendid examples were found in the royal tombs at Tanis. The substantial weight of gold, in the collars meant their recipients were made wealthy by the gift and by the public recognition of their exploits by the pharaoh.

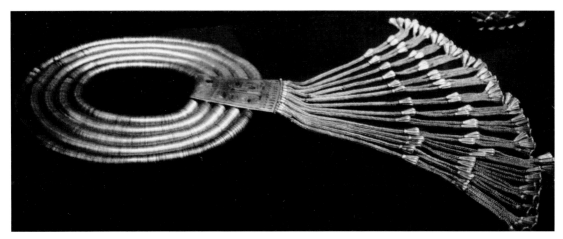

172. Shebyu *collar found in the royal tombs at Tanis.*

The prospects for the defeated enemy were less good. If prisoners were captured they were usually taken back to Egypt, where they were often led in manacles before the king, in the obligatory victory parade. Many prisoners were then given as slaves to soldiers and officers who had distinguished themselves in action.

Some prisoners, usually those of high status or rank, were executed and their bodies displayed as a "warning" to others. Execution was usually by impaling on a wooden stake. Representations of this are rare and it is not shown in any of the battle scenes. A hieroglyphic determinative appears on the Amada stela of Merenptah and depicts the body of a man, face down, supported in the centre of his torso by the point of a stake. (See fig. 135). If the stake pierced a major organ then death would have been quick, but otherwise the victim would suffer a slow and agonising death. It is possible that in military executions, with plenty of suitable weapons to hand, death was swifter.

Execution does seem to be the exception, rather than the rule, and, generally speaking, the Egyptians were far less brutal in their treatment of prisoners and captives than many other

173. Manacled prisoners being led in triumph. Scene from the Tomb of Horemheb at Sakkara.

civilisations. Most prisoners were taken to Egypt, where they seem to have been quickly integrated into the community, with many marrying Egyptian spouses.

Some captured foreign soldiers were "persuaded" to join the Egyptian army in return for their lives' being spared – the proverbial "offer that cannot be refused".

There was a distinct advantage to the Egyptian army in this, for the captured soldiers' local knowledge of their homeland could be used on future campaigns (although one has to question the obvious divided loyalties of such mercenary soldiers fighting for the Egyptian army and possibly against their own countrymen).

THE DANGERS AND DRAWBACKS OF LIFE IN THE ARMY

As we shall see later, one specific type of warfare, common not just in Egypt, was the siege. This technique, whilst avoiding a short, but probably bloody, pitched battle, could be particularly stressful for the participants on both sides. The Egyptians laid siege to many towns and cities on numerous campaigns and each siege could last for many weeks. It was simply a question of who could hold out the longest, those on the inside or those on the outside. Whilst the immediate and most obvious dangers of a pitched battle were not present in a siege, the dangers and difficulties faced could, ultimately, be just as serious.

Often the conditions inside the towns were dire, if water and food was in short supply, when there would have been little alternative to surrender. However, the besiegers would also have had to cope with poor supplies of water and have had to rely upon whatever food could be scavenged from the surrounding countryside. Often the victors of a siege were only in a slightly better physical state than the vanquished. After a successful siege, the victors may well have captured the town, but have had to face the prospect of finding no food within. The motivation of plunder may have been enough to keep the soldiers going, but it might explain why Papyrus Anastasi describes the soldier returning "like a stick"!

A good supply of food was essential to the soldiers, but no more so than to the civilian population. For most of the time the food enjoyed by soldiers was probably identical to that of their civilian counterparts, but occasionally their standard and quantity of food were probably much less.

Egypt was generally well provided with food for its population and even in times of famine or poor harvests, the prudent storage of food in the plentiful years meant that the population could survive relatively easily.

The main diet for most Egyptians was bread, and a number of varieties were made from both barley and wheat. Within Egypt the raw ingredients were readily available and bread was probably cooked as required. On campaign either loaves or the ingredients would have needed to be carried, but that pre-supposes that ovens were available or could be made in the army camp to cook them. If an army was camped for some days, then there would probably have been time to make simple ovens, but if it was just an overnight stop, then this would have been more difficult and the army would probably have had to rely on bread carried with them (unless there were local supplies available from towns or villages nearby). The bread may well have been stale, but in a dry climate this would not necessarily be a problem as the bread would be hard and more biscuit-like than when fresh. Stale rations are nothing new for most soldiers.

Interestingly, badly stored bread or grain can produce natural antibiotics which can actually give protection (albeit unknown to anyone at this time) from many minor diseases. However, the soldiers would have undoubtedly suffered from worn teeth, a problem faced by every ancient

Egyptian from pharaoh to farm worker. The bread contained a high level of grit, introduced either into the flour as it was milled, or by wind-blown sand and dust. Over a period of time this wore down the enamel of teeth, causing at best some discomfort and pain, and at worst, serious abscesses and infections, which could prove fatal.

174. Egyptian bread.

Onions were another part of the Egyptian's staple diet and they have the advantage that they store and travel well. Other vegetables and fruits such as beans, figs and dates were also dried and could be easily transported.

175. A basket of fruit.

Fish and meat were eaten, either salted or sun dried, although the main diet for most Egyptians was predominantly vegetarian. On campaign within Egypt, fish would have been readily available and soldiers may have been able to catch some themselves. Enemy livestock would also have been considered fair game so the soldiers may sometimes have eaten as well as their officers and commanders. The spoils of war could include an improved diet (on occasions at least), too.

Apart from water, beer was the main Egyptian's drink, and was made from wheat or barley. It is believed that it did not keep well and may not have been taken long distances on campaign. However, if there was a "field kitchen" it is possible that some beer might have been brewed whilst on campaign, for the brewing process was short and went hand-in-hand with the baking of bread.

Wine was also drunk and could be transported, but was probably reserved for the officers. Again, if it was not carried with the army, local supplies (either obtained legitimately or plundered) may well have been acquired.

On campaign, the diet of the soldier could vary dramatically depending on what was taken with the army, but most importantly on what was available in the territory through which he was passing. There may have been times where his diet was substantially *better* than when at home, but equally many times when he had to survive on a subsistence diet only.

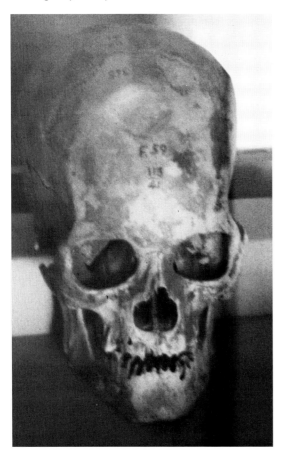

176. Skull showing possible evidence of a mace-inflicted injury.

"Wounded in Action"

During any battle, skirmish, siege or campaign, there was always the real risk of personal injury, whatever the rank of the individual from foot soldier to pharaoh. Physical evidence of injuries received in battle is rare as we have not discovered the bodies of many known soldiers, but one notable example is the mummy of King Seqenenre-Tao of the Seventeenth Dynasty, who clearly died in battle.

The skull of another individual (now in the museum at Aswan) has survived and shows a severe blow to the head, clearly depressing the front part of the cranium. The exact origin or circumstances concerning the infliction of the wound is not known, nor is its effect on the victim. He appears, however, to have survived the injury, which was possibly caused by a mace.

Amongst the entourage which would have accompanied the army would have been a team of physicians, who would have been able to deal with the more routine and simple injuries. Wounds inflicted in battles at this time fall into two distinct categories.

Firstly there were wounds involving blows to the body that were strong enough to break bones and cause severe bruising. The physicians could cope with most of these injuries well; but would have been unable to treat ones that caused internal injuries, which were not readily apparent.

Secondly, and perhaps more difficult to treat, were the puncture wounds, caused by arrows, spears and swords. Whilst simple flesh cuts might have been treatable, the physicians would have had limited or negligible success in dealing with deep puncture wounds to the body when the internal organs were damaged.

Relatively few bodies have been found that can be positively identified as belonging to soldiers. If flesh wounds had been received and had healed well, the process of embalming (which involves covering the skin in a thick layer of resin) and/or the natural decay of a body would render this visible indication of a military life invisible.

The remarkable survival, therefore, of a number of bodies of Middle Kingdom soldiers gives us a rare insight into the dangers they faced. With some detective work it is also possible to reconstruct exactly how they met their end.

Their tomb was discovered at Deir el Bahri on the West Bank of the river Nile at Luxor in 1923 AD, by H.E. Winlock, who was part of an Egyptian expedition from the Metropolitan Museum of Art in New York. The rock-cut tomb was found to contain a mass of bodies, believed initially to be those of Coptic monks. It was not, therefore, examined in any detail until 1926, when a study of some of the linen wrapping of the bodies revealed ink writing that indicated that the bodies were much older than initially thought. They dated to 2060 BC in the Middle Kingdom and specifically to the reign of Nebhetepre-Mentuhotep I.

At least sixty bodies had been buried in the tomb, possibly more, but robbers had disturbed the contents a few hundred years after the burial and before the tomb was sealed by a rock fall until modern times.

The bodies were all of men with an average height of five foot six inches and of robust build. They were taller than many Egyptians today and their age was between thirty and forty, with only three individuals showing any sign of greying hair or baldness. All the men had dark hair, dressed into tight curls and covered in some type of grease.

It was soon apparent that the bodies belonged to soldiers and that they had all died in battle. Many appear to have been veterans, as there was evidence of old wounds that had healed. Most of them were to the head and to the left side in particular, the most likely area for any injury when facing any enemy. Much of the soft tissue in the bodies had, however, been lost and evidence of any cuts and flesh wounds had not survived.

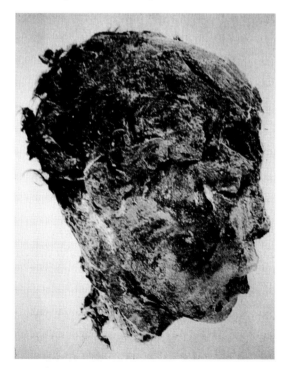

177. The head of one of Mentuhotep's soldiers from the tomb at Deir el Bahri, showing a wound to the forehead.

121

Ten of the soldiers had been killed by puncture wounds caused by ebony-tipped arrows. Only fragments of the arrows remained, as after any battle spent arrows (even those that were still embedded in bodies) would have been collected for re-use. One arrow fragment was found lodged in the hair of a soldier; other fragments were still embedded in the flesh of the victims, and in one instance in an eye.

One soldier had been felled by an arrow that had entered his back and which, from the angle of impact, had been fired from a great height, possibly from battlements. It had penetrated the lungs and heart, and its tip protruded from the man's chest. When he fell forwards, the impact of his body's hitting the ground broke the end off the arrow. The amount of bleeding from the wound shows that death was not instantaneous.

Many other soldiers appear to have received wounds from blunt objects, also falling from above, possibly stones thrown from battlements.

Not all the injuries had in themselves been fatal, but a number of the bodies showed additional wounds which clearly were. It was apparent that many of the soldiers had been clubbed to death, for their skulls had been hit by a blunt object with considerable force. Most wounds were to the left side of the head, as if the men had been held by their hair then hit with a club in the right hand of their attacker. This is the position seen on the many traditional smiting scenes.

All the bodies had been simply wrapped in a few layers of linen with no evidence of any embalming. Those who had prepared the burial had extended the arms of the men by

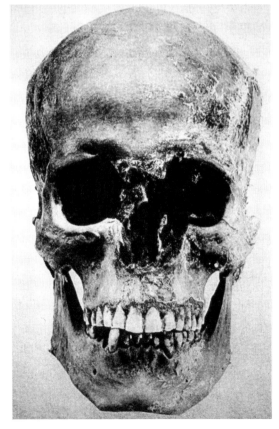

179. Skull of one of Mentuhotep's soldiers, showing severe injury to the nasal area.

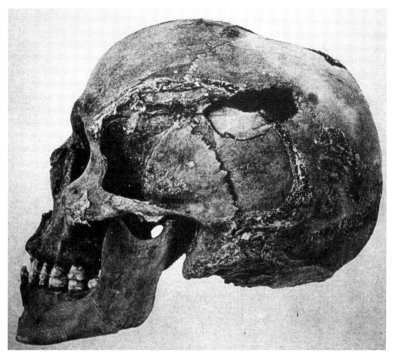

their sides, although this was not possible with some of the bodies, as *rigor mortis* appears to have set in before they were wrapped. Many of these particular bodies appeared also to have been attacked by scavenging birds.

All these men died at a time when there were no campaigns outside Egypt, so they must have died during the series of civil wars when the Princes of Thebes were trying to re-unify the country under their rule. From the evidence of the bodies, Winlock was able to reconstruct a likely scenario for the battle in which they died.

We know that the men were not killed in hand-to-hand combat, where they would have received wounds to the torso and particularly to the arms and hands if they had been fending off an attack. The soldiers of Mentuhotep were possibly injured in an attack on a well-defended town, with high defensive walls.

In the first attack on the town, a number of the soldiers were killed or wounded by arrows and stones fired or thrown from the battlements. The attack faltered and the soldiers were called back. More of them were killed as they retreated, receiving arrows in their backs.

The surviving soldiers and walking wounded retreated, possibly some distance from the town, leaving the bodies of their fallen comrades behind. It was then that the soldiers inside the town made a sortie to retrieve their arrows and anything else of value on the fallen bodies. It was at this time that those fallen soldiers who were wounded but still alive were clubbed to death. (This may sound barbaric and could have been an act of pure revenge, but consider the circumstances: the men left behind must have been those most severely wounded since those with less serious injuries would have walked or been helped away. The fallen men faced a slow and agonising death with absolutely no hope of any medical help and little chance of survival, so their enemy may have regarded their killing as purely humane. Such "mercy killing" has occurred in similar circumstances during military campaigns throughout history).

The defenders then withdrew back into their town, leaving the bodies of their enemy outside the city walls. There they lay for a while, at least long enough for the bodies to begin to decompose and for many of them to be attacked by vultures or other carrion birds who stripped off much of the soft tissue.

A second assault was then made on the town, which this time was successful. However, many men were killed in this attack too. The victorious Mentuhotep collected all the bodies, those that had lain there for some time and those fallen more recently, and arranged for them to be taken to Thebes for burial. There they were given the singular honour of a burial in a tomb that was close to the planned burial place of the king himself, and indeed overlooked it.

That the king chose to honour these soldiers in this way indicates that this particular battle was of great significance, perhaps the capture of the last remaining town opposed to his rule and his aim of a re-unified Egypt.

It must be supposed that Mentuhotep arranged for the bodies of all the soldiers who fell to be treated in this way. If this is the case, a fatality rate of just sixty or so is relatively small in an attacking force that must have been several hundred strong. Although battles were sometimes fought with hundreds and thousands of men throughout history, even with primitive medical support the casualty list of those killed outright in battle was often surprisingly small. We must imagine an equally large number, possibly more, of wounded men, some with minor wounds but many much more severely injured.

This was the reality of life for an Egyptian soldier, indeed for any soldier, and it is important that it is not forgotten or overlooked. Reports of such an event might just say that "Mentuhotep attacked the town, was initially driven back but it was captured in a second attack." That is only *part* of the real human story.

As convincing and compelling as this scenario may be, it is my no means certain that this is actually what happened. Dr. Carola Vogel of the University of Mainz has questioned if the wounds exhibited by the bodies were actually caused by arrows fired from battlements. The angle of the arrows in the bodies could be explained another way, for if arrows are fired from ground level high into the air, they will descend to the ground almost vertically.

Dr. Dorothea Arnold, of the Metropolitan Museum of Art in New York has questioned the dating of the bodies to the reign of Mentuhotep (as has Dr. Vogel). It is now thought that the bodies could date to the reigns of either Amenemhat I or Senuseret I, some ten to eighty years later than the reign of Mentuhotep.

Nevertheless, regardless of the actual date and exact circumstances, the injuries received by the soldiers and the treatment of their bodies still illustrates most graphically the dangers and brutal reality of ancient warfare.

Even if individuals came out of action alive but wounded, their survival was by no means certain, for many would have died from infected wounds. More men are likely to have died from their wounds after a battle, than during the conflict itself. Some of those who survived their wounds faced a life where they were severely disfigured or handicapped.

The survival of any individual would have owed more to chance, physical condition and age, than to the skills of the physician. The physicians had a wealth of practical experience and a limited range of ointments and drugs to call upon. The antiseptic properties of honey on wounds was well known and drugs such as opium, whilst not available to all, could have been used for pain relief. Medicine was still in its formative years and apart from relatively simple cures and remedies for basic problems the physicians' skills would have been defeated by many of the ailments and injuries presented to them. When their skills were insufficient, they could do little more than try to make their patients as comfortable as possible and invoke the services of the priests.

However, perhaps earlier accounts have done the ancient physicians an injustice by underestimating their skills, for in recent years human remains have been found that indicate more advanced treatment for wounds and ailments than we had previously known.

At Giza, in the tombs of the builders of the pyramids, there is evidence of successful limb amputation, where the patient appears to have survived for some time, and also for treatment of bone fractures that had been expertly splinted to aid recovery.

At Thebes, remains from the Eighteenth Dynasty and later also show that amputations were successfully carried out. There is a rare survival of a prosthetic big toe, carved from wood, which we can tell was used in life and not just provided for the afterlife.

We know that the physicians encountered some horrendous wounds and that they occasionally kept records of what they saw of internal parts of the body, even if they did not fully understand their workings. One surviving account, perhaps of a war wound, is the earliest recorded description of the human brain:

> "When you examine a man with a … wound on his head, which goes to the bone; his skull is broken; broken open is the brain of his skull ... Something is there ... that quivers and flutters under your fingers like the weak spot on the head of a child which has not yet grown hard … Blood flows from his two nostrils."

In addition to war wounds, the physicians would also have been expected to deal with any number of complaints and aliments, which would have occurred either on campaign or in the barracks. It is apparent from research on mummified remains from the Theban necropolis that around 15% of the bodies have suffered some form of trauma that has left clear evidence on the skeleton. In many cases soft tissue has not survived, so we do not have an estimated figure for any injuries in this area. Soldiers could expect a much higher injury rate, either caused in combat or simply from the day to day accidents they suffered when on campaign or undertaking other duties.

The level of injuries may have varied through Egyptian history. In the early times and into the Middle Kingdom, bows, arrows and spears were the main weapons – which were not designed for close combat. By the New Kingdom swords were used – and these were close-combat only weapons. Casualty rates in the New Kingdom appear to have been higher and to have risen as swords became more widely used. Thutmose III recorded only eighty or so casualties at the battle of Megiddo, but by the reign of Ramesses III, casualties (amongst the enemy at least) ran into thousands.

Soldiers (and indeed any ancient Egyptian) would also have been plagued by gnats, midges and sand flies and, if they were living on the edge of the desert, would have had to cope with scavenging dogs, jackals and poisonous snakes. Travel on the river was also a risky business, with crocodiles along the length of the Nile; hippopotami were also present, which even today in central Africa cause more deaths than any other wild animal.

Schistomiasis, caused by a parasite that invades the body, was (and still is) a major disease in Egypt. Tuberculosis appears to have been endemic too, with perhaps as much as 40% of the population affected. Recent studies have also indicated that there were cases of vitamin C deficiency (scurvy), and the severe dental problems already mentioned could lead to abscesses and more serious infections. Ancient Egypt was a dangerous place for both soldiers and civilians.

We do not know where most soldiers were buried, especially those who died away from Egypt. Small burial sites have been found at some of the fortifications, but it must be presumed that those of high status would have had their bodies returned home for burial. On campaign, most soldiers who were killed in action were probably buried close to the place they died.

Life in any army has *never* been easy, and it was rare indeed for a soldier to survive to a ripe old age and to be able to relate the stories of his campaigns to his grandchildren.

5 FORTIFICATIONS AND SIEGE WARFARE

The earliest representations of settlements in Egypt clearly show them with strong, fortified walls, circular, rectangular or square in shape.

The hieroglyphic symbols of "city" and "enclosure" are plans of circular and rectangular enclosure walls.

181. The hieroglyphs for towns and fortifications.

The earliest defences were probably simple fences made of reeds designed to keep livestock in and wild animals (particularly jackals and lions) out. By the early Dynastic Period towns were enclosed within walls built of mud brick and were a suitable defence against military attack too.

Most settlements in Egypt were built on higher ground. This was essential because most of the country was flooded by the river Nile once a year and houses needed to be located well above the rising water level. This also gave them a good defensive position.

Any fortifications or defensive measures were probably initially parochial in nature, and not part of any national strategy to protect Egypt's frontiers. The building of walls around a town shows high organisational skills for it would have needed a communal effort to erect and maintain them.

Defensive walls were made from simple mud brick. The raw material, Nile mud, was readily available and mud bricks were used for most domestic architecture throughout the whole Dynastic Period. The mud was strengthened by the addition of chopped straw, which prevented the bricks from cracking when they dried in the sun. Thick walls were reinforced with wooden beams built into them at regular intervals and were built with a wider base than top, which meant that inner and outer surfaces were not vertical, but sloped inwards. They were built with crenellated battlements, which gave protection to defenders who could fire arrows through the gaps at the top of the wall. The rough surface of the wall was finished with a smooth mud coat and sometimes also with an additional fine layer of white plaster.

The scale of some of the early mud brick building is impressive. A rare example can be found at Hierakonpolis, where a huge building, known erroneously as the "Fort", still survives substantially intact today. The structure was built by Khasekhemwy around 2686. Its exact

182. The mud brick walls of "The Fort" at Hierakonpolis.

purpose is unknown, but it was probably not a fort, nor a tomb as was first believed, but was perhaps used for a religious or ceremonial purpose. Nevertheless it is worth examining this site, as such large-scale walls were undoubtedly also built for defensive purposes around the larger settlements. At the "Fort" the mud brick walls survive in places to almost their original height of around ten metres and they are nearly five metres thick. They are constructed with the typical recessed panel "palace façade" decoration and would have originally been plastered and painted white. The "fort" measures around sixty-five metres by fifty-seven metres, and there is just one entrance into the enclosure.

183. The great mud brick enclosure walls at Elkab.

We know that the great city of Memphis was built with similar large defensive walls, which were probably also plastered and painted – the "White Walls", described by the early kings. Similar huge walls survive at Nekhen (Elkab), enclosing a vast area, and also at temple sites, such as the Temple of Amun at Karnak and the Temple of Ramesses III at Medinet Habu.

As the centralised control over a unified Egypt grew, and especially when the borders of Egypt were under threat, fortresses were built at strategic points in the country. Egypt has distinct natural borders: the western desert, and the Sinai along the western and eastern edges of the Delta, the western and eastern deserts along the length of the Nile and the First Cataract of the river itself just south of modern Aswan.

These geographic features formed natural barriers which were more than sufficient for many centuries to isolate and protect Egypt and to allow its culture to develop and become established. They were strengthened with forts in the Early Dynastic and Old Kingdom, but when the Egyptian Empire expanded further into enemy territory, new and artificial defensives were created.

One of the oldest forts in Egypt was built during the Old Kingdom on the southern tip of Elephantine Island, which sits in the middle of the Nile just north of the First Cataract. A small settlement grew up around the fort and this important site was further developed and inhabited for the whole of the Dynastic period and beyond.

During the Middle Kingdom a new string of fortresses (known as the "Walls of the Prince") was built in the eastern Delta to protect the trade routes into the Levant. A fortress was also built in the Wadi Natrun to protect the Western Desert from the Libyans.

The southern border with Nubia was at this time further strengthened. The island of Elephantine marked the border between Egypt and Nubia. To get around the Cataract, which could not be navigated by ships, all goods had to be unloaded and transported along the riverbank. This route was open to potential attack by the Nubians, and was protected by a huge mud-brick wall, built in the Twelfth Dynasty. This wall ran for seven and a half kilometres. Further south at the Second Cataract, the land route around the natural obstruction was similarly protected.

184. View of the First Cataract at Aswan.

During the Old Kingdom a series of small trading posts had been established in Nubia, and in the Middle Kingdom these settlements were substantially fortified. The fortresses were located at strategic points along the river and were situated on high ground with a commanding view of both the river and surrounding land. Many were enormous, and completely enclosed the original settlements. The garrisons may have been small, but these were also major trading centres and storage areas.

The fortresses contained huge storerooms, workshops, housing for the garrison and burial sites too. Designed and located to be a visible symbol of Egyptian control over the area and a deterrent to any potential invader, they dominated the landscape.

Evidence recovered from these sites shows that the storage capacity in terms of grain in each location was sufficient to feed between three and five hundred people a year. The number of soldiers present on a permanent basis may well have been only about fifty, with the remainder of the inhabitants being officials, bureaucrats and traders. At the fort of Mirgissa, there is evidence that spears, arrows and javelins were actually manufactured on site and this may well have been the case at the other fortresses too.

The walls and ramparts were built of mud brick, to complicated and very sophisticated designs. Ramparts and ditches around the fortress proper formed the first obstacle to any attackers. The high mud brick walls that overlooked the ditches and ramparts gave a clear line of fire on any attackers, whilst giving the defenders superb protection.

The military design of such fortifications is remarkable. It has rarely been surpassed and would have been recognisable and appreciated by military engineers throughout the ages. These Egyptian fortresses, and castles built three thousand years later in mediaeval Europe, were designed to withstand attack from similar weapons and their almost identical design and layout is probably no coincidence. Only with the introduction of gunpowder was this type of defensive fortification made obsolete. The great Nubian forts may well have influenced Greek and Roman military engineers and some of the architectural details and defensive structures may have been copied, influencing fortifications for the next two thousand years.

Ten large-scale fortresses were built in the area of the Second Cataract, where the river Nile is at its narrowest and any convoys of goods are at most risk of attack.

From the north to the south, they were Buhen, Kor, Dorginarti, Mirgissa, Dabenarti, Shalfak, Uronaroti, Semna, Kumma and Semna South. Walls, bastions and ditches were all of the same design.

A large number of these forts were built in a relatively short space of time. Between the reigns of Senuseret I and III, at least seventeen were constructed in a period of one hundred and thirty years. It is likely that just one or two expert military architects designed them, for they show a certain uniformity of design and an ability to make the most of any natural defences, using the local topography to best advantage. The forts of Buhen and Mirgissa, for example, were rectangular in layout, whereas the fort of Semna was built on an "L" shape in order to fit on the rocky outcrop upon which it was built. Uronaroti was triangular in shape for a similar reason.

One of the most important features in each fortress was a protected stairway giving a direct link with the river, providing both access and also a ready supply of fresh water.

Within the fortress, the town and any military buildings were laid out in a regular geometric grid pattern. A clear space ran around the inside of the defensive walls to enable rapid movement of troops in the event of any attack.

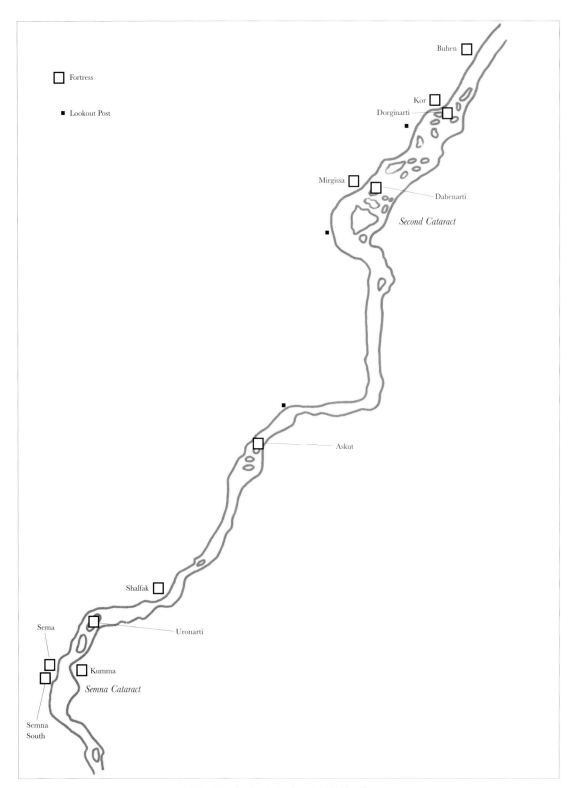

Fortress

Lookout Post

Buhen

Kor

Dorginarti

Mirgissa

Dabenarti

Second Cataract

Askut

Shalfak

Sema

Uronarti

Kumma

Semna Cataract

Semna
South

185. Map showing the location of the Nubian Fortresses.

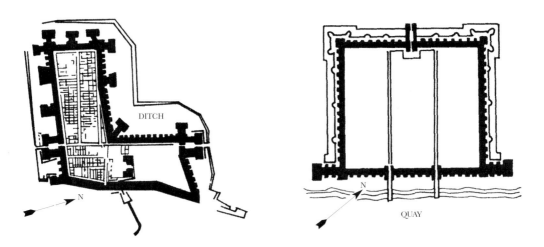

186. Plans of the Fortresses of Semna (left) and Buhen (right).

The Fortress of Buhen was one of the largest and its dimensions were impressive. Built entirely of mud brick, the outer enclosure walls that surrounded the site were over seven hundred metres long and four metres thick. The walls were strengthened at regular intervals by semi-circular bastions. The western wall had five large towers and an enormous central tower measuring forty-seven by thirty metres protected the double gateway, which was sealed by double wooden doors and a movable drawbridge.

187. The remains of the Fortress of Buhen.

188. View of the outer battlements of the Fortress at Buhen.

The inner walls of the fort were five metres thick and at least eleven metres high, reinforced by square towers at the corners, and also with bastions at regular intervals. The walls were made with loopholes for the archers and with crenellated battlements. Such defences would have been truly formidable.

189. View of the outer and inner fortress walls at Buhen.

190. Reconstruction of the original appearance of the Fortress of Buhen.

There is no record that any of the Nubian fortresses actually came under attack, and in fact they could easily have been by-passed in the desert by anyone seriously intent on invading Egypt. If they *had* been attacked they would probably have proved impregnable, but as a deterrent they served their purpose and they were not put to the test. The fortresses would have been used as a base for short-term "smash and grab" raids by the Egyptians at times when the permanent garrison would have been strengthened. These raids were sufficient to subdue any rebelliousness in the area, or at least to prove who was in control; but the fortresses were there primarily to protect the trade route and the king's monopoly on the precious commodities imported into Egypt from Nubia and Africa. It is evident that the kings of the Middle Kingdom were very successful in this respect, for during this period the whole of Nubia and the land as far south as the Third Cataract came under Egyptian control.

Other fortresses were built to the north of Buhen in lower Nubia. These seem to have been connected primarily with the diorite quarries (at Aniba) and the copper and gold mines (at Kubban). They appear, however, to have played no strategic role in the defence of the area, nor to have been associated with any large centres of population, but to have been little more than architectural propaganda.

A series of lookout posts, located to overlook the river Nile, was established between the larger forts. Remains of stone huts show their location and help us to see that good and rapid communications could be maintained along the chain of forts.

In the New Kingdom, the kings needed to re-establish their control over Nubia following the period of unrest and disorder of the Second Intermediate Period, when many of the Middle Kingdom fortresses in Nubia had fallen into disrepair. (Mud brick buildings require regular maintenance.) The fortifications along the Nile in Nubia were repaired and in many cases enlarged, as trade with the centre of Africa was re-established.

Some of the improvements made to the fortresses were in response to technological innovations: access had now to be provided for chariots, and the horses required stabling. The fortresses in the New Kingdom became more like small towns than garrisons and trading points, although that was still their main function. Defence, however, now appears to have become almost a secondary consideration, as the Egyptians felt secure in the completely subjugated land of Nubia. Temple building replaced the building of new fortresses

At the old fortresses, new stone temples were erected inside and outside the strong walls. Fortifications erected at new towns such as Soleb were much simpler, often little more than a simple mud brick wall with towers at intervals.

Sadly none of these magnificent fortresses survive today; they are now under the waters of Lake Nasser, created by the building of the High Dam at Aswan. Before they were flooded, they were excavated and the resultant published reports and limited number of photographs are the only evidence now available to us. Many of the temples were, however, moved to new sites.

In the north of Egypt a series of forts was built in the New Kingdom, to protect both the eastern and western approaches to the Delta. Many still survive at sites such as Tell el-Heir in

191. *Map showing the location of the Nubian temples, both historically and today.*

the east and Zaiwat Um el-Rakham in the west. Like the Nubian forts, they also appear to have been centres for trading, but the scale of the fortifications is much smaller. Mud brick was used for the main walls with only some of the more important buildings being made from locally quarried stone.

In times of unrest or invasion, the forts were the first lines of defence and, certainly by the time of the New Kingdom, there is little evidence that the major centres of habitation were themselves fortified. True, few town sites have actually been excavated as many today lie buried directly under modern towns and villages; but the few that do survive, even if they are enclosed by a wall, are certainly not fortified. It was the temples of the gods that provided a place of refuge when necessary. Always enclosed by a huge perimeter mud brick wall, the temples could be easily defended. The high and thick walls enclosed a large area and there was room for the local inhabitants and their livestock.

192. Mud brick enclosure walls at the Temple of Dendera.

The rulers of the New Kingdom and later periods erected temples in Nubia rather than forts. Many of the temples were massive stone constructions surrounded by mud brick enclosure walls. Although centres of religion, these buildings could also be used as havens in times of unrest. Many of these temples survive, although most are now located at new sites, having been moved to escape the rising waters of Lake Nasser in the 1960s.

In Egypt, the Mortuary Temple of Ramesses III at Medinet Habu was used as a refuge when Libyans were raiding from the desert. The temple complex, which comprised not just the temple, but a royal palace, houses for the priests and storerooms, is completely enclosed by substantial brick walls and there are only two entrances to the enclosure. The eastern and western gateways of the temple (only the eastern one survives) are copies in stone of fortifications seen by the Egyptians in Syria. Known as a *migdol*, the stone gates have wide-based walls, windows high up in the walls and crenellated tops. Each gateway had two gates, both open from above to allow any attackers to be fired upon, in the event of their actually reaching that far. These gates may have been built simply as an architectural novelty, but many years after they were completed, they were to prove their worth as the complex of Medinet Habu was used as a safe and well-stocked fortress when Thebes was under attack.

193. The outer wall of the Mortuary Temple of Medinet Habu, showing crenellations.

194. The Migdol gateway in the Mortuary Temple of Ramesses III at Medinet Habu showing the strength of the outer walls.

195 and 196. Two views of the Migdol gateway in the Mortuary Temple of Ramesses III at Medinet Habu.

137

For a town (or temple) to be successfully defended, especially in a siege, strong walls were not enough. Stores of food, for the inhabitants and livestock, would have needed to be kept within the town, and a ready access to a water supply from wells, protected access to the river, or nearby canals, was absolutely essential.

Many temples were provided with several wells and a sacred lake within the enclosure walls of the complex. Food was stored in large granaries, and particularly fine examples of large, mud-brick vaulted stores survive at the rear of the Ramesseum, the Mortuary Temple of Ramesses II at Thebes.

197. Granaries at the rear of the Ramesseum at Thebes.

In many places, settlements were built on elevated ground, which gave defenders an advantage: it is always more difficult to attack uphill. The space immediately outside the walls would have been kept clear of buildings and trees and any attack would have had to have been made across open ground with no cover, whilst the defenders would have been secure behind their walls and have been able to fire arrows spears and other missiles down on any attackers. In these circumstances, an adequate stock of weapons was also essential.

The art of siege warfare is completely different from that of a pitched battle. Some sieges could be over very quickly. A short but sustained full attack could quickly weaken defences and demoralise the defenders to the extent they soon surrendered. If an initial onslaught failed to take the town, the defenders, given a suitable time to reflect on their circumstances, might decide that they were not able to hold out and that they had no alternative but to negotiate a surrender. If, however, the defenders had a good food and water supply, morale was high and there was sufficient manpower, then a siege could last much longer. The attackers would have had to starve the defenders into submission.

The logistical problems of feeding an army on campaign could cause problems for the besiegers too, and often it would have been simply a case of who could hold out the longest. There must have been many occasions where those inside the besieged town had adequate food, water and good defences and where they could watch their attackers suffer from lack of food and water and ultimately be forced to raise the siege and leave.

One of the earliest representations of what was probably a series of successful sieges comes from a ceremonial palette dating to around 3000 B.C and now in the Egyptian Museum in Cairo. It shows a series of animal deities or symbols, attacking walled towns with mattocks. The towns are shown enclosed in thick, buttressed walls and the name of each town is recorded. It is presumed that the palette represents the victorious outcome of a series of campaigns by an unknown early king. This is from a time when the separate nomes of Egypt were still in the process of being united as a nation state.

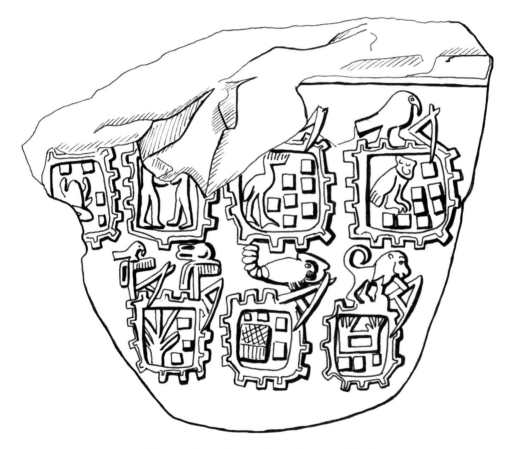

198. Captured towns shown on a fragment from a ceremonial palette.

The mattock, essentially an agricultural implement, was actually a very effective siege weapon. Walls of sun-dried mud brick are soft and could relatively easily be cut through or undermined with the use of mattocks.

Before the mining could begin the attackers had first to reach the base of the walls, in itself a difficult task. Once there, their aim was either to cut a way through the walls by tunnelling, or just to undermine parts of the walls sufficiently to cause them to collapse. This was always a lengthy job, however, and a dangerous occupation.

An Eleventh Dynasty tomb of the Middle Kingdom at Thebes, already mentioned, contained the bodies of soldiers who had clearly died in battle. All the men had been injured by arrows and the angles of the wounds indicate that the arrows had been fired from above the men, perhaps from town walls during a siege.

If walls could not be breached or tunnelled through by the use of mattocks, the only alternative for the attackers would have been to attempt to force a way in over the walls or through any gateways.

With high defending walls, the only way to get *over* them was to use ladders. A wall-scene in the Tomb of Khaemhesy of the Fifth Dynasty shows a scaling ladder in use. The strong wooden ladder has wheels at its base, to enable it to be rolled swiftly into position before being raised vertically against the walls of the town. Soldiers at the base of the ladder wedge poles against the ladder to prevent the base rolling away from the wall whilst their colleagues swarm up the ladder to the top of the wall, their axes tucked into the waistbands of their short kilts, ready for action.

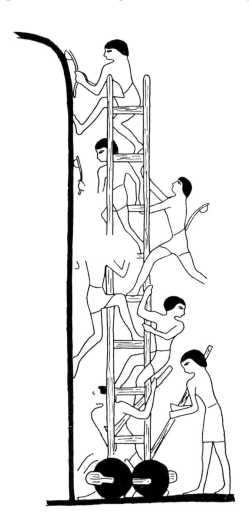

This too was a very risky operation for the attackers. Firstly, the ladder had to be manoeuvred into position, whilst under enemy fire. Secondly, it had to be raised against the wall, an exercise that would logically have met some resistance, and thirdly, the ladder then had to be scaled by the soldiers. Only one soldier would reach the top of the wall at a time and he had to climb, defend himself, and fight from a precarious position to gain a foothold on the wall. Only when he was on the wall (or had been pushed off the ladder) could the next soldier in turn try his luck.

A rare scene of a siege survives in the Old Kingdom Tomb of Anta at Dishasha in Middle Egypt. Anta lived around the middle of the Old Kingdom, about 2340 BC. The wall scenes are fragmentary and whilst the inscription is too badly damaged to tell us exactly what is happening, the images themselves speak volumes and they are the oldest battle scenes to survive from Ancient Egypt.

The eastern wall of the tomb is decorated with a scene showing a battle between Egyptians and foreigners, most probably in the area of southern Palestine.

199. A siege ladder fitted with wheels.

200. Battle scene from the Tomb of Anta at Dishasha.

The Egyptians are attacking a walled town, and it is clear that the enemy have sent out a force to fight the Egyptians outside the town. The Egyptians fight with battle axes and maces, and this part of the battle was clearly preceded by an attack by archers, for the enemy are shown pierced with arrows.

The main part of the scene shows the walled town under attack. Soldiers are climbing up scaling ladders in an attempt to climb over the walls, whilst others are digging away at the mud brick walls in an attempt to make a breach. Men inside the walls are shown listening carefully for the sound of digging, in order to defend any breach.

What is especially fascinating is that the inhabitants of the town are shown, and that they are mostly women, as the men had left the town to fight. Far from being shown as defenceless, the women are shown fighting the Egyptian soldiers who entered the town, using daggers and their bare hands to defend their homes and children.

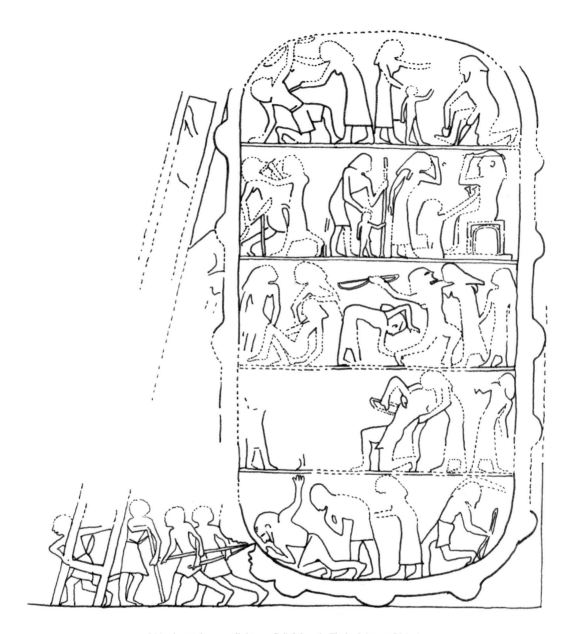

201. An attack on a walled town. Relief from the Tomb of Anta at Dishasha.

The Egyptian attack was ultimately successful and a small group of women, clearly in distress, are shown announcing the fall of the town to the local chief, who sits on a stool in his house within the city.

To the victor goes the spoils of war, and a line of tethered captives, including women and children, is shown being taken from the captured town. One Egyptian soldier is shown carrying off a woman over his shoulder.

This rare survival of an early battle scene is superior in execution to other rather stiff scenes from the Twelfth Dynasty at Beni Hassan. It shows great invention and detail and a real glimpse of the realities of siege warfare. The action of the women is particularly interesting, and their combatant role is likely to have been common in such events, albeit as a last resort.

During any campaign, few commanders would ever have risked the lives of their men unless there was a good chance of success. Each town being besieged would have had its defences carefully evaluated by the attacking force. If the fortifications looked vulnerable, or poor, and the defenders not able to put up much of a fight, then a direct assault might be launched.

The usual approach was a full-scale attack and an attempt to force the town gates. In the Middle Kingdom, we see for the first time battering rams being used to break open the gates. A wooden covering, known as a *testudo*, is used to stop the enemy arrows and other missiles reaching the men. The use of a battering ram was probably the first tactic in any siege, as entry into a defended town through the gateway has always been the easiest way.

If, however, the town defences were well maintained and substantial, then the attackers would settle in for a long siege, rather than risk losing men in an attack.

From the New Kingdom onwards we have written descriptions of sieges. Ahmose I, the founder of the Eighteenth Dynasty, drove the Hyksos out of Egypt by attacking many of the Delta cities. One of his soldiers, Ahmose, the son of Ebana, recorded his own exploits on the walls of his tomb at El Kab.

Ahmose I captured Avaris, the Hyksos capital in the Delta, then moved on to the city of Sharuhen, a Hyksos base in north Sinai.

"Then Sharuhen was besieged for three years. Then his majesty took it."

Clearly such sieges could last a *long* time and the defenders would have effectively prevented a sizeable contingent of Ahmose's army from campaigning elsewhere. The tactic of withdrawing into a fortified town was useful, not just for the immediate benefit of self-preservation. Once inside a town, the defenders, if adequately stocked with food and water, had a chance to rest and regroup, and might even be able to plan and execute an attack from the town against the besiegers.

The Mortuary Temple of Ramesses III at Medinet Habu, in effect a fortified town, had access to several wells and a large sacred lake, which meant a constant supply of fresh water was available from within the walls. Safe inside the walls, the defenders could simply wait for a relieving force to arrive whilst at the same time hoping that the enemy would grow weaker and leave.

202. The sacred lake within the Mortuary Temple complex of Ramesses III, along with several wells, meant a constant supply of fresh water was available.

Sieges of several months would not necessarily cause a problem to the defenders of the best-prepared of the large cities. There would be an adequate supply of stored food, but if a siege was protracted, then the fields around the town could not be worked, which meant no fresh supplies would be available as stocks diminished.

The bulk of information about sieges comes from the New Kingdom and from the reigns of two pharaohs in particular, Thutmose III and Ramesses II.

Thutmose III made seventeen separate campaigns into West Asia, (which are recounted more fully elsewhere in this volume). He captured a great number of cities during his campaigns, the names of which are recorded in the inscriptions on the pylon he raised in the temple of Amun at Karnak.

The most important city to be besieged was Megiddo. From the narrative which is preserved we know that the Egyptian army under Thutmose III "... invested [this] city, surrounding it with a ditch and enclosing it with fresh timbers of all their pleasant trees."

The King had ordered the building of siegeworks. He denuded the area surrounding the city and encircled it with fortifications, both to contain the city and its occupants and protect the attackers.

Thutmose III's Gebel Barkal stela records that the siege lasted for "... a period of seven months before they came out into the open, pleading to my Majesty and saying 'Give us breath, O our Lord'."

Thutmose also attacked the city of Kadesh, where the Egyptians successfully breached the city walls.

The Egyptian policy of cutting down the enemy's trees and digging up their corn is noted in many accounts of this time. This served two purposes: firstly it deprived the enemy of their use, but more importantly, it enabled the attacking army to survive. Whilst a defending town might have a good supply of food and water, the attackers had to literally live off the land. They ate the enemy's crops, and his cattle, and used his timber to construct siege works and palisades for their own encampments. If a siege lasted longer, then soldiers would become farmers and would work the fields, planting and harvesting crops for themselves and the animals and ensuring the fields were constantly irrigated. The necessary skills would have been readily available, as many of the soldiers would have come from farming backgrounds.

One slightly unusual tactic, which is alluded to in the accounts of Thutmose III's campaigns, is the successful capture of the city of Joppa by Djehuty, a General of Thutmose III. The general liaised with the defenders and it was agreed that some supplies would be allowed to enter the city. Djehuty was devious and clever and the defenders were far too trusting: a small body of commandos was carried into the city hidden in large wicker baskets.

Djehuty tells us that Thutmose "... caused two hundred baskets, which he had fabricated, to be brought and caused two hundred soldiers to descend into them ... They were told – as soon as you enter the town you shall ... seize hold of all persons who are in the town and put them in rope bands straight away."

The people of the town were tricked into believing the baskets contained plunder belonging to the prince of Joppa. At night the men crept out of the baskets and opened the town gates from the inside, allowing a larger Egyptian force to enter. This was an early pre-cursor of the Trojan-Horse tactic and one that worked (at least on the first occasion it was used!)

Djehuty was a successful general and he seems to have prospered. We know this, for his burial at Sakkara survived intact until 1824 AD. His mummy was found "cased in solid gold" and many other precious objects survived too. The contents of the tomb were dispersed to various collections around the world and no detailed records were made of the discovery; even the location of the tomb is not known today. Many of the gold objects appear to be personal gifts from Thutmose III showing the high regard the king had for his general.

Detailed written accounts of sieges from the Ramesside period are lacking, but we have a series of monumental scenes carved on the walls of the temples which give a wealth of information.

Like Thutmose III, Ramesses II led a number of campaigns and placed himself at the head of his troops. His capture of the Hittite city of Dapur is shown on the exterior walls of the temple of Luxor and also on the walls of his Mortuary Temple, the Ramesseum.

The city was taken by Ramesses and the text tells how the king "... hurls down their possessions ... makes all of their places into desolate mounds". One of the Luxor temple reliefs illustrates this well. The captured city is completely empty of people, dead or alive. The doorways are leaning at crazy angles; lintels and bricks fall from the walls and in the surrounding

203. *Attack on the town of Dapur in the reign of Ramesses II.*

145

countryside, even the trees and shrubs have been destroyed. The scene is one of absolute destruction and desolation, the city having been completely sacked by the might of the Egyptian army. There was obviously no intent, on this occasion at least, to capture the city intact and occupy it. Nothing less than complete destruction would serve the Egyptian purpose (presumably only after the city had been plundered of anything of value by the victorious army).

Ramesses II also had his battle scenes carved on the walls of his small temple at Beit el Wali in Nubia, where the various stages of his campaigns are shown in detail.

Ramesses III did the same with his own exploits on the walls of his great fortified Mortuary Temple at Medinet Habu on the west bank of the river Nile opposite the city of Thebes. The victorious Egyptian soldiers are shown on top of the walls of the captured cities, triumphantly waving their battle standards and blowing their trumpets. Below them, other soldiers are demolishing the gateway, felling trees and burning hayricks.

Most of the scenes of the battles of Thutmose III and Ramesses II show the heaps of bodies of slain enemies. Ramesses III's scenes show the counting of the severed hands (or the phalli) of the slain enemy. These gruesome trophies of the victory are arranged in huge heaps to show the magnitude of the defeat.

It was obviously important to record the number of the slain, and severed body parts could be taken away from the battlefield and accurately counted later. In this instance Ramesses III appears to have been more than usually ruthless. If the claims from the temple reliefs are correct, and not purely propaganda, then most of the male inhabitants of the captured cities were killed, especially those who had borne arms against the Egyptians.

205. Ramesses II attacking a walled town. Cast of a relief from the
Temple of Beit el Wali in Nubia.

Feelings would no doubt have run high amongst besiegers who had to suffer almost as many hardships as the besieged. When a siege was successful, relief and the prospect of plunder may have made the victors more ruthless than they would otherwise have been. What became of any captured women and children can only be a matter of conjecture, but many may have been given as slaves to the victorious officers and been taken back to Egypt.

In the later periods of Egyptian history, not all sieges were against foreign cities. In the Twenty-Third Dynasty, Piye managed to bring Egypt back under his unified rule, after

206. *The trophies of victory: scenes from the Mortuary Temple of Ramesses III at Medinet Habu showing the counting of severed hands.*

207. *The trophies of victory: scenes from the Mortuary Temple of Ramesses III at Medinet Habu showing the counting of severed phalli.*

a period of disorder and the failure of national government. With rebellion still rife throughout the country, a prince of Sais laid siege to Herakleopolis and news of this soon reached Piye further in the south at Napata. The report tells how the prince "... is now assaulting Herakleopolis. He has completely ringed it around, allowing neither reinforcements to enter nor refugees to depart, but rather fights daily. He has invested it in its entire circumference. Every leader knows [his own sector of the] rampart, that he may cause every man among the leaders and tribal sheikhs to lay siege from his own sector."

Piye sent an army to raise the siege and the besiegers fled. Piye's troops pursued the fleeing army, but they too had to lay siege to several towns themselves, which dramatically slowed their progress. Piye came to Egypt himself to take control of the situation. He issued instructions to "... surround Hermopolis – capture its people, its herds, its ships which are on the river. Do not let the field hands go into the fields and do not let the ploughmen plough ..." The siege was established and "... they surrounded Hermopolis on its four sides, without letting reinforcements enter or refugees depart." A protective wall was made to cover the city wall and a 'wooden servant' (a siege engine or tower, or possibly just some protective covering for the troops working underneath) was raised up high against it.

For each day of the siege archers shot arrows into the city, slaughtering the people trapped within. Days passed and the city "... gave forth a foul stench to the nose ... Then Hermopolis prostrated itself."

This account illustrates well another aspect of siege warfare. Walled up within a city with many wounded, dying and dead, and perhaps with little or no fresh water, conditions would soon become very unsanitary and the prospect of disease a real threat.

Part of Piye's army also attacked the nearby stronghold of Tatehen, which they found to be, "... filled with soldiers and with all the valiant men of the Deltaland. Then a battering ram was made and used against it. Its walls were demolished and a great slaughter was made among them."

208. *A protective cover, used by soldiers attacking a walled town.*

Piye advanced still further into Egypt towards the Delta and reached the great ancient city of Memphis. He saw that the city was "... a stronghold, the rampart having been heightened with a new wall and the bastions equipped with strength that no toe hold for fighting against it might be found."

Different advice was forthcoming from his officers: "Some men said, 'Come let us assault it'; others said, 'Let a ramp be raised against it. Let us raise the earth against its ramparts. Let us tie a 'wooden servant' together. Let us erect towers. Let us place hangings upon the sides against it.' "

Piye, however, saw the weak link in the otherwise almost impregnable defences. The city was well prepared to withstand an attack from the landward side, but not one from the river. Piye first attacked the harbour and "... carried away every ferry, every yacht, every barge and every transport which had been anchored at the harbour of Memphis, their prow ropes being tied at its buildings." Using these boats, Piye then launched his attack from the river and the city was taken.

From this period onwards there were no other major *recorded* sieges, although there will undoubtedly have been sieges made by the Egyptians and also against them, as towards the end of the Dynastic Period, Egypt was increasingly invaded by Eastern Mediterranean armies.

Maintaining existing defences or building new fortifications can be a lengthy process and one that involves a great deal of organisation. In the latter years of Egyptian history, central control and organisation was lacking and once the main border fortifications had been passed, any invader of Egypt probably found little in the way of physical defences and fortifications to block his progress.

Sieges, rather than pitched battles were the most common type of military action seen by the Egyptians throughout the Dynastic Period, and, as we have seen, could be both dangerous and unpleasant for forces either attacking a town, or defending it.

6 CAMPAIGNS, BATTLES AND FIGHTING PHARAOHS

The Ancient Egyptians developed the art of writing at the beginning of what we now call the Dynastic Period, around 3150 BC. Within a relatively short period of time their deeds, thoughts and beliefs were being recorded – carved and painted on the walls of temples and tombs or written on objects and papyrus.

THE EVIDENCE

For some periods the surviving information is sparse, whilst for others we have a tremendous amount of detail, but from the earliest times we have written records of the military activities of the Egyptians from minor border patrols to full-scale battles and sieges.

The pharaohs were keen to record their military deeds and their own personal bravery, and some of the accounts appear to us to be bombastic, boastful and exaggerated, so much so that military disasters are actually portrayed as significant triumphs. At least the Ancient Egyptians are not alone in this; throughout the ages Kings, Emperors and Generals have realised the power of the written word as propaganda, to emphasise their own importance and to inspire, impress or intimidate their subjects.

The ancient records from Egypt have, therefore, to be interpreted with care, but occasionally we have written evidence from other contemporary civilisations, which can clarify or confirm some of the details.

Whilst the written word can give us a good understanding of events, nowhere is the saying "a picture paints a thousand words" perhaps more true than for Egypt. Many of the texts are accompanied by detailed depictions of the battles and actions of the pharaohs, scenes of victor and vanquished providing a wealth of detailed information about the campaigns. These scenes are, however, very stylised and most date from a relatively small period in the span of Egyptian history, the New Kingdom.

In the following pages we shall look in detail at some of the military campaigns beginning with the early Dynastic Period and ending three thousand years later when Egypt was conquered by the Romans.

In Egypt, official records known as Annals were kept for the reigns of each pharaoh, but only fragments of two have survived the centuries. The first survivor is the *Palmero Stone* which is part of a record that covers the earliest period of Egypt's history until the Sixth Dynasty; the second is the *Annals* of Thutmose III of the New Kingdom. These two records are over a thousand years apart and cover only a fraction of the Dynastic Period. We have to look elsewhere for other evidence of the military history of Egypt.

Fortunately for us, many inscriptions were made on the walls of monuments, although even many of these seemingly "permanent" records have been lost to us. In some cases these accounts have survived on far less likely writing surfaces. Senuseret II of the Middle Kingdom erected a large stela in a new temple he built at Heliopolis. The temple was destroyed centuries ago and the stela lost, but the inscription survives because a scribe copied it, possibly to practice his writing, on a roll of leather.

From the time of the Old Kingdom the custom of building stone tombs means that we have many inscriptions preserved on their walls. In the earliest tombs these texts tell us little more than the owner's name and his titles, but gradually over the centuries texts became more biographical. By the Sixth Dynasty we have details of the careers of some individuals and their services for pharaoh.

With a growing Empire, the pharaohs of the Fifth Dynasty and their successors left inscriptions on outcrops of rock in the territories they conquered. Many examples survive, such as those in the alabaster quarries of Hatnub, behind Tell el Amarna and on the quarry walls of the Wadi Hammamat in the Eastern Desert on the road to the Red Sea.

Similar texts also survive in the south of the country in the area of the First Cataract at Aswan. Many of these can still be seen today carved on the granite boulders by the river Nile. The earliest inscriptions *above* the Cataract date from the reign of Amenemhat I of the Middle Kingdom and are evidence that the Egyptians had taken firm control of the area. These inscriptions initially proclaimed the names and titles of the pharaohs, but the royal officials often added their own, more detailed, inscriptions. Most of our knowledge of military activity during the Middle Kingdom is drawn from accounts carved on the rocks in and around Aswan.

209. Inscriptions on rocks at Aswan.

From the time of the Middle Kingdom we also have many memorial stelae, erected by individuals at the holy site of Abydos. The inscriptions on the stelae record the visit to Abydos, give biographical details of the individual concerned, and crave the favours of the god for the recently deceased and their families. Biographies for this period are also found in the well-preserved tombs at Beni Hassan.

There are some surviving Middle Kingdom royal monuments where the inscribed records are more plentiful. Papyri also survive from this period, although their subject matter is often more domestic, such as letters, bills and accounts rather than covering great affairs of state.

It is not until the New Kingdom that a variety of documents of quality and quantity survive, which give us a far more detailed view of the affairs of the country. Royal monuments are particularly plentiful and well preserved. They contain scenes and inscriptions that detail the victories of the kings and the presentation of prisoners and spoil to the Theban god Amun. In many cases the same text was inscribed at more than one site, so where one version has been damaged any gaps can be filled by referring to other surviving examples. Walls, stelae and obelisks, erected to the glory of the god Amun, but also to the glory of the pharaohs, are covered in texts, written in poetic and highly coloured language.

210. The pylon of the Temple of Luxor, decorated with scenes of Ramesses II at the battle of Kadesh.

Other than the temple texts, official royal records are rare, but we do have some surviving international royal correspondence from the time of Akhenaten and also a peace treaty between Ramesses II and the Hittites.

From the New Kingdom onwards, private monuments and records are more numerous. In the painted scenes on the walls of tombs and accompanying texts we have records of the work of generals and the administrative officials of the Empire. In some instances the *only* record of foreign wars is from these biographical texts, as all other official State records have been lost.

Towards the end of the New Kingdom the site for the governing of the country was moved

211. Shattered temple remains at the Delta site of Tanis.

north from Memphis into the Delta. In the great new cities such as Per Ramesse and Tanis, temples were raised to the gods, palaces built and the state archives housed.

Unfortunately, these Delta sites are not well preserved: first in line for later invasions of Egypt, the many great cities were left in ruins. Buildings which *did* survive such attacks have, over the passing centuries, been systematically robbed of their stone (which is a precious commodity in the area) leaving only traces of their existence today. The dampness of the Delta has meant that little organic material has survived, and the fact that the region has been continually inhabited and farmed has resulted in the almost complete loss of many sites of archaeological importance.

These are the cities which would have witnessed the departure of the Egyptian armies and their return, either victorious or defeated and which would have felt the first impact of invading armies. The lack of archaeological evidence from the Delta sites does mean that our knowledge of ancient Egypt is somewhat one-sided and is based mainly on our knowledge of the history of Upper Egypt.

Despite the apparent abundance of New Kingdom evidence, the texts that do survive invariably have portions missing. These are almost inevitably the most important parts, the last few lines, giving the outcome of a battle or a dispute. Sadly much has been lost in relatively recent years, where tombs and exposed sites have been damaged, either by the hand of man or by exposure to the elements. Today, Egyptologists are keen to record the texts and this on-going recording is of great importance as some ancient texts are known to us today only because they were carefully recorded by early Egyptologists and travellers to the country. *Every* text is important, for even texts that may be incomplete, or whose meaning is obscure to us, may suddenly become important if missing fragments or other copies are found in the future.

THE PREDYNASTIC PERIOD

Up to 3150 BC

Geographically, Egypt is like no other country: there are no great mountain ranges and no plains, just narrow strips of fertile land along the edges of the great river Nile, in the Delta in the north and in a few desert oases.

   The prosperity and survival of the Egyptians depended entirely on the river, which provided a constant supply of water and whose annual inundation deposited a fertile layer of mud each year in which the crops were grown. No wonder that the Nile valley attracted settlers in Prehistoric times – certainly as far back as 5000 BC and probably before. This area had a wetter climate than today and supported a host of wild animals, such as wildfowl, antelope, gazelles, hyenas and lions, all now found only further south in Africa. The land was fertile enough to support a permanent population of humans and wildlife and the previously nomadic hunter-gathers established settlements, which ultimately were to form the basis of the Egyptian civilisation.

212. The successful hunter.

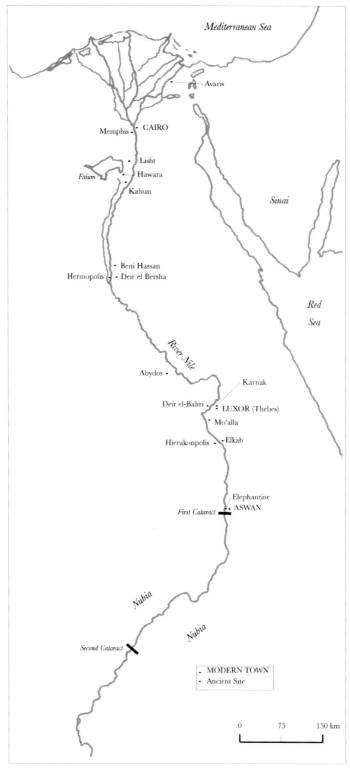

213. Map of Egypt covering the Predynastic and Archaic Periods to the Middle Kingdom.

We know that the climate in Egypt in the very early periods was different from today. The whole area was savannah-like, but this gave way to desert as the climate became warmer, forcing the population to concentrate along the Nile valley, where the water supply could support them.

As we have already seen, many of the weapons used by the Ancient Egyptians derived from those used for hunting. From the earliest times, the abundance of wildlife along the banks of the river Nile meant that there was always a plentiful supply of food, if it could be caught.

Spears and bows and arrows are shown in the earliest rock paintings. Many Egyptians would, of necessity, be familiar with the use of such weapons, and skilled in their use. Slings and throw sticks could bring down wild birds, and knives were needed to dismember the catches.

With a veritable arsenal of weapons available for domestic purposes, it was a simple transition for them to be used as weapons against neighbouring settlements if the need arose. Strength meant power and those villages that could field a large number of either hunters or warriors could enforce their control over others.

In a country with plentiful supplies of food, wildlife and cultivated crops, rivalry between villages was probably initially minimal, but with permanent settlements and a growing population, the pressure on these limited resources may have led to local disputes. Threats to the food supply or to personal territory could cause anger, jealousy and at worst, open conflict. Defence of property and family ultimately fell to the young and the fit. The natural leaders of the early settlements would have been the fittest and bravest of the men from the village. A brave and successful hunter could also be an effective head of the community and others would rely on his leadership and guidance.

214. Detail from the "Hunter's Palette" showing early Dynastic warriors with a variety of weapons.

When the leaders grew older, younger and fitter men may have challenged their position and it is probably from this time that the origins of the *Heb-Sed* festival were established. During the *Heb-Sed* festival the old leader had to prove he was still able to lead the group, with the emphasis on physical fitness. Part of the ritual appears to have required the ruler to run a set distance to prove his fitness and ability to continue as leader of the community. In later Egyptian history, during the *Heb-Sed* (which was usually celebrated during the thirtieth regnal year of the king, but often whenever the king wished) the royal powers were *magically* renewed and re-invigorated. In the earlier times, failure presumably meant the loss of status and the selection of a new leader.

215. Amenhotep III at his Heb Sed *festival, on a block from a now lost building at Karnak.*

There has been much debate over the centuries about the ethnic origins of the first rulers, who, some would argue, were not native Egyptians; although the idea of a "Dynastic Race", moving into Egypt and swamping the native population, is now generally dismissed. There is evidence during this very early period of trade links with Sumer, the civilisation which lay far to the east of Egypt, between the great Euphrates and Tigris rivers. There are some clear and

216. The Gebel el Arak
knife.

217. Detail of the handle of
the Gebel el Arak knife.

obvious similarities between the early art of the two countries and a number of Mesopotamian objects have been found in Egypt. This may well simply be because of a sophisticated and organised trade between the two countries, and may not necessarily indicate any formal invasion of Egypt in the earliest times.

A superb flint knife found at Gebel el Arak and now in the Louvre, has a decorated ivory handle carved with scenes showing men fighting and also boats.

It is not clear if this scene represents a Mesopotamian or an Egyptian event. It does, however, illustrate well periods of conflict in evolving civilisations. It is easy to understand how the Nile valley would seem to be a very attractive location in which to settle and perhaps early traders from Mesopotamia settled in Egypt, and became "Egyptian".

The Egyptians concept of "foreigners" throughout the centuries is interesting: it would appear that those who lived in Egypt and drank the waters of the Nile were regarded as Egyptians, even though their ethnic origins lay outside the country. Marriage with the local inhabitants would also have ensured a speedy integration. Perhaps Egypt was gradually infiltrated this way, and the early settlers were more ambitious and organised than were the native Egyptians. Egypt may well have been the first truly multi-racial society, with fewer problems caused by ethnic origins than we face today.

The complete absence of any written records before 3150 BC means that we can only guess at the nature of life in Egypt before this time. Many of the very early sites have never been fully excavated and it is only in recent years that we are beginning to get a true picture of this formative and important period of Egyptian history. Information can be gleaned from simple objects found in the tombs, such as pottery and beads, and from crude paintings found on rocks and pieces of pottery. Sometimes the interpretation of this evidence is difficult.

The Neolithic Egyptians were a stone-age people using stone tools and weapons for hunting, which included axes, knives, spears and arrows tipped with flint.

The social structure of Egypt probably began with independent villages and tribes scattered in settlements along the banks of the river, which over a period of time grouped together and evolved into small kingdoms. One tribe might be in dispute with another and open conflict would ensue, with ultimately one victor. Other tribes might be united by alliances based upon mutual need, perhaps shared agricultural work, or diplomatic alliances to deter potential aggressors. These groups of villages were known as "nomes" and there were forty-two nomes or local administrative areas. (The term "nome" is Greek; the Egyptian name was *sepat*.) This nome-structure never completely disappeared from Egypt throughout the Dynastic Period.

We know that even at this early stage in Egyptian history, goods were being traded between nomes and also over larger distances, indicating a well organised society.

THE ARCHAIC PERIOD
3150-2686 BC

Dynasty "0": 3150-3050

King Scorpion
Horus Narmer

A king called Narmer (also known as Menes) is credited with the unification of Egypt under his sole rule, around 3150 BC. The two separate kingdoms of Upper and Lower Egypt (themselves formed by the grouping together of individual nomes) were combined for the first time into a united Egypt. The distinction between the original two kingdoms was, however, never entirely lost: for the next three thousand years, the rulers of Egypt had, as one of their many titles, "Lord of the Two Lands".

Evidence for any formal battle that resulted in the final act of unification is minimal and it is likely that it was not achieved by one event, but was the end product of a more gradual and longer-term process. The only real evidence we have is a stone palette showing King Narmer, wearing the crowns of both Upper and Lower Egypt; he is the first ruler known to have done this. The "Narmer Palette" is believed to be ceremonial, although much simpler palettes (usually smaller) were used to grind malachite, as a cosmetic to decorate the eyes. The palette was found at Hierakonpolis and seems to have been deliberately buried there late in Egyptian history. The information available from the palette is open to interpretation and although the decoration includes writing, the early hieroglyphs that accompany the carved scenes are limited to names only and do not constitute a narrative text.

218. The decoration of the "Narmer Palette" showing the king wearing the White Crown of Upper Egypt and smiting his enemy.

219. The decoration of the "Narmer Palette" showing the king wearing the Red Crown and standing before rows of decapitated prisoners.

The largest figure shown on the palette is that of Narmer, who is shown in act of smiting his enemy. In his raised right hand he holds a heavy mace and in his left hand the hair of his vanquished enemy. This mace is presumably about to be used to deliver a fatal blow.

A servant who carries the king's sandals accompanies Narmer and in front of the king is a large falcon above a prostrate figure. The figure is bound and the falcon (a symbolic representation of the god Horus of Hierakonpolis) holds the end of a piece of rope used to tie him. It is presumed that the captive is the king of Lower Egypt (the Delta area). The scene at the bottom of the palette shows two vanquished enemies, along with hieroglyphs that represent the names of captured cities.

On the other side of the palette, scenes show a large bull demolishing the walls of a fortified town. This is one of the first representations of the king as a "Mighty Bull", another royal title that appears throughout Egyptian history. Narmer is shown wearing the crown of Lower Egypt, the Red Crown; before him are military or nome standards and a line of decapitated bodies of slain enemies.

Another important object to survive form this period (and found with the Narmer Palette at Hierakonpolis) is a large ceremonial mace head. Stone-headed maces were used as weapons from the earliest times, but this one appears to be too large to use as a practical weapon. It was probably made for ceremonial purposes, (perhaps in the same way as the maces used today in the British Houses of Parliament and by local authorities).

220. The decoration on the ceremonial mace-head of Narmer.

The decoration on the mace appears to show the marriage or union of Narmer, possibly to a princess of the captured Northern kingdom. The king again wears the crown of the north. Perhaps Narmer followed up a military victory with a diplomatic and tactical marriage. The use of military force may have be sufficient to achieve his goal, but the establishment of a *lasting* peace and the ability to consolidate and strengthen the unification was also important and he may well have been one of the first monarchs to realise this.

Both these objects appear to commemorate a victorious military campaign, which was essentially a civil war. On the mace head, Narmer tells us he captured 120,000 men, 400,000 oxen and 1,422,000 goats.

Unification of the country was important to Narmer. The Delta was the most fertile area of the country. Most of the food for Egypt was grown there and the pastureland was excellent for cattle and goats. Most importantly, it was via the Delta that trade links were established with other countries around the Mediterranean; and the routes to the quarries for turquoise and copper in the Sinai Peninsula ran through it. Even in the earliest times, trade was important and a strongly unified and organised country established trading routes that were to last for centuries.

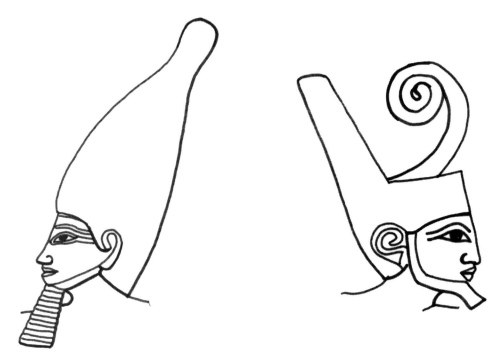

221. The crowns of the Two Lands: the White Crown of Upper Egypt, as worn by the Third Dynasty pharaoh, Djoser (left) and the Red Crown of Lower Egypt, as worn by Narmer. (right).

The First and Second Dynasties: 3050-2686

Horus Aha
Horus Djer
Horus Djet
Horus Den
Horus Hotepsekhemwy
Seth Peribsen
Horus and Seth Khasekhemwy

Narmer's successor was a king called Hor Aha, whom some Egyptologists have also identified with Menes. Possibly it is Hor Aha who should be known as the first king of the First

162

Dynasty. He was able to consolidate the Unification of Egypt under the rule of one sovereign. Any military threat to his position at this time would have come mainly from within the country, as the borders of Egypt were secure and protected by great natural barriers. As has been noted, to both the east and west of the river Nile lay vast expanses of empty desert, which would have been (and still are to some extent) difficult to cross.

One slate cosmetic palette depicts vividly the aftermath of an early battle and is probably the most graphic and accurate of the representations to survive from antiquity. Known as the "Battlefield Palette" it is now in the British Museum. The victorious king is shown as a lion devouring his defeated enemy. All around lie the dead and dying enemy soldiers, their bodies surrounded by carrion crows and a vulture. Perched in some cases on the corpses, the birds peck at the eyes and flesh of their victims.

222. *The Battlefield Palette, showing the king as a lion defeating his enemies, probably Libyans.*

223 A cast of the Palmero Stone.

224. King Den smiting his enemy, shown on a small ivory plaque.

Other information about this formative period of Egyptian history comes from the *Palmero Stone* (named after the museum in Italy which has housed it since 1877, even though parts of the stone are held in other Egyptian collections). It is a fragment of what was once a large slab of diorite, which originally measured some seven feet long by two feet in height. Only a portion of the middle remains, but even in its fragmentary state it has provided the basis for our chronology of the earliest Dynasties. Many of the names of the kings are lost, but recorded are details of jubilees of the kings and also a "numbering of all people of the nomes of the west, north and east" – presumably a census of the population, which shows how organised the country was at such an early time. Tantalisingly brief statements are included such as "… voyage to Sahseteni. Smiting of Werka."

We know from the earliest Dynasties that turquoise and copper were obtained, possibly through trade, from the Sinai area, and gold from Nubia. Nubia was also important for it was through this country that the route lay for the importation of goods from the heart of Africa, such as the precious commodities of ebony, ivory, ostrich feathers and eggs. Whilst there was no concerted Egyptian invasion or conquest of these areas at this time, the trade routes and trading expeditions often fell prey to nomadic groups and needed some military protection.

There is evidence of more military action within Egypt during the reign of Khasekhemwy, which indicates that at the end of the Second Dynasty the strength of the Union may have faltered. Possibly there continued to be minor conflicts within Egypt, but the early pharaohs clearly saw themselves as the defender of Egypt against foreign enemies and no longer against an "enemy" within the country.

THE OLD KINGDOM
2686-2181 BC

The Third Dynasty: 2686-2613

Nebka	2686-2668
Djoser	2668-2649
Sekhemkhet	2649-2643
Kaba	2643-2637
Huni	2637-2613

There is little information available about some of the earliest rulers of the Old Kingdom. This is perhaps surprising, for rulers such as Djoser of the Third Dynasty are well known to us for their impressive surviving monuments. Djoser constructed a vast mortuary complex of stone at Sakkara surrounding his huge six-stepped stone pyramid. It is unfortunate, however, that whilst such splendid monuments survive, we know very little about the lives and activities of the people who built them.

225. Statue of Djoser from his Step Pyramid complex at Sakkara.

226. King Djoser of the Third Dynasty, shown smiting his enemy. Rock carving from Wadi Maghara in the Sinai.

Only fragments of information survive, often found on the very borders of Egypt: in the Sinai desert, inscriptions on rocks show various pharaohs in the already-classic "smiting of the enemy" scenes as seen on the earlier "Narmer Palette".

227. *King Sekhemkhet of the Third Dynasty, shown smiting his enemy. Rock carving from Wadi Maghara in the Sinai.*

Djoser's successor, Sekhemkhet, planned an even larger pyramid complex for his burial, also at Sakkara. He ruled only for a short time and we know little about his reign. His tomb and surrounding buildings were never completed and when the sealed burial chamber and intact and sealed sarcophagus of the king were discovered in the last century, his body was not there.

The Fourth Dynasty: 2613-2498

Sneferu	2613-2589
Khufu	2589-2566
Djedefra	2566-2558
Khafra	2558-2532
Menkaura	2532-2504
Shepseskaf	2504-2500

By the time of King Snefru of the Fourth Dynasty the few surviving inscriptions are more specific.

"Building of one hundred cubit *dewatowe*-ships of meru wood, and of sixty barges of the king. Hacking up of the land of the Negro. Bringing of 7,000 living prisoners and 200,000 large and small cattle." The subjection of Nubia by the Egyptians had begun in earnest. It was during the Old Kingdom that a fort and small settlement were established on the island of Elephantine. Situated below the First Cataract it was the ideal location to protect and control the vital trade route into the heart of Africa.

Inscriptions in Sinai, dating to the reign of Senefru, indicate that the military activities were not confined to the south. These inscriptions contain only the names and titles of the King, "King of Upper and Lower Egypt, Favourite of the Two Goddesses, Lord of Truth, Golden Horus: Snefru. Snefru, Great God, who is given Satisfaction, Stability, Life, Health, all Joy forever. Horus: Lord of Truth. Smiter of Barbarians." The importance of the pharaoh as a great defender of Egypt and a slayer of its enemies had by now been well established, and inscriptions similar to this can be found for all periods of Egyptian history. The borders of the country to both the north and south were secure, and whilst there may not have been any major threat of invasion, a military presence and occasional "flexing of muscles" ensured that the trade routes were kept open. Precious commodities, not available from within Egypt, crossed the northern and southern boundaries.

229. Sneferu smiting his enemy. Stela from Wadi Maghara in the Sinai.

167

More inscriptions in the Sinai were made by Sneferu's successor, Khufu, who is described there as "Smiter of the Troglodytes," a reference to the fact that the inhabitants of that area lived in caves.

Evidence for any military activity is rare, but blocks from the Pyramid Complex of Khufu at Giza have recently been found at Lisht, re-used in Middle Kingdom buildings dating to the reign of Amenemhat I. Fragmentary reliefs, of superb quality, show archers, probably soldiers rather than hunters, drawing their bows

230. Stone marker at Wadi Maghara in the Sinai, showing Khufu, smiting his enemy.

231. Small ivory figure of Khufu.

It is from this period of Egyptian history that the greatest of all the surviving monuments were built, the pyramids. Whilst pyramid building stretched across many dynasties, the pyramids from the Fourth Dynasty were the largest ever built, notably those at Meidum, Dahshur and Giza.

The bulk of the workers who built the pyramids were Egyptian peasants (not, as is often related, slaves) who helped move the blocks during the time of the year when the river flooded the land and their fields could not be cultivated. Villages were built to house these temporary workers, who were provided with food and drink in return for their labours. A more permanent workforce would include the stone masons and master builders who would remain at the site all year round. Logistically, the movement of people and building materials was a massive undertaking and shows how well organised the Egyptians were at this time.

232. The Pyramids of Giza. View from the south.

Whilst the stone for the core blocks of the pyramids were quarried locally, the fine casing limestone came from further afield, from quarries on the opposite bank of the Nile. The granite, used for parts of the pyramids and their accompanying buildings, came all the way from Aswan in the south.

We know from later periods of Egyptian history that the army was used to provide manpower for some building works and it would perhaps be surprising if the army and its soldiers were not also used during some of the building work at the Pyramids. Modern estimates of the workforce needed to complete the Great Pyramid of Khufu, indicate that around twenty thousand men were used. About five thousand of them were probably a full-time workforce of specialist workers and artists. The remaining fifteen thousand or so were brought to the site as needed for the basic work of moving the stones into place.

A special village for these workers (probably the permanent workforce) has recently been discovered at Giza, along with their tombs. DNA testing on the bodies has shown that the workers (who had their families with them) came from all parts of Egypt and also that the ancient population was genetically very similar to modern Egyptians.

From surviving Old Kingdom tomb furnishings, we know that timber was imported from the Lebanon. Great quantities must have been imported. The amount of cedar needed to construct the boat of Khufu, found buried next to his pyramid at Giza, is impressive, and this was only one of several such boats buried at the site, although only two have survived. One boat has been excavated and restored and is now on display in a special museum next to the Great Pyramid. The second boat still lies, for the time being undisturbed, still sealed in its pit.

The size of the restored boat shows that such vessels would have been capable of carrying large cargoes and many passengers. It is not clear if Khufu's boat was actually used, but vessels of this size and construction must have been used on the river Nile and also the open sea. By the reign of Khufu, important trade links had been well established and journeys to places such as the Lebanon, to bring back the much-prized cedar, must have been common.

233. Composite photograph of the cedar boat of Khufu at Giza.

Other major imports included turquoise and copper, obtained from the Sinai, and gold, ebony and ivory from Nubia. Such trade links would have warranted some limited military protection. However, a military presence does not *necessarily* mean actual conquest, unless you are an early Egyptian pharaoh, and have subjects in Egypt to impress!

Khufu's successors, Khafra and Menkaura, also built large pyramids at Giza, which would have needed the organisational and administrative skills developed under Khufu. The trade routes clearly remained open but there is little if any hard evidence of military activity, other than perhaps the usual border garrisons and routine patrols.

The immense size of some of the building blocks used in the Giza pyramids and temples would have needed organised teams of workmen to move them from the quarry sites (including granite quarried at Aswan in the south). A military presence at Aswan was probably necessary and perhaps provided an escort when the blocks were transported south.

234. Khafra, builder of the second pyramid at Giza.

The Fifth Dynasty: 2498-2345

Userkaf	2498-2491
Sahure	2491-2477
Neferirkare	2477-2467
Neferefre	2460-2453
Niuserre	2453-2422
Djedkare-Isesi	2414-2375
Unas	2375-2345

The Sixth Dynasty: 2345-2181

Teti	2345-2333
Pepi I	2332-2283
Merenre	2283-2278
Pepi II	2278-2184

The kings of the Fifth and Sixth Dynasty inherited a secure and well-organised country. There are few records of any serious military activity in this period. One relief, in the mid-Fifth Dynasty tomb of Anta at Dishasha, has already been mentioned (see Chapter 5 on Fortifications and Siege Warfare).

The military activity documented by Anta may have been a record of one of the few campaigns of this period. This was probably because the "enemies" of Egypt were not actually posing any direct or consistent threat at this time, but may also have been because the country was experiencing a period of drought. It is believed that such a natural disaster happened towards the end of the Fifth Dynasty; this would have meant that all the efforts of the state were diverted to dealing with this domestic problem.

The kings still built pyramids, but perhaps they simply did not have the manpower to build on as large a scale as their predecessors. Their pyramids built at Sakkara and Abusir are smaller and of inferior construction. The great age of pyramid building had passed, although the mortuary temples connected to the pyramids became much larger and more elaborate than ever before. Perhaps this indicates an increase in the power of the priesthood vis-à-vis the pharaoh.

235. Head from a statue of Userkaf.

171

Nevertheless, stone for pyramids and temples still had to be cut and transported. Userkaf erected a huge statue in his mortuary temple at Sakkara. Cut from a single piece of Aswan granite it is the largest portrait of a king to survive from the Old Kingdom, and may even have been the first colossal statue to be made in Egypt.

Apart from tombs and mortuary temples, there was also other major building work at this time. At Abu Roash, just north of Abusir, both Userkaf and Sahure erected sun temples – large monuments built of stone. There may well have been other construction work around Egypt at this time, but most Old Kingdom temples have not survived,

In the Sinai, inscriptions made by Sahure, the second king of the Fifth Dynasty, record some military activity: "The Great God smites the Asiatics of all countries." Lack of hard evidence does not discount the possibility that the other Fifth Dynasty kings also led such small expeditions.

236. Granite blocks bearing the names and titles of Sahure. From his pyramid complex at Abusir.

There is evidence of a period of famine in Egypt by the end of the Fifth Dynasty. This includes carved reliefs from the pyramid causeway of Unas at Sakkara showing emaciated men. If the population were suffering, there would not have been the manpower available for state building works such as pyramids.

In the reign of Pepi I, one of the army officers of the king's expedition, the Commander Ibdu, added his own inscription to that of the king. It tells us that Ibdu's father was also a "Commander of the Troops", and lists the names of fifteen subordinate members of the expedition. The *profession* of a soldier had been established and sons were happy and proud to follow in their fathers' occupation. The position of an officer in the royal army was one of considerable status and Ibdu was able to record his name and, thereby, ensure his own immortality.

An inscription from the tomb of Uni at Abydos details the work he undertook for Pepi I. Uni organised a campaign against the Bedwin (Bedouin?) people to the north of Sinai and five times he was sent to quell revolts in this area. He finally pushed his army up into southern

Palestine, which is the first known Egyptian invasion of that country. At the same time, military power was still needed in the south of the country to quell any unrest in Nubia. The trend was now well established and successive Pharaohs had to maintain an army presence in both the north and south of the country.

Uni tells how "His Majesty made war on the Asiatic Sand-dwellers and His Majesty made an army of many ten thousand ... His Majesty sent me at the head of this army ... I was the one who made for them the plan." He tells how well his soldiers behaved "... not one thereof took bread from any city, not one thereof took any goat from any people", and how "... this army returned in safety after it had hacked up the land of the Sand-Dwellers ... after it had overturned its strongholds, after it had cut down its figs and its vines; this army returned in safety after it had slain troops therein in many ten thousands ... after it had carried away therefrom a great multitude as living captives. His Majesty praised me on account of it above everything."

Pepi I had a long reign, during which there is evidence of a weakening of the royal authority. Uni also tells of an unsuccessful assassination plot made against Pepi towards the end of his reign.

237. Copper statue of Pepi I, found at Hierakonpolis.

In the reign of King Pepi II, a nobleman from Elephantine called Pepi-Nakht led two campaigns in Nubia. In the first he "... slew a great number there, consisting of chief's children and excellent commanders. I brought a great number of them to the court as living prisoners, while I was at the head of many mighty soldiers as a hero."

In the second Nubian Campaign he "... brought the two chiefs of these countries to the court in safety, together with chief's children and the two commanders who were with them."

Pepi-Nakht also led a remarkable expedition to the northern Red Sea, to rescue the body of a nobleman bound for Punt, who had been killed by the sand-dwellers whilst building ships for the voyage. The expedition was successful and the body was recovered and returned to Egypt for burial.

Another account records a similar expedition, whose sole purpose was also to recover a body. This shows how important the Egyptians regarded a burial in Egypt. In his tomb at Aswan, Sabni describes the expedition into Nubia to rescue the body of his father, Mekhu. This time force was not the solution and some delicate negotiations were needed, for Sabni tells how he "... pacified these countries", having taken with him "... ointment, honey, clothing, oil ... in order to make presents in these countries".

238. Decoration in the Tomb of Sabni and Mekhu at Aswan.

Most of the campaigns at this period are little more than border disputes, with the Egyptians periodically asserting their authority. Short, sharp and occasionally brutal campaigns kept the borders secure. It would appear, though, that the Nubians were becoming more organised and the Egyptians began to regard them for the first time as a *real* threat.

Pepi II, who was only six years old when he came to the throne, had the longest recorded reign in Egyptian history. The decline in royal power, which had commenced in earlier reigns, continued. Some of the important state positions became, in effect, hereditary for the first time and the control of large sections of the administration remained within the same families for generations. The power shifted from a central control to such officials, who were all keen to expand their status and wealth, unchecked from above.

THE FIRST INTERMEDIATE PERIOD
2181-2040 BC

At the end of the Old Kingdom central control and organisation of the country collapsed and power reverted to the individual nomes, ruled by nomarchs. We know this time as the First Intermediate Period. Conflict between the nomes was common, especially between the northern nomes and the Theban Princes, but for the most part, the country probably functioned well with everyone adopting a more parochial attitude and paying close attention to local, rather than national affairs. The crops were still planted and harvested, and for most Egyptians life continued unchanged. The nomarchs ruled their own area as kings in all but name and many lived well and very comfortably.

Inscriptions of the nomarch Tefibi at Assuit record his military success over the combined forces of the southern nomes that had united together. Tefibi apparently defeated two armies and one battle fleet, driving the enemy south as far as Abydos.

Using descriptions of his actions worthy of a pharaoh, Tefibi recounts how he "... hastened to battle like a bull going forth," and attacked the enemies' ships. The southerner "... fell in the water, his ships ran aground, his army were like bulls when attacked by wild beasts."

The victorious soldiers were rewarded and promoted by Tefibi. "When a man did well I placed him at the head of my soldiers." He goes on to say that "... the land was under the fear of my soldiers."

Tefibi was succeeded as nomarch by his son Kheti, whose titles included that of "Military Commander of the Whole Land". Despite this military title, his rule seems to have been peaceful, for in his own tomb he tells that "... there was no one fighting, nor any shooting an arrow. The child was not smitten beside his mother, nor the citizen beside his wife."

Clearly military action, at this time, was sporadic rather than continuous, with periods of conflict alternating with periods of relative peace. Local officials acted on their own initiative and to fulfil their own aims.

THE MIDDLE KINGDOM
2040-1782 BC

The Eleventh Dynasty: 2060-1991

Mentuhotep I	2060-2010
Mentuhotep II	2010-1998
Mentuhotep III	1997-1991

During the Eleventh Dynasty the intermittent wars between the Theban princes and the northern nomarchs continued. Under a prince called Intef from Thebes part of the north was captured. On a stela dedicated to Intef, it is recorded that Intef "... captured the entire Thinite nome … opened all her fortresses ... made her the door of the north."

The final and full conquest of the north and re-unification of the country under the rule of one king was completed in the reign of Mentuhotep I. In a fragmentary relief from the temple of Gebelen, the king is described as "... binding the Chiefs of the Two Lands, capturing the south and northland, the highlands and the two regions, the Nine Bows and the Two Lands."

There are many references to outbreaks of fighting in the earlier years of his reign. It is interesting that on some reliefs, local officials are shown with weapons, rather than their insignia, and that burials of ordinary men were equipped with weapons as well as the usual grave goods. By the end of his reign, the indications are that the country was more peaceful.

239. The Tomb and Temple of Mentuhotep I at Deir el Bahri.

175

240. *Statue of Mentuhotep I, found at Deir el Bahri.*

It was during the reign of Mentuhotep I that a number of his soldiers were killed in battle and were buried in a communal tomb at Thebes. Their story has already been mentioned (in Chapter 5, on Fortifications and Siege Warfare).

If large-scale building is evidence of the onset of more peaceful times, then this is demonstrated in the buildings of the King, principally at Thebes, which became a city of importance for the first time, joining the older northern cities of Memphis and Heliopolis. The most impressive surviving monument is the large tomb and mortuary complex Mentuhotep constructed at Deir el Bahri. Built against the cliffs on the West Bank, and today overshadowed by the later temple of Queen Hatshepsut, his tomb was elaborate and decorated with reliefs and statues cut in fine limestone.

Mentuhotep I bequeathed to his son, Mentuhotep II, a stable and flourishing country. Mentuhotep II was relatively elderly when he became king and ruled for just twelve years but he was the first king for many years to rule over a firmly united Egypt. He re-established Egypt's overseas trade and arranged an expedition (to restore trade rather than for conquest) to the land of Punt (probably modern Eastern Sudan). An official of the king, Henu, who helped to organise the expedition, records that "... there was with me an army of the South. The army cleared the way before, overthrowing those hostile to the King." He goes on to say, "I went forth with an army of three thousand men. I gave a leathern bottle, a carrying pole, two jars of water and twenty loaves to each one among them every day. The asses were laden with sandals." Soldiers normally went barefoot, but perhaps the terrain they were expected to cross was particularly rough.

The army reached the Red Sea coast, where Henu supervised the building of a ship to sail to Punt. The ship may have been carried there in pieces, to be assembled by the members of the expedition, no doubt using the manpower of the soldiers.

The expedition returned successfully loaded with gifts for the king. "Never," recorded Henu, "was brought down the like thereof for the King's court."

Under Mentuhotep III, the last king of the Eleventh Dynasty, the internal wars within Egypt were forgotten. Inscriptions from the quarries at Wadi Hammamat record how the army was put to practical and peaceful work and that three thousand men from the Delta area helped with the transportation of a large block of stone for the lid of the King's sarcophagus.

The main block of stone for the body of the sarcophagus needed another expedition, this time with an accompanying army of ten thousand made up of men from the southern and middle Egyptian nomes. The block was transported successfully and in an inscription of Mentuhotep, he records that "... my soldiers descended without a loss, not a man perished, nor a troop was missing" – words that make it sound like a full military campaign even though the soldiers were, on this occasion, not facing a hostile enemy.

A contemporary inscription of a man called Senekh, Commander of the King's Troops, records how the soldiers were "... equipped with water skin buckets, with bread, beer and every fresh vegetable of the south." It is clear that at this period the army was organised, well equipped and provisioned.

The man responsible for the organisation of these expeditions was called Amenemhat. Both expeditions for his king were successful, but it is possible that the quarried stones were never

241. Relief from Gebelen showing Mentuhotep III smiting his enemy.

used for the burial of Mentuhotep III, whose tomb or sarcophagus have never been found. It seems likely that Amenemhat, with the backing of his ten thousand men, seized the throne for himself, and founded a new dynasty.

The Twelfth Dynasty: 1991-1782

Amenemhat I	1991-1962
Senuseret I	1971-1928
Amenemhat II	1929-1895
Senuseret II	1897-1878
Senuseret III	1878-1841
Amenemhat III	1842-1797
Amenemhat IV	1798-1786
Sobekneferu	1785-1782

In the reign of Amenemhat I, the first ruler of the Twelfth Dynasty, an inscription of Khnumhotep I in his tomb at Beni Hassan records how he accompanied his king on an expedition, in which twenty ships of cedar were engaged in expelling a certain foe from Egypt. The inscription is fragmentary and the exact enemy is uncertain. It could have been Asiatics in the north or Nubians in the south or even another Egyptian claimant to the throne, as there appears to have been some minor dispute over the succession at this time.

242. Statue of Senuseret I.

In the year twenty-four of his reign, an inscription of Amenemhat records that he led a campaign against Asiatics on the northern frontiers of Egypt. The king tells how he "... defeated the Asiatic Troglodytes, the sand-dwellers. I overthrew the strongholds of the nomads as if they had never been."

Amenemhat created a new fortified royal residence at a place called Itjtawy, (possibly near Lisht, although the precise location has never been established). Itjtawy became the effective administrative centre of the newly-unified Egypt, with many of the functions of the state moved northwards from Thebes. Itjtawy remained the administrative capital of Egypt for the remainder of the Middle Kingdom. The location was, however, far from ideal, for it was still remote from the Delta, especially when compared to the earlier administrative capital, Memphis, which lay further to the north. Having a more remote capital may have contributed to the difficulties that arose in the Delta in later dynasties.

243. *Relief of Senuseret I from his White Chapel at Karnak.*

During the reign of Senuseret I the south of Egypt was under attack and he secured the boundary after a successful campaign. To ensure a longer-term stability in Nubia, he started the construction of a chain of forts in the area.

A prince from Beni Hassan, Amenemhat, recorded how he "... followed my Lord when he sailed southwards to overthrow his enemies ... I advanced the boundary of the land. Then His Majesty returned in safety having overthrown his enemies in Kush. ... There was no loss among my soldiers."

There does not seem to have been any major battle and the Nubians no doubt beat a hasty and sensible retreat.

Further expeditions followed, although these were mainly for trade, with gold being the most sought-after commodity, and all were accompanied by soldiers. One commander recorded how he "... sailed southward with a number, four hundred, of all the choicest of my troops who returned in safety having suffered no loss."

Egypt began to prosper and the kings were soon building extensively. Much work was done in the Theban area, to the glory of the Theban god Amun, whose principal cult temple was there. The temple was embellished with statues of the king and a new barque shrine was erected at the entrance. Few of the Middle Kingdom buildings from Karnak survive, but the ones that do are impressive for their quality and artistic skill. The barque shrine of Senuseret I is one of these, but only because it was demolished in the Eighteenth Dynasty and its blocks were used as the foundations of new buildings. It has now been reconstructed in the Open Air Museum in the Temple of Karnak and is known as the "White Chapel".

During the Middle Kingdom all the arts flourished and many of the finest objects, including jewellery, date from this time. The written language developed too and for the first time we have substantial texts that have survived. From the reign of Amenemhat I comes the *Tale of Sinuhe*, which sheds some light on this period.

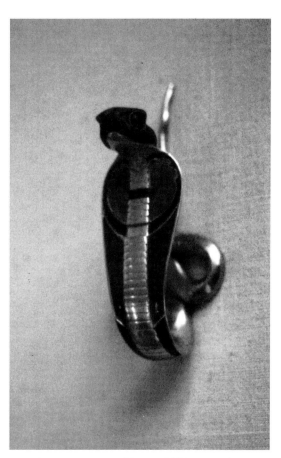

244. Gold and inlaid uraeus of Senuseret I. This was probably the very one which the king wore on his crowns.

Sinuhe was an officer in the Egyptian army who was involved in fighting against Bedouin tribesman. Whilst travelling back to Egypt he heard that Amenemhat had died and that his son Senuseret had taken command of the Egyptian armed forces. It is possible that there was some dispute amongst the royal princes over who should succeed Amenemhat I and perhaps there were plots to remove the rightful heir.

For reasons which are unclear, Sinuhe decided that it was unsafe for him to return to Egypt and he fled from the country, avoiding all the towns and cities, the known river crossings and the frontier posts. From his description it is possible that he was near Dahshur when he heard the news. There he crossed the river to the eastern bank, headed south to Meidum and then made for the Sinai. The journey was difficult and Sinuhe was on the point of collapse when he met up with some Asiatics who appear to have known him. He travelled with them, finally ending up in Byblos.

Sinuhe settled in Byblos, and soon made himself at home there. He must have achieved a position of some status and influence, for it appears he married the daughter of the ruler and was a commander of the army.

During his self-imposed exile, Sinuhe clearly pined for his native land and made a point of entertaining visiting Egyptians whenever he could.

Sinuhe led several campaigns for the ruler of the land of Retenu and he must have been a considerable asset with his practical Egyptian military experience. He seems to have been a successful warrior and was honoured above the local officers. This caused some dissent as he received a personal challenge to a duel from a local man who resented Sinuhe's wealth and status.

The night before the day set for the combat, Sinuhe prepared by practising with his bow and polishing his weapons, making sure his dagger would draw easily from the scabbard. He describes the duel in detail and tells how his opponent was armed with "… his shield and his battle axe and his armful of javelins ... Now after I had let his weapons issue forth, I made his arrows pass by me uselessly, one close to another. He charged me, and I shot him, my arrow sticking in his neck. He cried out and fell on his nose. I felled him with his own battle-axe and raised my cry of victory over his back while every Asiatic roared. I gave praise to Montu, while his adherents were mourning over him. This ruler Ammienesh took me in his embrace. Then I carried off [the enemy's] goods and plundered his cattle. What he had planned to do to me, I did to him. I took what was in his tent and stripped his encampment."

Sinuhe had had a lucky escape thanks to his own skills, but perhaps he realised that he had outstayed his welcome in Byblos. Hearing that Senuseret was secure on the Egyptian throne he decided it was time to return. Leaving all his possessions to his family, he left his wife and children and sailed for Egypt. There, dressed as a Bedouin, Sinuhe met Senuseret, with some concern about the reception he might receive, but the king seems to have accepted him back into Egypt. He was given a fine apartment and allowed to spend his last years in some luxury in his native land.

It was under Senuseret III that the complete subjugation of Nubia was undertaken. He led four full campaigns occupying and subduing totally the area between the First and Second Cataracts. He finished the building of many huge fortresses at strategic points along the river Nile, which protected the river route into Egypt. Not only were these forts garrisons for troops, but they also served as major trading posts for the importing of produce into Egypt, goods which included gold, ebony, ivory, ostrich eggs and feathers.

From this period and for over a thousand years, Nubia was to be a permanent possession of the pharaohs, apart from a brief interval during the Hyksos Period (1663-1555).

In order to improve communications in Nubia, Senuseret had a canal dug that allowed his ships to travel south above the First Cataract. This was a major engineering feat, one which had been started but abandoned in the Sixth Dynasty. Until the canal was completed, the fast-flowing water and the rocky rapids had meant that ships had had to be either manhandled out of the water and carried, pulled around the obstruction, or have their cargoes unloaded and carried to new vessels higher up on the river.

In a campaign in the eighth year of his reign, Senuseret III pushed further southwards to some thirty-seven miles north of Wadi Halfa above the Second Cataract. There he set up a boundary stela "… in order to prevent that any Negro should cross it by water or by land with a ship, or any herds of the Negroes, except a Negro who shall come to do trading ... or with a commission." The boundaries of Egypt had been secured and no one could cross without specific permission or the requisite permits.

Despite this successful campaign and the new fortifications with their permanent garrisons of men, relations with the Nubians remained uneasy, and in year twelve, "… his Majesty journeyed to overthrow Kush," again, followed by another campaign in year sixteen, where another boundary stela was erected. The King was able to state "I have made my boundary beyond that of my fathers."

Nubia was plundered. Senuseret tells how he "… captured their women … carried off their subjects, went forth to their wells, smote their bulls … reaped their grain and set fire thereto."

Senuseret urged his sons to protect and preserve this new boundary of Egypt. "Now as for every son of mine who shall maintain this boundary which My Majesty has made, he is my son, he is born to My Majesty, the likeness of a son who is the champion of his father who maintains the boundary of him that begot him. Now, as for him who shall relax it and shall not fight for it, he is not my son, he is not born to me!"

245. Senuseret III: Red granite head from the Temple of Amun at Karnak.

Year nineteen of Senuseret, however, saw yet *another* campaign to "overthrow the wretched Kush". The Nubians probably conducted a guerrilla-type warfare against the Egyptians; small raids here and there were more of an annoyance than a *serious* attempt to drive the Egyptians out of the country. The chain of manned forts and good communications meant that Senuseret could, and did, react swiftly to any disturbance.

Sebekhu, an attendant of the King, accompanied him on one of the campaigns to Nubia. He was rewarded for his gallantry by the King, who promoted him to the position of commander.

Whilst Nubia proved troublesome in the south, all was not quiet on the northern frontier, and Senuseret III also had to lead campaigns there. Sebekhu accompanied Senuseret to Syria, where, in a battle fought there, Sebekhu personally captured a prisoner who was given to him by the king as a reward.

246. Statue of Amenemhat III, successor to Senuseret III.

This is the only record of any invasion of Syria in the Middle Kingdom. It appears to have been only a small campaign, possibly motivated by the prospect of plunder and not a serious attempt to capture and then hold any territory.

The army at this time was clearly effective and well organised, although possibly achieving its main success as a deterrent rather than a fighting force. The strong, well-equipped presence in Nubia effectively stopped any serious attempts by the Nubians to drive the Egyptian invaders from their land.

Senuseret III was succeeded by his son, Amenemhat III, who reigned for a remarkable forty-five years. Despite the length of the reign there is a great lack of inscriptions detailing the exploits of the king. Clearly Amenemhat benefited from the successful campaigns of his father and his own reign seems to have been one of peace and economic growth.

Amenemhat exploited the quarries of Egypt and the turquoise mines in the Sinai. Agriculture prospered, particularly in the area of the Faium.

He built two pyramids, one at Dahshur and a second at Hawara in which he was buried. The pyramid complex at Hawara included a massive mortuary temple adjoining the pyramid, built with fine stone and with granite and limestone columns.

Both of Amenemhat's pyramids were built mainly of mud brick, with a casing of stone. The burial chamber of his Hawara Pyramid was made of one enormous block of quartzite twenty-two feet by eight feet, which was hollowed out like a lidless box. A second large block formed the lid or top of the chamber. Undoubtedly, Amenemhat had followed the example of

247. *Relief from the Tomb of Djehutihotep, showing the moving of a colossal statue.*

Mentuhotep III and would have needed a large detachment of his army to move such enormous blocks of stone.

It is evident that the manpower and organisation of the army was put to good use for civilian and engineering tasks and also for more peaceful purposes. A scene from the Tomb of Djehutihotep at el-Bersha in Middle Egypt, shows the transportation of a colossal statue, pulled by one hundred and seventy-two men in four rows. The accompanying inscription tells how the second row is made up of soldiers.

Amenemhat III was succeeded by his elderly son, who became Amenemhat IV. Amenemhat was married to Sobekneferu, who may have been his sister, and when Amenemhat died after a short reign, Sobekneferu took on, and held, the role of Pharaoh for four years. She used male titles and had herself portrayed with the male trappings of power. With her death the Twelfth Dynasty came to an end.

THE SECOND INTERMEDIATE PERIOD
1782-1570 BC

Following the death of Sobekneferu, there was a succession of pharaohs, all reigning for short periods. As had happened before, during this period power devolved from a central point to the local rulers of the nomes of Egypt.

It is easy to see how local governors could take control of their own local area because of the geography of Egypt. With the river Nile being the main highway of Egypt, *anyone* powerful enough to control the movement of vessels and trade on the river could easily bring the unified country to a standstill.

248. View of the river Nile at Beni Hassan.

For example, at Beni Hassan in Middle Egypt, the town sits on a broad sweep of the river. With the mountains on the east bank as an ideal vantage point, any movement on the river, from north or south, could be spotted whilst it was still miles away, and intercepted.

What perhaps is surprising is that the central control worked so well for most of Egyptian history and that local nomarchs were not constantly looking after their own interests rather than the country as a whole.

Around this time, in addition to disruption within the country, invaders from Asia, known traditionally as the Hyksos, swept into the Delta and effectively took control of this area. At the same time, the Egyptian hold over Nubia was lost and the native Egyptian princes found themselves with hostile forces to both the north and the south.

The Jewish historian Josephus described the Hyksos as "shepherd kings" and that title is still given to them today, but the Egyptian name for them was *Hekau Khasu*, which translates as "princes of foreign countries". The Hyksos were far more than simple shepherds and were probably Canaanites from Syria and Palestine (the area known to the Egyptians as Retenu). They came in search of land, trade and food, and one of their main reasons for heading towards Egypt may have been a period of famine and poor crops in their own country. As many Biblical accounts tell us, in times of famine Egypt was seen as the land of plenty and was frequently the destination for hungry refugees.

249. Middle Kingdom painting from the Tomb of Khnumhotep at Beni Hassan showing Asiatics in Egypt.

The "invasion" of the Hyksos was probably not an invasion as such, but is more likely to have been a series of opportunistic encroachments over a number of years, and in sufficient numbers to enable the Hyksos eventually to assume control over their new territories. They came with good military training, better metal weapons and more powerful bows. Their arrival coincided with the introduction of the horse and chariot, which had not been seen in Egypt before.

The Hyksos established their capital at the fortified city of Avaris in the Delta. Evidence found at Tel el Daba, believed to be the site of Avaris, shows that a large Canaanite temple was built there and that Egyptian statues already in this area were deliberately defaced at this time. The Hyksos seemed to have adopted a mixture of their native ideas with those of the Egyptians, and some earlier monuments were usurped by the new rulers, whose names were superimposed on the cartouches of Middle Kingdom rulers. Sphinxes of Amenemhat III were re-used in this way (and were later to be usurped by Ramesses II in the New Kingdom).

250. The newly introduced horse and chariot. Painting from the Tomb of Nebamun.

251. The "Hyksos" sphinxes, usurped from the earlier pharaoh, Amenemhat III.

It is unclear exactly how much of Egypt the Hyksos actually controlled. They established an alliance with the Nubians in the south, so clearly had good lines of communication through the country and in areas over which they did not exercise complete control. This implies that there must have been, initially at least, some co-operation between the Hyksos and the native Egyptians. Perhaps the Egyptians realised too late the hold the Hyksos had over them. Before long, Egyptian resentment of the new rulers grew. The Hyksos exacted tribute from the Egyptians, whom they seemed to regard with some contempt. Their language was strange to the Egyptians and, worse still, they worshipped foreign gods (apart from the Egyptian god Set).

Little is known about the Hyksos sites, as their settlements in the Delta have, until now at least, not been studied in detail. Gradually, as a result of new excavations in the area of Avaris, a better picture is beginning to emerge. At Tel el Daba, evidence of the military activity at this time includes the tomb of a soldier. He had been buried with pottery containing the usual food and drink offerings, but also with his weapons, which included a dagger and a copper scimitar, the kepesh (the oldest example yet found).

The Seventeenth Dynasty: 1637-1570

Sakhenenre-Mentuhotep IV	c1633
Seqenenre-Tao	c1574
Kamose	1573-1570

The Egyptians moved their own seat of power and the court south to Thebes and it was there that the old values were preserved. The Egyptian princes there realised that they faced a formidable foe in the Hyksos, who had become well established in the Delta towns and cities. Learning from their enemies, the Egyptians began to use the horse and chariot, to improve their own metal-making skills and to adopt the new Hyksos weapons. The simple bows used by the Egyptians were gradually replaced by the more powerful composite bows. Some of these weapons were difficult to make and the Egyptians must have had some help from Hyksos weapon-makers. They no doubt had captured some weapons in minor disputes, but making them and then becoming practised in their use took longer.

The Egyptians were, however, well motivated. Their goal was nothing less than the re-unification of the country and under the leadership of the Theban princes who were determined to drive out the worshippers of Set, there was an outbreak of patriotic fever. The princes, with the image of their god Amun carried with them, wanted to see Egypt rise and prosper again and that meant the expulsion of the Hyksos from Egypt.

A surviving, if fragmentary, document shows that there was some communication between the Hyksos rulers and the princes of Thebes. The Hyksos king Apophis wrote to Seqenenre-Tao II, demanding that he should give up his hippopotamus pool, at Thebes, as the noise of the animals was keeping him awake at night (notwithstanding the intervening distance of several hundred miles!) Seqenenre's reply is not recorded, but was no doubt couched in similar terms.

The situation eventually deteriorated past mere exchanges of flippant correspondence and the princes of Thebes considered the time was right to lead a major revolt against the Hyksos.

We know that Seqenenre himself died a violent death, undoubtedly in battle, fighting the Hyksos. The head of his mummy (found in the Royal Cache at Deir el Bahri in 1881 AD) clearly shows the wounds that killed him. He had been struck repeatedly by an axe and by arrows.

252. The head of the mummy of Seqenenre-Tao II. The arrows indicate the many serious wounds.

Examinations of the axe wounds in particular indicate that they were inflicted by an Asiatic axe, the type used by the Hyksos.

Recent research on the mummy of Seqenenre-Tao indicates that the king may have received his wounds in two separate events. In the first, he was injured when standing and he appears to have survived these wounds for a while, as there is evidence of bone re-growth. The second set of wounds appears to have been inflicted when the king was in a prone position, possible still recovering from the first wounds. It was this second set of wounds that were directly responsible for his death. The position of the hands of the king indicates he may have been partially paralysed after receiving his first wounds.

We do not know where Seqenenre fell, but the Egyptians were able to recover his body, possibly after it had lain on the field of battle for some time, and to arrange for it to be returned to Thebes for burial. The body was inexpertly and poorly embalmed, and when discovered in the Royal Cache of mummies, still lay in the contortions of death.

Seqenenre had not succeeded in defeating the Hyksos who were still in control, but this first, failed attempt to drive them out proved an incentive for the Egyptians to continue their armed resistance to Hyksos rule.

Seqenenre's son and successor, Kamose, led a flotilla of boats to the north. On his journey he overcame resistance in Middle Egypt, over which the Hyksos had more control, and his army slowly advanced towards the Delta. Before long, all of Egypt to the south was under Kamose's control and the stage was set for the final military thrust.

In the far south, the Nubians, who were allied to the Hyksos, were prevented from rebelling by allies of Kamose, the Medjay tribes. The Medjay were nomads who supplied mercenary troops to the Egyptian army and who were to prove useful in Kamose's campaign.

Kamose never saw the successful completion of his campaign against the Hyksos; that task fell to his son, Ahmose. It was Ahmose who is regarded as the founder of the Eighteenth Dynasty and the period we know as the "New Kingdom".

THE NEW KINGDOM
1570-1070 BC

The Eighteenth Dynasty: 1570-1293

Ahmose	1570-1546
Amenhotep I	1551-1524
Thutmose I	1524-1518
Thutmose II	1518-1504
Thutmose III	1504-1450
Hatshepsut	1498-1483
Amenhotep II	1453-1419
Thutmose IV	1419-1386
Amenhotep III	1386-1349
Amenhotep IV/	
Akhenaten	1350-1334
Smenkakare	1336-1334
Tutankhamun	1334-1325
Ay	1325-1321
Horemheb	1321-1293

Information on early New Kingdom military exploits is limited. One of the most informative is preserved on the walls of the tomb of a naval officer, Ahmose, son of Ebana, at Elkab. Ahmose served under three kings (Ahmose, Amenhotep I and Thutmose I) during the time when the Hyksos invaders were finally driven out of Egypt and the foundations of Egypt's great Empire were being laid.

The early kings secured their position by being generous to their trusty servants and Ahmose, son of Ebana, benefited greatly from royal gifts of land and servants.

Under King Ahmose I, Ahmose son of Ebana took part in a siege at a city called Hatwaret in the Delta where the Hyksos made their last stand in Egypt. The city fell only after a long siege. The fleeing Hyksos were pursued into Syria as far as the city of Sahuren, which was also captured after a siege. Ahmose then pursued the Hyksos still further into Syria and well away from Egypt. The Egyptian army had learnt well, having successfully adopted the military innovations of the Hyksos invaders and used them with great effect against them.

During the attacks on the Hyksos, Ahmose "… showed valour on foot before his majesty; then I was appointed to [the ship] 'Shining in Memphis'. One fought on the water in the canal. Then I fought hand to hand; I brought away a hand. It was reported to the Royal Herald. One gave me the gold of valour." After the capture of Avaris, Ahmose, son of Ebana was rewarded with the gift of one man and three women as slaves.

Having secured the northern borders, King Ahmose returned to Egypt to deal with a rebellion in Nubia. Ahmose, son of Ebana, accompanied his king on this campaign too,

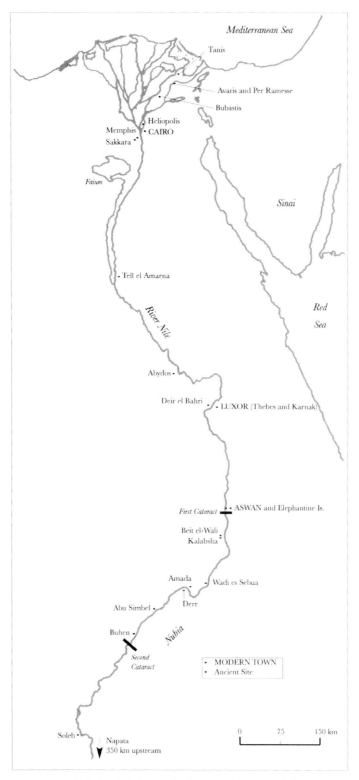

Mediterranean Sea

Tanis

Avaris and Per Ramesse

Bubastis

Heliopolis
Memphis · CAIRO
Sakkara

Faium

Sinai

Tell el Amarna

River Nile

Red
Sea

Abydos ·

Deir el Bahri · · LUXOR (Thebes and Karnak)

First Cataract ━━ · ASWAN and Elephantine Is.

Beit el-Wali
Kalabsha

Amada
· Wadi es Sebua
Derr

Abu Simbel ·

Buhen ·

Nubia

Second
Cataract

· MODERN TOWN
· Ancient Site

0   75   150 km

Soleb ·
Napata
350 km upstream

253. *Map of Egypt in the New Kingdom and Third Intermediate Period.*

254. Ahmose, son of Ebana: Relief and inscription from his tomb at Elkab.

recording that, "… after his majesty had slain the Asiatics, he ascended the river … to destroy the Nubian Troglodytes. His Majesty made great slaughter against them. His Majesty sailed downstream, his heart joyous, with the might of victory, for he had seized Southerners and Northerners."

In Nubia, King Ahmose found many of the great Middle Kingdom fortresses in a state of disrepair. At sites such as Buhen, he gave orders for the reconstruction and expansion of the fortresses and ensured that the garrisons were fully equipped and manned.

Nubia was still really regarded as a natural extension of Egypt and whilst successive Egyptian rulers had led series of campaigns to subdue the Nubians, many of these may have been for appearance only. The real threat to Egypt was now Asia, which with many new emerging powers was also a great unknown.

Once the Hyksos had been driven out, the Egyptians were determined to *keep* them out, and for the first time the Egyptian army moved deep into the land of Retenu. There they encountered an alien landscape, so different from their own familiar Egypt. The roads in Retenu ran over high mountains and through thick forests, difficult to penetrate. Foreign towns were protected not with mud-brick walls, as in Egypt, but with walls of stone and they were facing not just one enemy, but many small kingdoms. Sometimes these kingdoms worked together and at other times independently and actually knowing *who* the enemy was could be difficult.

In Phoenicia, the Egyptians encountered heavy rain, which is relatively rare in Egypt. They found foaming rivers, with torrents of water rushing through deep gorges, all so different from the placid and predictable river Nile. The water was freezing cold, sometimes too cold for the Egyptians to drink unless it was allowed to stand for a while. On the mountaintops, snow fell and

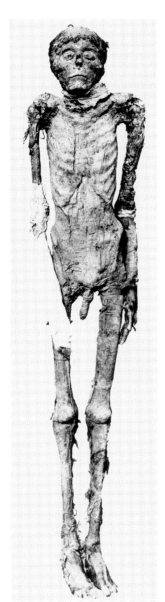

255. *The mummy of Ahmose.*

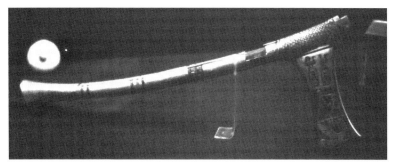

256. *The gilded axe found with the body of Ahotep, and bearing the name of her son, Ahmose.*

257. *Image of Ahotep from her gilded coffin.*

bears stole food from their camps and attacked the men. Maintaining morale and discipline in such an environment must have been a challenge for the military commanders.

To the west of Egypt, the Libyans were also causing some concern. Cattle-farmers for the most part, like the Hyksos, they were attracted to the fertile farming area of the Delta. Trade routes with Libya through the desert oases had been established for some time, but in the early New Kingdom large numbers of Libyans began to move into the Delta. Ahmose strengthened the borders and was determined that Egypt would not suffer any further invasion and take-over by foreigners.

There may have been some residual trouble in Thebes too at this time, for we know that Queen Ahotep, mother of Ahmose, called out the garrison there to put down a dispute and restore the stability of the area. It is probably for this reason that the king awarded her the "Gold Flies of Valour". It is obvious that Ahotep had a strong military connection, for in her tomb, along with the gold flies, were elaborate gold axes and daggers.

Other military evidence is rare, but only recently Dr. Stephen Harvey, from the University of Memphis, has discovered the remains of a large funerary monument of Ahmose at Abydos. Only fragments of the fine reliefs that decorated the building have survived, but they include representations of chariots (the earliest to have been discovered so far in Egypt) and other scenes, clearly of warfare, showing archers and walled towns with defenders in the battlements. These are very similar to many scenes from the end of the New Kingdom, and are unique in that they record the campaigns right at the beginning of this important period of Egyptian history.

Ahmose made himself the master of the two kingdoms of Upper and Lower Egypt and founded a dynasty that was to last for over two hundred years, a period that was to see great expansion and empire-building.

Under the next pharaoh, Amenhotep I, Ahmose son of Ebana was again in Nubia putting down another minor rebellion there. The start of any new reign (if we can believe the propaganda) seemed to occasion minor revolts on all of Egypt's frontiers to test the strength and organisation of the new ruler.

Amenhotep I, with his northern and southern borders secure, was able to devote his energies to ensuring that the unified Egypt prospered and that the previously separated parts worked well together.

Amenhotep is believed to have been the first pharaoh to cut his tomb in the Valley of the Kings at Thebes, although its location is not known. The earliest royal tombs in the Valley of the Kings were undecorated and have no inscriptions, and with no surviving funerary equipment, even fragmentary, the identification of many of them is not possible.

The Reign of Thutmose I: 1524-1518

Disturbances in Nubia also marked the accession to the throne of Amenhotep I's son, Thutmose I, at the age of almost forty. In his second year as king, Thutmose defeated a Nubian rebellion and fortified his boundaries. In the north, his Empire extended to the Euphrates river. No account of any Asiatic campaign survives from this reign and it must be supposed that his predecessors had pushed the boundaries to this extent, although more precise information as to who and when has not survived.

After quelling the rebellions, Thutmose was able to enjoy the rewards of his Empire. "All the Southerners come down-river, the Northerners come up-river, and all lands are bringing their tribute to the Good God, Thutmose, who liveth forever, the mighty one. He hath overthrown the chief of the Nubians; the Negro is helpless, defenceless in his grasp. He hath united the boundaries … there is not a remnant among the curly-haired who come to attack him."

258. Thutmose I and Thutmose II before Amun. A relief from the Mortuary Temple of Hatshepsut at Deir el Bahri.

In Nubia, Thutmose cleared the canal of Senuseret III at the First Cataract, which had become silted up and unusable, and he was able to reinforce his control over the area south of the Second Cataract, having destroyed any Nubian resistance.

Under Thutmose I, the city of Thebes was effectively made capital of the expanding Empire, although in practice this role was probably shared with the older city of Memphis in the North. Certainly Thebes became one of the most important religious sites in the country. It was the princes of Thebes who had re-united the country and it was their god, Amun, who received much of the credit. The spoils of war and the inflow of tribute benefitted the coffers of the god as well as those of the king.

Thutmose spent much of his time away from Egypt on campaign, being one of the first pharaohs who was confident enough to do this. It must be remembered that this was only a short time after a long period of unrest in Egypt and it must have taken a brave man to leave the country in the hands of officials who, only a generation before, might well have tried to usurp the throne for themselves. Thutmose realised that a good, loyal administration in Egypt was essential and specific powers were delegated from the king to viziers and provincial governors, who owed their position entirely to him.

The Temple of Amun at Thebes was greatly extended and Thutmose erected two huge granite obelisks at the new gateway of the temple. (One obelisk still stands on the site today.) Thutmose began the process (which was to continue for generations) of replacing the earlier, smaller temple, with a larger, completely stone built structure, worthy of the new-found prominence of the Theban god.

The Valley of the Kings at Thebes was also chosen by Thutmose I as the location for his tomb, following the example of his father Amenhotep I. Thutmose established a tradition for royal burials that would continue for the next four hundred years.

259. One of the obelisks erected by Thutmose I in Temple of Karnak to the glory of the Theban god Amun.

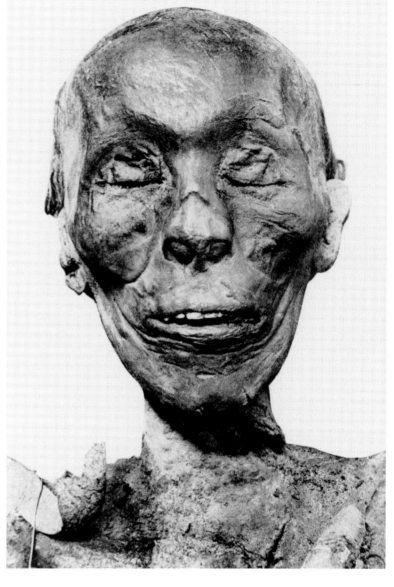

260. The head of the mummy of Thutmose II.

The amount of building work that Thutmose I instigated at Thebes, and possibly elsewhere, indicates a period of stability after the re-unification of the country. There was, however, still a threat to the security of Egypt in the north and the next pharaoh, Thutmose II, in his short reign, made at least one expedition into Asia.

Despite the efforts of Thutmose I, the Nubians in the south were still not subdued, for Thutmose II also records an expedition south to quell a Nubian rebellion. One must wonder if the Nubians were really as rebellious as they are portrayed or if they were just gluttons for punishment! Perhaps every new ruler found that it was politic, useful and *easy* to lead a military expedition south, find a few Nubians to kill, a village or two to plunder, then to return to Egypt with tales of great victories!

This period appears to be one of apparent conflict and uncertainty as members the Thutmoside royal family vied for control. Thutmose II may have ruled alongside his father before a period of sole rule, but his reign was only to last for fourteen years. On his death he was succeeded by his son Thutmose III, but as the latter was still a child, it was Thutmose II's sister and Great Royal Wife, Hatshepsut, who effectively took control. She ruled as regent for the young Thutmose III, then as ruler in her own right before Thutmose III assumed sole control on her death. Perhaps she realised that to hesitate might allow additional family disputes to arise.

The situation is confused and is not helped by Hatshepsut's inscribing monuments to her father Thutmose I, and her husband, Thutmose II, then by Thutmose III's adding his name to earlier monuments and erasing Hatshepsut's name. The complexities and clash of personalities evident from the records are outside the scope of this book.

Hatshepsut ruled as pharaoh (there was no Egyptian term for queen regnant as we know today) and, in most of her monuments, is shown as a man, and referred to in inscriptions as "he". She was not the first (nor the last) female to reign as pharaoh, but the male representation

261. Hatshepsut as Pharaoh. Statue from her Mortuary Temple at Deir el Bahri.

is unique, although whether she *actually* wore male attire will perhaps never be known. It should be realised that most Egyptians would have been relatively unconcerned and ill informed about their ruler – as long as there *was* a pharaoh – and relatively few Egyptians would have seen her in person. It is only in relatively recent times that rulers have been public figures, whose features are well known to all. Interestingly, in the inner parts of her Mortuary Temple, which would have been accessible to very few people, Hatshepsut had statues of herself shown as a woman.

The Reign of Hatshepsut: 1498-1483

Hatshepsut's reign is mainly famous for a well-recorded trading expedition to the land of Punt (probably located in the area now occupied by the Eastern Sudan and on the Red Sea coast). This expedition is recorded in considerable detail on the walls of her great Mortuary Temple at Deir el Bahri and is generally hailed as a demonstration of the peaceful nature of Hatshepsut's reign. This may be too simplistic, for the expedition was accompanied by a large military presence, clearly recorded in the inscriptions and reliefs. Interestingly the reliefs show the soldiers carrying their axes, but also small branches of foliage, perhaps meant to symbolise their peaceful intent.

In the land of Punt the army camped in the myrrh terraces, and was present when the chief of Punt delivered his "tribute". This expedition was an invasion in all but name and returned "with ships laden with myrrh trees, woods, resins, ivory, apes, monkeys, with panther skins and with natives and their children" – all depicted in carved relief on the walls of Hatshepsut's Temple. If the expedition was indeed just a "trading venture", one must wonder what the inhabitants of Punt received in return for their exotic produce.

The expedition was a remarkable feat, for the Egyptian boats had to be carried or dragged across the eastern desert from the river Nile to reach the Red Sea. The boats could have been

262. Soldiers of Hatshepsut, with spears, shields and kepesh.

263. Soldiers of Hatshepsut, with axes and walking sticks.

264. The King and Queen of Punt. Scene from the Mortuary Temple of Hatshepsut at Deir el Bahri.

pulled on sledges over the desert and the larger boats may well have been dismantled and moved in sections. The method of construction of Egyptian boats, with their timbers lashed together with rope, meant that they could easily be dismantled. Even so, the manpower needed would have been considerable, with the army probably providing most of the resources needed.

Hatshepsut's ruined Mortuary Temple at Deir el Bahri contained many fragmentary scenes and inscriptions relating to battles, and one of the 19th Century AD excavators of the temple,

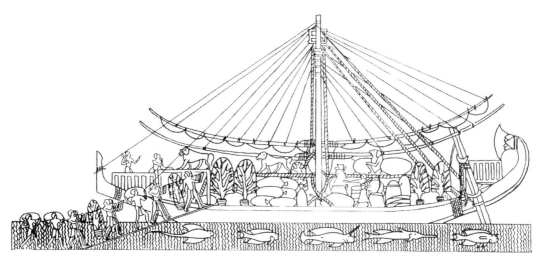

265. A boat loaded with items from the land of Punt. Scene from the Mortuary Temple of Hatshepsut at Deir el Bahri.

Edouard Naville, was convinced that she had actually led campaigns herself.

There was a reference to wars against the Nubians (a traditional enemy and easy target at the start of any reign) and also in Asia. Blocks recorded the names of captured towns and one scene shows Hatshepsut as a human-headed sphinx, trampling the enemies of Egypt underfoot. In an account of a Nubian campaign, Hatshepsut is described as acting "… as was done by her victorious father, the King of Upper and Lower Egypt, Aakheperkare [Thutmose I] who seized all lands in Nubia … a slaughter was made among them, the number [of dead] being unknown."

Whilst these accounts may be part of the official propaganda, another survives, which appears to be an eyewitness account of Hatshepsut on campaign. Written by a nobleman called Ti, we are told how he "… followed the Good God, the King of Upper and Lower Egypt, Maatkare, may He live. I saw him [i.e. Hatshepsut] overthrowing the Nubian nomads, their chiefs being brought to him as prisoners. I saw him destroying the land of Nubia, while I was in the following of His Majesty."

Other hard evidence for a warrior-Hatshepsut is lacking, but one ostraca survives from this period, which appears to show a female ruler in a chariot, firing arrows at her enemies. Does this represent Hatshepsut?

266. *Drawing on a flake of limestone, showing a female monarch in battle; perhaps meant to represent Hatshepsut.*

Some modern accounts of the reign of Hatshepsut have concentrated on the peaceful and benevolent aspects of a female pharaoh. The truth, however, may well have been different. Whether or not Hatshepsut herself led any active military campaigns, she did not appear to have neglected the state of the boundaries of Egypt. She had an organised army, whose officers would have included the young Thutmose III, who, because of his status, probably had a senior role in operations.

Hatshepsut built extensively at Thebes, where many of her monuments still survive. She erected four huge obelisks in the Temple of Amun at Karnak, one of which is still standing near the fallen remains of a second. The cutting of the stone for them in the granite quarries of Aswan was a truly monumental undertaking, as were their successful transportation by river to Thebes and their erection within the temple.

The organisation called for would have been phenomenal, and the army played a vital role. Hatshepsut had an account of the cutting and erection of the obelisks portrayed in her Mortuary Temple at Deir el Bahri. She ordered the building of a "very great boat", perhaps one of the largest vessels built in the ancient world, to transport the obelisks downstream. Orders were issued to "… the whole army, in order to load the two obelisks." Once the loaded barge arrived at Thebes, the soldiers and mariners were again assembled to land the obelisks and to help raise them into place, to the glory of the god Amun and to their pharaoh, Hatshepsut. The court rejoiced at the successful completion of this enterprise. "The companions, the dignitaries, the soldiers of the whole land, say, 'Happy is the heart; this thy desire, it has come to pass.' "

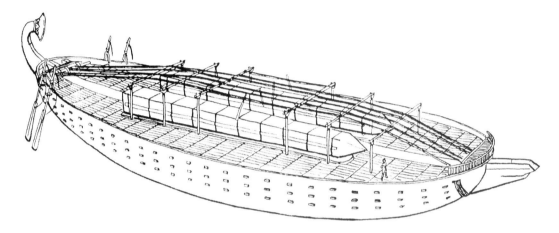

267. Reconstruction of the appearance of the colossal obelisk barge of Queen Hatshepsut, loaded with two obelisks.

The use of the army for such an enterprise was not surprising, for the queen needed to call on a large body of strong, fit and disciplined men to move the colossal stones. Hatshepsut was not the first to raise large obelisks, for her father Thutmose I had also erected two Aswan granite obelisks at Karnak (although he was more modest about his exploits!). The techniques of moving and erecting obelisks and the detailed planning and organisation required had been well tested and perfected.

It was not just obelisks that needed moving. Hatshepsut, and later Thutmose III, used great quantities of Aswan granite for their buildings. Some of the stones were massive, especially those used for the many colossal granite statues erected in the temples. At any given time, there must have been a constant procession of heavily loaded barges from Aswan. The strength and organisation of the army would have been needed to load and unload the massive blocks and to move them into place.

The reign of Hatshepsut (female pharaoh or not) appears to have been a great period for Egypt. Exactly what the Egyptians themselves thought of their ruler may perhaps never be known. It has been argued that behind every great woman, there is a great man, and in Hatshepsut's case the man in question was Senenmut, her adviser, tutor to her daughter and possible architect of the great temple at Deir el Bahri. Senenmut was certainly an important man, but there is no real evidence that he was anything other than a loyal subject. However a contemporary obscene graffiti at Thebes does appear to show a female ruler in a compromising position with a man, perhaps it is meant to represent Hatshepsut and Senenmut.

The Reign of Thutmose III: 1504-1450

Thutmose III appears to have been kept somewhat in the background, certainly for the early years of Hatshepsut's rule when he was still a boy. It is presumed that like many of his contemporaries, he received military training from an early age, and may have been involved in minor campaigns during the period when he was co-regent with Hatshepsut. It is obvious that he had strong control over the army and that it had been maintained in a state of readiness, well trained and equipped, and ready for action.

Hatshepsut and Thutmose III are shown on surviving monuments as joint pharaohs (although Hatshepsut is always shown first). Both wear the same royal insignia and bear the usual royal titles, neither one otherwise being given any obvious seniority over the other. Exactly *how* the royal duties were split between them is, however, unclear. It is also not known if this arrangement was imposed by Hatshepsut on the young Thutmose, or if it was by mutual consent.

Control of the army would have been sufficient for a successful coup to depose Hatshepsut, but perhaps Thutmose was just waiting for the right time, or the division of power between them

268. *Hatshepsut (left) and Thutmose III (right) as joint pharaohs. Scene from the Red Chapel of Hatshepsut at Karnak.*

worked well. This meant that each ruler could concentrate on the role for which he or she was best suited, with Hatshepsut running the administration and Thutmose pursuing his military interests.

Thutmose III became the sole occupant of the throne of Egypt in year twenty-three of his reign and immediately embarked on the first of what was to be a long series of military campaigns. As a military commander, Thutmose led from the front and by example and appears to have had the support of the army from the earliest years of his reign.

Thutmose led seventeen campaigns in total and recorded them in his *Annals* inscribed on the walls of the Temple of Amun at Karnak. Perhaps, after all, Hatshepsut had let things slip and the new monarch, now in complete control, had to re-establish the boundaries of Egypt and ensure that the tribute continued to flow into the royal coffers.

Thutmose III, however, did far more than simply re-establish the boundaries of Egypt, for he pushed them further than any other pharaoh had done before him, and further than any other pharaoh would ever accomplish. His really was the time of the great Egyptian Empire, and his status as the greatest warrior pharaoh is justly deserved.

The *Annals* are fragmentary, but enough information survives to give us an excellent account of Thutmose III's military activities, more so than for any other Pharaoh.

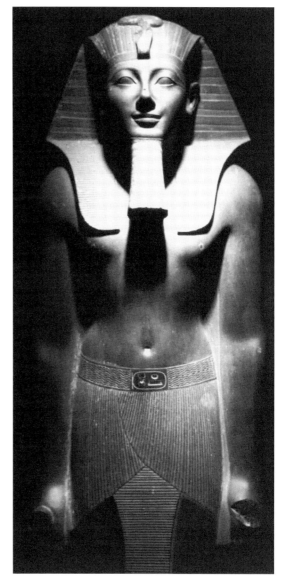

269. *Statue of Thutmose III from Karnak.*

"His Majesty commanded to cause to be recorded his victories which his father, Amun, gave to him ... setting forth each expedition by its name, together with the plunder which His Majesty carried away."

The first campaign, which was also the most important, is, luckily for us, the one of which the physical records are best preserved. It dealt with a general revolt amongst the Syrian conquests of his father, perhaps occasioned by the death of Hatshepsut and the belief that Egypt was weakest at a time of transition of power. The reality was the exact opposite, for no new ruler had perhaps been quite as ready as Thutmose III.

The *Annals* contain a detailed record of this campaign, almost on a day-to-day basis, ending with the overthrow of a coalition of his enemies led by the King of Kadesh, at Megiddo.

270. Map of the Levant at the time of Thutmose III.

Carcemish

Aleppo

River Euphrates

Ugarit

Mediterranean
Sea

Tunip

Kadesh

River Orontes

Simyra

Byblos

Damascus

Tyre

Megiddo

River Jordan

Joppa

Gaza

Dead
Sea

   In a period of just over five months Thutmose captured Megiddo, marched on to the
Lebanon, captured a further three towns there and built a fortress, before returning to Thebes
for the great victory celebrations. He had left Egypt in mid-April and was back in Thebes early

in October. The speed with which the Egyptian army was mobilised and marched into Syria appears to have taken the enemy completely by surprise.

The Egyptian soldiers were led into unknown territory by Thutmose and they encountered a land very different from Egypt, with snow-capped mountains, thick forests and raging rivers, all of which must have been a daunting experience for many. It says a lot for the discipline and organisation of the army and the loyalty of the troops that they followed the king without question.

The viceroy of Kush recorded Thutmose's exploits. "The King himself led the way of the army, mighty at its head, like a flame of fire, the King who wrought with his sword. He went forth, none like him, slaying the barbarians, smiting Retenu, bringing their princes as living captives, their chariots, wrought with gold, bound to their horses."

271. Egyptian soldiers from the time of Thutmose III. Relief from the Mortuary Temple of Queen Hatshepsut at Deir el Bahri.

This is a typical Egyptian account, similar to others we have seen many times before, but Thutmose does seem to have had a particular quality of leadership that inspired his army. The victories of Egypt were as a direct result of his leadership.

The *Annals* tell how Thutmose called a council of war of all his officers when major decisions needed to be made. The enemy was established in the city of Megiddo and there were several routes that the Egyptian army could take. Two were considered to be safe, but longer than a third route, which was through a narrow mountain pass. Whilst the mountain pass was the shortest route, it was so narrow the Egyptian army would have been spread out along it whilst making the journey and vulnerable if attacked. The generals believed this route would be well guarded by the enemy and they favoured one of the longer, but much safer routes.

Thutmose recorded the comments of his generals and their advice to him against taking the mountain pass route. "The enemy is there waiting, holding the way against a multitude. Will not horse come behind horse and man behind man likewise. Shall not our advance guard be fighting while our rear-guard is yet standing … not having fought? There are yet two other roads … so that we shall come out to the north of Megiddo. Let our victorious Lord proceed upon the road he desires, but cause us not to go by a difficult road."

Thutmose did indeed choose the road he desired, but it was the difficult one. He told his generals, "… let him who will among you go upon those roads you have mentioned, and let him who will among you come in the following of My Majesty."

There was obviously great debate about the route to take, but Thutmose showed superb leadership skills and having first sought the opinion of his officers, then convinced them that they should follow him on the road that *he* believed would give him a strategic advantage and the element of surprise.

If his officers were still doubtful, Thutmose led by example and showed his own resolve and bravery and he "… went forth at the head of his army himself, showing the way by his own footsteps; horse behind horse, his majesty being at the head of his army."

There was a brief encounter with a small detachment of the enemy in the mountains, which led to the officers' calling for the straggling rear of the army to catch up with the main force and join in the fighting. The Egyptians managed to defeat the small force in the mountain pass, who had clearly not expected the Egyptian army to take this route. Thutmose was proved right in his choice and he finally emerged from the mountains in the evening with his army relatively unscathed.

Thutmose immediately set up his camp and urged his troops to be ready for battle in the morning, when "His Majesty went forth in a chariot of electrum, arrayed in his weapons of war, like Horus, the Smiter, Lord of Power, like Montu of Thebes, while his father Amun strengthened his arms. … Then His Majesty prevailed against them [the enemy] at the head of his army, and when they saw His Majesty prevailing against them they fled headlong into Megiddo, abandoning their chariots of gold and silver."

Exactly what happened in the battle is unclear. It is likely that the Egyptian army advanced *en masse* towards the enemy who were camped in the open ground before Megiddo. The enemy were unprepared and thoroughly intimidated, and simply crumpled before the Egyptians. The battle was probably over almost before it started!

The enemy fled back to the city and the gates were rapidly closed to keep the Egyptians out. Many fleeing enemy troops and their officers were caught outside the gates and they were hastily hauled up over the city walls by their clothing and ropes made of lengths of material knotted together.

The prospects of spoil in the unprotected and now empty enemy camp proved too much for the Egyptian soldiers and they immediately fell to plundering. A vast amount of booty was captured and the army was jubilant. Thutmose himself was none too pleased as he realised that the capture of the city would now be difficult. The delay in following up the initial attack, caused whilst his soldiers looted the enemy camp, enabled the enemy to establish itself behind the city walls and the momentum of the Egyptian attack was lost.

Thutmose ordered an enclosure wall to be built around Megiddo and settled in for a long siege. The city finally fell, but the siege lasted seven months. Yet more spoils were then recorded in the *Annals*. The list of captured booty is long, impressive and very detailed. It includes weapons, armour, male and female slaves, "… various drinking vessels, three large kettles, eighty-seven knives … six chairs of the foe of ivory and carob wood, vessels of bronze …" and much more.

During the siege, the captured land was divided into fields and the Egyptian soldiers became farmers, to grow crops to feed the army and the animals.

Despite a frustratingly long siege, which must have been hard on the Egyptian soldiers, Thutmose exercised considerable restraint in dealing with the captured city and its occupants, and took few lives in reprisal. Some of the Syrian leaders were taken back to Egypt as hostages, but most were allowed to return to their homes. They were, however, forced to return riding on donkeys, for Thutmose took all their valuable horses. Some two thousand horses returned to supplement and re-stock the royal stables.

Thutmose's return to Egypt, and to Thebes in particular, must have been spectacular, as a large proportion of the plunder was dedicated to the Theban god Amun.

The campaigns of the next few years saw limited military action and appear to have been organised to enable the king to re-assert his control over the captured lands and to receive his tribute in person. The lesson of the fate of Megiddo had been well learnt and many enemy states submitted easily to Egyptian authority, rather than risk direct conflict.

In year thirty of his reign, in his sixth campaign, Thutmose headed for the city of Kadesh, which had been the centre of disturbances against Egyptian rule. His army travelled most of the way on this occasion by sea, probably landing at Simyra on the coast. This campaign too was a success and the city of Kadesh, which occupied a strategically important position giving access to territories to the north, fell to the Egyptian army.

An officer on the campaign, one Amenemhab, recorded in his own tomb details of this campaign. As is usual in such accounts, he tells of his own bravery, that he personally killed and

273. Thutmose III as the victorious pharaoh, smiting his enemy. Large relief from his pylon in the Temple of Amun at Karnak.

captured many of the enemy and that the king personally rewarded him. He particularly mentions the award of "two flies" the equivalent of a bravery medal, presented by to him by Thutmose.

During the siege of the city, the enemy, who were perhaps more used than the Egyptians to warfare using chariots and horses, employed an old trick. The Egyptian chariots were pulled by stallions, and in an attempt to disrupt the disciplined and feared Egyptian chariotry, the Prince of Kadesh sent out a mare which was in season to run in front of the arrayed Egyptian chariot lines.

Amenemhab quickly realised what might happen if the stallions reacted and he went after the mare in his chariot. When he had caught up with her he leapt off and pursued her "… on foot, with my sword and ripped open her belly and cut off her tail." In an act of great panache, Amenemhab returned to Thutmose and presented the severed tail which he "… set before the king, while there was thanksgiving to the god for it."

When not fighting battles or laying sieges, Thutmose entertained himself by hunting, as no doubt did many of his officers. Amenemhab describes one elephant hunt where one hundred and twenty elephants were hunted for their tusks. Perhaps not surprisingly, it was Amenemhab who apparently hunted and killed the largest of all the elephants!

He tells us, "… I engaged the largest which was among them, which fought against his Majesty. I cut of his hand [presumably the trunk] while he was still alive … while I stood in the water between two rocks."

When Thutmose returned to Egypt he took with him the children of the native prince so that they could be raised and educated in Egypt as Egyptians. This was a clever ploy, as the children were effectively hostages, but Thutmose also hoped that they would consequently be well disposed to the Egyptians and Egypt, so that when their fathers died and they returned to their native lands to rule, there would be peace between the countries and an end to centuries of hostility. Thutmose perhaps realised military campaigns alone were not enough and was looking for a more permanent solution. He had discovered the advantages of diplomacy.

Thutmose went even further to establish closer links between Egypt and the newly conquered parts of his Empire, for he married the daughters of foreign princes to cement a diplomatic alliance. The burials of three of Thutmose's minor wives were found at Deir el Bahri, all of whom had been provided with fine jewellery and funerary equipment.

The eighth campaign saw Thutmose conquer the lands of the Euphrates. His successful previous campaigns in Asia, and the fall of Kadesh in particular, enabled him to establish garrisons to sustain his army and to help his stretched lines of communication. Again the King sailed to Simyra and marched down the river valley of the Orontes, possibly fighting three battles before erecting his new boundary stela.

The campaigns Thutmose III led into Asia are evidence of the incredible Egyptian logistical skills: boats were built or requisitioned and loaded with men, military equipment and all the supplies needed to support the army.

The Egyptian intelligence service was effective too: advance units of troops and paid spies gave Thutmose much better information about his enemies than they had about him. On many of his campaigns there were often times when his army was vulnerable, but the enemy never seems to have been in any position to take advantage of this.

The far-off King of Babylon, possibly concerned about how far Thutmose intended to lead his army, sent presents to Thutmose, as did the leaders of the Hittites. Both hoped the Egyptian army would stop well short of their borders and were anxious to ensure friendly relations. Thutmose, typically, describes the gifts as "tribute", even though the lands of the Hittites and the Babylonian Empire were to remain well beyond his new boundaries.

The result of this campaign too was a vast amount of tribute and long, detailed lists of the individual items received appear in the *Annals*. As well as receiving tribute and plunder from captured nations, Thutmose sent a "trading expedition" to Punt as Hatshepsut had done before him, and the *Annals* list the exotic supplies brought back to Egypt.

Egypt, the pharaoh and the temples of the gods had never before seen such wealth, nor would they ever again. Tribute from the land of the Retenu, received on an annual basis, kept Egypt supplied with slaves, timber, cattle, horses, plundered valuables and minerals of all sorts. Even complete ships were received "Behold all the harbours of his majesty were supplied with every good thing … consisting of *Keftew* ships, Byblos ships and *Sektu* ships of cedar laden with poles and masts, together with great trees." One remarkable present was a crate, which

274. List of the names of the towns and cities captured by Thutmose III on his campaigns. From the pylon of Thutmose III in the Temple of Amun at Karnak.

contained four domestic chicken that "… lay eggs every day" and was a real marvel to the Egyptians, who had not seen the like before.

Nubia, which appears to have been surprisingly free of the usual rebellions at this time, continued to pour tribute into Egypt, "… oxen, vessels laden with ivory, ebony and all products of this country, the harvest of Kush likewise."

275. Tribute being presented from Asia.

Thutmose's sovereignty over Nubia extended south well beyond the Fourth Cataract of the Nile. He marked his control over these lands by the erection of large stela at strategic points, such as one found at Gebel Barkal, and he built temples there, such as the one at Amada.

Thutmose's last military campaign, his seventeenth, which occurred in the forty-second year his reign, saw the elderly king re-tracing the route of his earlier campaign and heading towards Kadesh yet again to subdue a rebellion there.

The city was strongly defended, but fell to the Egyptians, only to be recaptured by the enemy, and then falling to the Egyptians and being plundered a second time. Thutmose returned again in triumph to Thebes, but this was to be the last of his many victory parades.

Towards the end of his long reign Thutmose III ruled without making any more long Asian expeditions, although he continued to make expeditions into Nubia until the end of his reign.

Nubian gold was essential to Egypt and something like ten thousand troy ounces of gold was extracted from the Nubian mines each year. Mining the gold was laborious

276. The Gebel Barkal boundary stela of Thutmose III.

work; quartz containing the gold was crushed and the gold washed out. The bulk of this work was undertaken by gangs of prisoners and criminals, overseen by small garrisons of soldiers.

Most military activity in Nubia was limited to dealing with any tribesmen who tried to interfere with the mining and to ensure that the trade flowed unhindered. Thutmose III had the old Middle Kingdom canal of Senuseret III at the First Cataract cleared to aid navigation. This canal obviously needed frequent and regular maintenance, for it had been cleared relatively recently in the reign of Thutmose I.

Thutmose concentrated on building works, notably at Karnak, where he erected obelisks, new entrance pylons and his "Festival Hall". The latter is unusual in that many of its columns are representations in stone of wooden tent-pole columns. This is unique, and perhaps Thutmose, who must have spent a large part of his life in tents on his campaigns, wanted his temple to reflect this.

Thutmose also showed, on the walls of one of his new buildings at Karnak, the variety of wildlife and flora that he encountered whilst on his campaigns. The artists successfully recorded a number of species of animals, birds and botanical specimens that were not native to Egypt, showing that the king took a real interest in his new territories.

When Thutmose was abroad on campaign, he received almost daily reports from his officials in Egypt (although by the time they actually reached him, the news was probably

277. The Festival Hall of Thutmose III in the Temple of Amun at Karnak, showing the unusual tent-pole columns.

278. Detail from one of the botanical scenes in the buildings of Thutmose III at Karnak.

considerably out of date). The bureaucracy had grown and improved from that established by Thutmose I and now there was not just one vizier in Egypt but three: one for Lower Egypt at Memphis, one for Upper Egypt at Thebes and one for Nubia.

The position of vizier was one of great trust and held real power. It seems invariably to have been passed down through members of the same family. The vizier was answerable to pharaoh for the administration of justice, for security and the gathering of taxes. The vizier was urged by the king to be fair in all his dealings, to treat everyone the same way, and to be honest and truthful in all matters, preserving the ancient virtues of Truth, Justice and Order, the concept known to the Egyptians as *Maat*.

Towards the end of his reign, Thutmose also diverted his attention to erasing from the records any reference to the reign of his aunt, Hatshepsut. Figures of the queen were hacked from temple walls and her name removed and replaced with that of Thutmose III. Thutmose must have employed a considerable number of workmen and skilled artists to complete this particular undertaking. We have no idea what his motives were for this vendetta against Hatshepsut, or why it occurred so long after her presumed death and after Thutmose's own long and very successful reign. Perhaps Hatshepsut had not died earlier after all when Thutmose assumed sole rule. She could have lived on in relative obscurity, but still respected, for a number of years, living to be an old lady. Only when she was finally out of the way did Thutmose commence his campaign to obliterate her name and memory.

It is possible that Thutmose believed that the reign of Hatshepsut was a disruption to the natural order of things, the concept of Maat, and that by erasing her name from the records he would appease the gods. Thutmose dated his reign from the moment his father died, and perhaps the parallel "reign" of Hatshepsut was simply not relevant. The truth, however, may never be known. It is possible that the removal of Hatshepsut's name from monuments was undertaken during the reign of Thutmose III's son, Amenhotep II, in an attempt to consolidate his own position.

Thutmose erected a great stela at Karnak, on which was inscribed a "Hymn of Victory", a summary of his exploits and reign, although written in the usual rhetorical style. In the hymn, the god Amun says how he had assisted Thutmose and declares:

"I worked a marvel for thee;
I have given to thee might and victory against all countries,
I have set thy fame even the fear of thee in all lands …
I have put the roaring of thy Majesty among the Nine Bows,
The chiefs of all countries are gathered in thy grasp … I have bound together the
Nubian Troglodytes by tens of thousands and thousands,
The northerners by hundreds of thousands as captives.
I have felled thine enemies beneath thy sandals …
The earth in its length and breadth, westerners and easterners are subject to thee …
Cut down are the heads of the Asiatics, there is not a remnant of them.
Fallen are the children of the mighty ones.
I have caused thy victories to be celebrated among all lands.
There is no rebel of thine as far as the circuit of heaven.
I have made powerless the invaders who came before thee;
Their hearts burned, their limbs trembling."

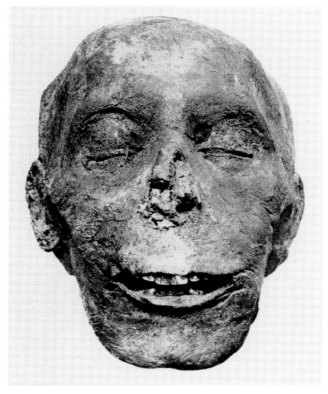

279. *The head of the mummy of Thutmose III.*

The hymn continues at length, extolling the virtues and the absolute power of the king over the Egyptian Empire and also the essential relationship between the king and god. The victories were not those of Thutmose alone, for it was Amun who had overseen the campaigns and the victories and spoils of war were his. The text of Thutmose's hymn was later copied, almost word for word, in the hymn of another warrior pharaoh, Seti I of the Nineteenth Dynasty.

Near the end of his reign, Thutmose III made his son, Amenhotep II, co-regent with him. The Eighteenth Dynasty was still new and it was essential for Thutmose to ensure that the succession was clear and uncontested, especially bearing in mind the confusion and problems at the start of his own reign.

The Reign of Amenhotep II: 1453-1419

At the age of sixteen, the young Amenhotep appears to have been a fit and athletic youth, five feet six and a half inches tall. Representations of him whilst still a prince show him being trained in archery and later, when king, he delighted in boasting that no man but him could draw his bow, and that he could shoot his arrows through copper targets three inches thick!

> "… He is a king very weighty of arm; there is not one who can draw his bow among his army … because his strength is so much greater than any other king who has ever existed; raging like a panther, when he courses through the battlefield."

Amenhotep actually gave his bow a name "Smiter of the Troglodytes" and it was taken with him to his tomb. This bow was actually found with the king's body in his quartzite sarcophagus in the Valley of the Kings when the tomb was discovered in 1898 AD.

280. Amenhotep II firing his arrows at a copper target. Scene on a granite block from the Temple of Karnak.

Amenhotep was also an accomplished charioteer with a passion for hunting lions from his chariot and also on foot. He claimed to be able to out-row two hundred men without stopping and be able to drink everyone under the table!

At the age of eighteen Amenhotep assumed the role of sole ruler on the death of his father. After a reign of fifty-four years, the death of Thutmose III, the great warrior pharaoh, was recorded by Amenemhab, who had served on many of the king's campaigns.

"Lo, the King completed his lifetime of many years, splendid in valour, in might and in triumph; from year one to year fifty-four, third month of the second season, the last day of the month under the majesty of King Menkheperre, Thutmose III, triumphant. He mounted to heaven, he joined the sun; the divine limbs mingling with him who begat him."

When news of the great pharaoh's death reached the Empire, the princes of Syria immediately rebelled by refusing to pay their tribute. This action was rapidly followed by attacks on the Egyptian garrisons in the area.

Amenhotep was furious and within a few months he led an army to put down the revolt. One enemy army was routed in Palestine in a battle where Amenhotep proved his worth as a soldier and commander by leading from the front, as his father had always done. Within two weeks he had crossed the river Orontes and defeated other enemy forces, capturing seven of the rebellious princes. Two weeks later, the rebellious city of Niy opened its gates before Amenhotep and invited the king to enter. The rebellion had been quashed.

Amenhotep set up new boundary stela, before returning to Memphis with over five hundred captive soldiers, two hundred and forty women, two hundred and ten horses and three hundred chariots. He also took away great quantities of gold vessels and copper ingots.

The king sailed to Thebes to celebrate his victory there, taking with him the seven captured Syrian princes. Their journey was less than comfortable, for they were suspended upside down from the bows of his royal barge. The prisoners were taken to the Temple of Amun at Karnak where the king personally slew them "… with his own weapons," in the presence of the god. Six of the decapitated bodies were displayed before the walls of the great temple, with the heads placed nearby.

281. Statue of Amenhotep II from the Temple of Karnak.

Amenhotep then travelled to Nubia. Not waiting for a rebellion there, he was determined to exert his control and authority. He took with him the decapitated and by then decomposing body of the seventh Syrian Prince and displayed it at the city of Napata below the Fourth Cataract. The Nubians were to be left in no doubt whatsoever that the new king would tolerate no rebellion and that he would act swiftly and mercilessly, if needed.

A large model boat found in the tomb of Amenhotep II shows on the bows a painted scene of prisoners. On the stern there is an image of the king as a sphinx, trampling his enemies and a representation of the god Montu shown in the act of killing the enemies of Egypt. If the model is accurate, then perhaps the full sized boats had similar scenes painted on them: an intimidating scene for any enemies of Egypt, a representation of the brutal, and by Egyptian standards rare, assertion of power and control that Amenhotep had made reality.

282. *Stern of a model boat found in the tomb of Amenhotep II, showing the god Montu killing the enemies of Egypt.*

Amenhotep had to live up to the reputation of his warrior father, but he lacked his father's shrewdness and believed that his enemies best understood ruthlessness and the power of the sword rather than diplomacy. The "Sphinx Stela" of Amenhotep II gives an excellent description of how he dealt harshly with his enemies: "He bound the heads of the Nine Bows. He has gathered them all into his fist, his mace has crashed down upon their heads."

By the seventh year of his reign, Amenhotep was again back in Syria to put down yet another revolt. The propaganda boasts of great victories, but in this campaign, Egypt effectively lost some of its control over the territories between the river Orontes and the Euphrates.

Another Syrian campaign in year nine of his reign may have followed, but his remaining years were peaceful and, like his father before him, Amenhotep carried out an extensive building campaign, much of it in the great Temple of Amun at Karnak.

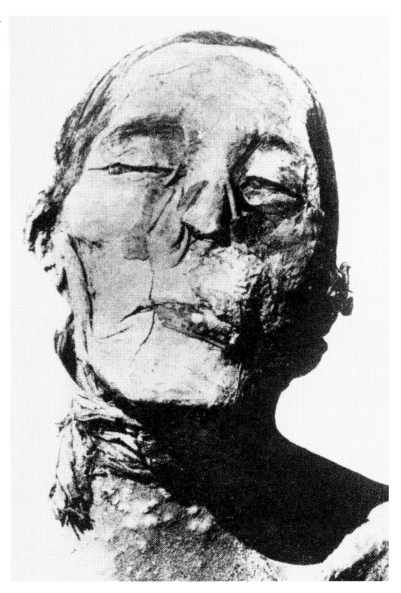

Amenhotep II's son and successor Thutmose IV received a military training when still young, and, like his father, is reported to have been skilled in the use of bow and chariot. As king, Thutmose conducted wars in Asia, but the records are scanty. He also conducted the obligatory campaigns in Nubia for which better records survive.

From a stela we learn that, in year eight of his reign, "news was brought to His Majesty ... the negro is invading the regions of Ouaouait. He has proclaimed a revolt against Egypt and has gathered around him all the vagabonds of other countries." Thutmose, who was in the Temple of Amun at Karnak when this message was received, continued with the ceremonies, asking the god for guidance, following which he immediately headed south. He travelled by river then on land, "his steeds pulling strongly the elite of his archers and all of his forces walking at his sides in two lines of young soldiers." The king landed briefly at Esna, where he was greeted by the inhabitants before stopping again at Edfu, where the ranks of his army appear to have been swelled by new troops from that area.

In Nubia Thutmose "slept not and scoured the mountains of the east, prowling along its paths like the jackal of the south in search of his prey, and he found the miserable negroes hidden in a valley known to no one … with their cattle and all their forage." Typically, the end of the text is lost, but it must be presumed that Thutmose successfully put down what was probably only a small scale uprising by a band of marauders, who had been harassing the tribes on the frontiers of Egypt and disrupting trade. His account, not unusually, makes it appear to be a far more impressive and important campaign that it actually was.

Thutmose probably maintained the Empire simply by making his presence felt and without any major military action. To counter the strength and threat of the growing Hittite Empire, Thutmose IV allied himself to the kingdom of Mittani, by marrying a daughter of the Mittanian king.

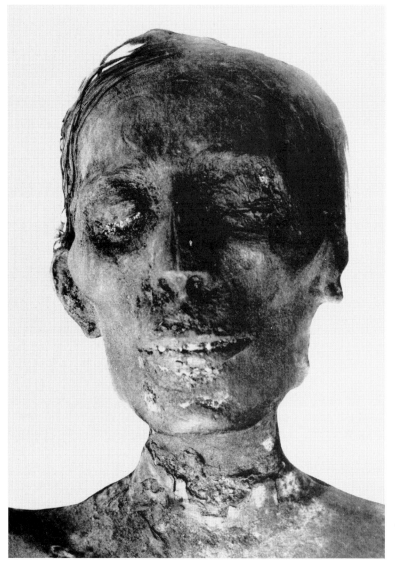

284. The head of the mummy of Thutmose IV.

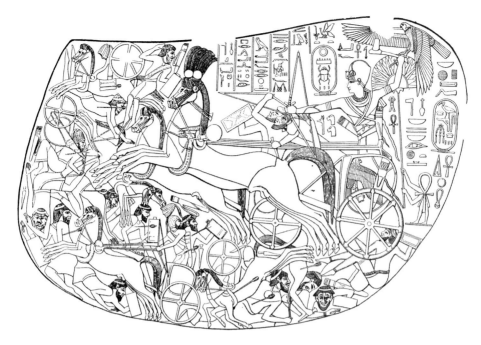

285. Drawing by Howard Carter of the decoration on the left side of the chariot of Thutmose IV.

One of the many damaged objects found in the plundered tomb of Thutmose IV in the Valley of the Kings was the body of a chariot. Decorated scenes on the sides of its battered body show the king in his chariot, fighting (symbolically if not in fact) the Asiatic enemies of Egypt.

Thutmose IV also built extensively at Karnak, although many of his structures have been destroyed or dismantled by later pharaohs. One of his principal monuments is the so-called "Dream Stela", which he erected between the paws of the great Sphinx at Giza. Thutmose recounts that, whilst still a prince, he fell asleep in the shade of the then-buried Sphinx, who asked him to clear away the sand and said that if he did so, he would be king. Thutmose did arrange for the sand to be cleared and he did become king, although, as the heir apparent to Amenhotep II, this should not have been in question. Perhaps

286. The Sphinx of Khafra and the "Dream Stela"
of Thutmose IV at Giza.

there were other potential claimants to the throne and Thutmose was clever enough to use his position and his relationship with the priests of Heliopolis to emphasise his divine right to succeed. Perhaps, also, Thutmose realised that the god Amun had received too much attention and credit for the successes of the previous reigns. It may be that this was his attempt to redress the balance and give the god Ra, who was associated with the Sphinx, some credit too.

287. Detail of the Dream Stela,
showing Thutmose IV offering to the Sphinx.

The Reigns of Amenhotep III: 1386-1349 and Amenhotep IV/Akhenaten: 1350-1334

Thutmose IV's son, Amenhotep III, was still a young boy when he became king; it must be supposed that in his early years he was guided by his ministers and advisers and perhaps a member of his family. In his fifth regnal year, Amenhotep led one campaign to Retenu and left detailed accounts of his victories there, although they read much the same as the accounts of previous pharaohs.

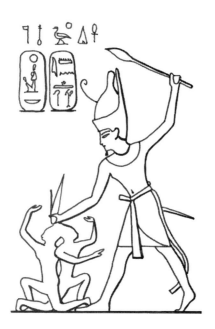

For the rest of his reign, however, the emphasis changed from battles with the enemies to treaties and the establishment of a network of diplomatic links.

Despite the lack of evidence for major campaigns, it is evident that Amenhotep did maintain the borders of Egypt and established good working relations with his subject states and neighbours. Trade and diplomacy flourished.

Part of the diplomatic archive of letters has survived from the time towards the end of Amenhotep's reign and they came from the kings of the Mittannians, Babylonians, Assyrians and Hittites. The monarchs greeted each other as brothers and as equals. They

288. Amenhotep III smiting his enemies. From a stela near Aswan.

agreed procedures for the handling of criminals convicted of offences in each other's territories and discussed each other's health problems. The King of Babylon, on hearing of Amenhotep's toothache, sent a statue of the goddess Ishtar to Egypt to effect a cure. Requests to Egypt more than often asked for gold (in return for toothache-relieving goddesses) and the qualified "thank you" letters, in response to the receipt of the presents, often complained of less gold being sent than had been expected!

One foreign ruler, Ribbadi of Byblos, sent many letters and Amenhotep actually complained about the quantity of letters he received. Egypt, however, maintained particularly good relations with Byblos, mainly to ensure that the important trade continued between the two countries. One particular request from Ribbadi was for some military assistance to reinforce one of his garrisons. Whilst on an international level there was a stable peace, it is likely that local disputes still flared up occasionally, which needed military intervention.

International marriages took place to cement alliances. Amenhotep's father, Thutmose IV, had married a princess from Mittani and Amenhotep himself took many foreign princesses into his harem, although his Great Royal Wife, Tiye, was Egyptian. The trade in royal brides was, however, one-way. Whilst Amenhotep seems to have actively searched for more foreign princesses to join his harem, he refused all the requests for Egyptian princesses to be sent abroad as wives of foreign rulers; possibly he believed that it might give those rulers a claim to the Egyptian throne.

Queen Tiye seems to have occupied a position of some influence, perhaps more so than earlier queen consorts of Egypt. In many statues she is shown, unusually, the same size as the king. Amenhotep seemed particularly keen to point out her Egyptian and "common" background. Her parents were Yuya (who was master of chariots for the king) and his wife Thuya. Their virtually intact tomb in the Valley of the Kings was discovered in 1905 AD, and contained splendid furniture and elaborate sets of gilded and inlaid coffins. As the in-laws of the king, they were given the rare privilege of being buried in a tomb cut in the royal necropolis.

Amenhotep appears to have enjoyed a peaceful reign and one that benefited greatly from the military exploits and successes of his predecessors. If ever there was a "Golden Age" in Egyptian history, then this was it. Tribute flowed into Egypt from the north and south and the country was rich and prosperous.

Amenhotep launched a truly massive building campaign throughout Egypt and was without doubt the greatest of all the royal builders. Thebes was transformed with

289. Queen Tiye.

221

290. The funeral mask of Yuya.

291. The funeral mask of Thuya.

massive building work for the god Amun.

The Temple of Amun at Luxor was completely re-built by Amenhotep. All traces of earlier buildings on the site were removed and a magnificent new temple erected. Many blocks from the Middle Kingdom temple were used as in-fill for the new walls. The Temple of Mut at Karnak was enlarged and new pylons, statues and a processional way were added to the great Temple of Amun. More colossal statues of the king were erected for Amenhotep III than for any other ruler (although many have been usurped by other pharaohs). Under Amenhotep the arts flourished and the whole country benefited from the years of prosperous peace.

In place of the great accounts of the military campaigns and warlike activities of

292. Foreigners shown in a scene from the reigns of King Amenhotep III and Akhenaten in the Tomb of Ramose at Thebes.

previous pharaohs, Amenhotep boasts of his bravery as a hunter and his success in hunting wild lions in particular. Instead of forts, in Nubia he erected temples such as the one at Soleb, intended to show the King was powerful even at a distance from Egypt.

Towards the end of his long reign, Amenhotep associated his son, also called Amenhotep, with him on the throne, although the exact length of this co-regency is a matter of debate. This is one of the most fascinating periods of Egyptian history. The new Amenhotep, the fourth of that name, favoured the worship of the sun god, the Aten, over that of Amun. He changed his name to Akhenaten (He who is useful to the Aten) and founded a new city dedicated to his god, which he called Akhetaten (the "Horizon of the Aten"), situated mid-way between Thebes and Memphis and now known as Tell el Amarna.

The religious capital of Thebes was virtually abandoned and the court moved to the new city, located on a virgin site. In the new city, temples open to the sky were erected to the sun god Aten, whilst at Thebes the temples of Amun were closed, the images of the god destroyed and any references to him

293. Statue of Amenhotep III from the Temple of Luxor.

removed. Hieroglyphs of the name of Amun were hacked from the temple walls. Even the name of Amun where it appeared as part of his father's name was carefully erased.

The reasons for this religious revolution are complex and probably began in the reign of Thutmose IV, grandfather of Akhenaten, for it is during this reign that the name of the Aten first appears. The importance of the new god had increased during the reign of Amenhotep III, who towards the end of his reign declared himself to be the "Living Aten". The term "revolution" to describe Akhenaten's actions is probably completely wrong, for latest research into this period indicates that Akhenaten was actually looking *back* to the true origins of Egyptian religion, and the earlier supremacy of the sun god Ra with his cult centre at Heliopolis. Perhaps Akhenaten should more correctly be called a fundamentalist, rather than a revolutionary.

Akhenaten was *not* a monotheist as is often claimed; he allowed the worship of many of the other ancient gods of Egypt to continue. It was specifically the god Amun and his priests who were persecuted. During the Eighteenth Dynasty the power of the priests of Amun had increased dramatically. The early warrior pharaohs had endowed the temples of the god with land and wealth and the priests were probably in a position of considerable power and influence.

At the end of the reign of Amenhotep III it is possible that the god Amun's coffers were still full, whereas those of the king were empty. Perhaps the dissolution of the temples of Amun

achieved a similar purpose to Henry VIII's dissolution of the monasteries in England in 1536 AD. The land, buildings and wealth of the god were confiscated and effectively returned to the state, and the king was able to exercise his absolute power.

Much archive evidence from this period has been lost to us, for the city of Akhetaten was abandoned after Akhenaten's death and the monuments erected by him elsewhere in Egypt were demolished by later pharaohs.

Akhenaten appears to have concentrated all his energy and resources on his campaign to establish his new religion and his new city. Correspondence continued with foreign heads of state, but it would appear that Akhenaten was less than enthusiastic about responding to their requests for assistance and he does not appear to have taken part in any military exploits.

This was a time when the Mittanian Empire was coming into conflict with the rising Hittite Empire and Akhenaten may have been keen to avoid any direct conflict himself with the Hittites. By adopting a "wait and see" policy, he either hoped the problem would just go away, or the Hittites would be stopped from expanding by their closer neighbouring countries.

Fragments of what may be battle scenes from the early part of Akhenaten's reign have been found at Medamud, but it is not clear if this is sufficient evidence of any Egyptian campaigns. The diplomatic records that survive from this period give no clear indication that there was any direct conflict at this time, whilst other records indicate that there may have been an unsuccessful Egyptian attack on the city of Kadesh.

Akhenaten, whilst still Amenhotep IV, is shown in a large-scale "smiting of the enemy" scene on a wall in the Temple of Amun at Karnak, but this may be more traditional than representational.

The Hittite king was keen to drive a wedge between the Egypt and Mittani. Both countries had enjoyed a period of peace and alliance against the threat of the Hittites. The Hittites attacked Mittanian possessions in the north of Syria, and Abdu-Nirari, the ruler of the area known as Nuhasse, sent a desperate plea for help to Akhenaten: "When Manahpiya [Menkheppere/Thutmose III] your forbear, made my father king in Nuhasse, he anointed his head with oil and spoke as follows, 'Whosoever the King of Egypt has made a king, let no-one depose'."

Akhenaten failed to respond and left Abdu-Nirari to his fate. The Hittites encouraged other vassal rulers in Syria to quarrel amongst themselves.

Ribaddi of Byblos sent over fifty letters to Akhenaten asking for help against the neighbouring state of Amor, its ruler Abdiashirta and later his son Aziru. Again Akhenaten failed to provide the forty horses and three hundred men Ribaddi had asked for and instead wrote a strongly worded letter to Aziru:

295. Amenhotep IV/Akhenaten, shown smiting the enemies of Egypt. Wall from a demolished building of his in the Temple of Amun at Karnak.

225

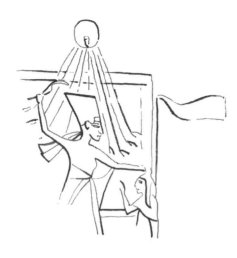

296. Image of Nefertiti , shown on the kiosk of a boat, smiting the enemy; on a block from Hermopolis.

297. Statue of Akhenaten.

"If for any reason whatsoever you prefer to do evil, if you plot to do evil, treacherous things, then you, together with your entire family shall die by the axe of the king. … Therefore perform your duty to the king your lord, and you will live. You know that the king does not fail when he rages against all of Amor."

Akhenaten summoned Aziru to Egypt to explain himself and, perhaps surprisingly, Aziru did as he was commanded. On this occasion Akhenaten had successfully exerted his authority without any direct military action, but other rulers, especially those more distant from Egypt, were not as compliant.

Hard evidence for any serious campaigns is lacking for this period and any scenes that do survive may have been the traditional "smiting" scenes, used to decorate temples and impress the Egyptians, without their being based on any actual campaigns. Images survive of Nefertiti, also in the traditional smiting pose, with a mace raised over the head of her subdued enemy. Images of queens in this role are rare and the interpretation of these scenes is difficult.

We do know that Akhenaten had some more than able officers, including one general, Horemheb, of whom we shall hear more later. It must also be presumed that the army was maintained, but that it was probably only used within Egypt, certainly for ceremonial use, but possibly as a police force too. One of his officials, Mahu, bore the title of "Chief of Police", which was recorded in his tomb at Akhetaten.

The exact role of the army within Egypt during the reign of Akhenaten is not recorded, although many surviving reliefs show it present when the king is depicted. It seems to have fulfilled a ceremonial role, not dissimilar to the military escorts seen in modern processions of heads of state, for in the reliefs, Akhenaten is shown with detachments of soldiers in front and behind

298. Akhenaten and Nefertiti in their chariots, escorted by the army, in a scene from the Tomb of Merere at Akhetaten.

his chariot and with a line of soldiers on either side. All the soldiers wear fairly elaborate uniforms, carry shields and are accompanied by standard bearers and musicians.

It is easy to dismiss Akhenaten as a "dreamer", "poet" or "visionary" as indeed many authors have done, and to assume that his entire reign concentrated on spiritual and artistic matters. Nothing was perhaps further from the truth.

Before the reign of Akhenaten the real day-to-day power in the land lay in the hands of the priests, particularly those of the Theban god Amun, who owned wealthy estates throughout the length of Egypt. It was the role of the pharaoh to preserve the ancient concept of truth, order and justice, the rule of Maat, and yet in the reign of Akhenaten, in the minds of most Egyptians, the rule of Maat was destroyed in one fell swoop by the person who should have been *protecting* it.

Akhenaten's treatment of the god Amun and the priests would have upset a large number of people, who would have been unwilling or unable to protest. It was not just the simple abandonment of the worship of Amun; the impact was much greater. Thousands of priests effectively became unemployed overnight, along with the huge number of people whose work supported the great temples. However, it is possible that some priests may have moved to the cult of Aten – it is not known if priests could, or did, move between cult centres.

Akhenaten ruled in what was effectively a police state. Evidence from private homes in Akhenaten's new city shows that personal objects that bore the name of the god Amun had had the name of the god removed. Removing the name from official buildings was one thing, but from private property is another. The implication can only be that it was an offence to possess anything bearing the name of Amun and if that was the case, there must have been some way of *enforcing* it and also seeking out transgressors. The only means available was the army, which was there to enforce Akhenaten's edicts on the population.

In a more serious and perhaps personal attack on his subjects, Akhenaten also had the name of Amun removed from the private tomb chapels (the part open to the family and priests)

299. Soldiers from the time of Akhenaten.

certainly in Thebes and probably elsewhere in Egypt too. Wherever the name Amun appeared it was removed, even if it was part of a private individual's name. The effect was to erase the name of the deceased person and this must have been regarded as a great offence and affront to the family members still alive.

Consequently, there may have been concern for Akhenaten's physical safety, and the ranks of troops we see in the reliefs may well have been there to keep the aggrieved people of Egypt away from their king. It would not be surprising if the powerful individuals whose livelihood had been ruined, and also a number of private individuals, saw it as their duty to the gods and to Amun in particular, to attempt to restore the rule of Maat. Akhenaten may have needed to watch his back, or at least have his army watch it for him.

While Amenhotep III was still alive his court was maintained at Thebes in the huge palace of Malkata on the West Bank of the river Nile, or at Memphis. Akhenaten seems to have formed a new, younger court at his new city, probably made up of the sons of his father's courtiers. These young men would have been more interested in the dramatic changes being made by their sovereign and their own lives within Egypt, rather than in international affairs. Under Thutmose IV and Amenhotep III, Egypt had enjoyed a long period of peace and prosperity and the military campaigns and struggles to establish the Empire, the benefits of which they were now reaping, were a distant memory to Akhenaten and his followers.

The Reign of Tutankhamun: 1334-1325

A ruler we know as Smenkhkare succeeded Akhenaten. Little is know about this period and Smenkhkare may have actually been Nefertiti, Great Royal Wife of Akhenaten, who ruled as pharaoh after her husband's death.

There is clear evidence, mainly from objects discovered in Tutankhamun's tomb, that there was a female pharaoh around this time. Smenkakare, whoever he or she was, only had a short reign, and was succeeded by a young boy called Tutankhaten.

The exact relationship between the new king who was aged only about nine, and his court, and indeed to his predecessors and successors is unclear and a matter of great conjecture. We know for certain he was married to one of the daughters of Akhenaten, but who his father was remains a mystery. Many suggest Akhenaten was his father, but in surviving reliefs Akhenaten is always shown with his family, which, if the reliefs are accurate (and there is no reason to suppose they are not) appears to have consisted only of *daughters*.

Tutankh*aten*, as he was first known, may have been a son of Amenhotep III and either Queen Tiye or another royal wife, but this depends on the much-debated length of the co-regency between Amenhotep III and Akhenaten. Tutankhaten would have to have been born before Amenhotep III died and Akhenaten is normally credited with a sole reign after the death of his father of considerably more than Tutankhaten's age of nine on his succession.

300. *Nefertiti, the famous painted bust of the Queen.*

301. *Nefertiti / Smenkhkare?*
Image from the Tomb of Tutankhamun.

Tutankhaten may have been a survivor of another branch of the Thutmoside family. We may never know, but we must assume he became pharaoh because of an important family connection and that, however he achieved it, he was the *rightful* and possibly only surviving male heir of the family. Tutankhaten's candidature for the throne must have been supported by the court, many members of which had served under both Amenhotep III and Akhenaten. These men included Ay, who acted as vizier to the king and regent and who may have been Tutankhaten's grandfather, and, also, general Horemheb.

The so-called "Amarna Revolution" of Akhenaten had a profound impact on Egypt and there were many who were keen to see the return of the old and established religion. Many had abandoned (officially at least) the worship of Amun under Akhenaten, but on his death, and possibly with some persuasion from the surviving priests of Amun, they soon decided to abandon the new god, and revert to the known order, the rule of Maat, without which, it was believed, Egypt could not prosper.

Probably under the guidance of Ay and other officials, the young king Tutankh*aten* returned to Thebes and changed his name to Tutankh*amun*. During his short reign he re-opened and refurbished the temples of Amun; he made new statues of the god to replace those that had been destroyed and re-carved the images of the gods on the temple walls. The work involved

302. *Statue of Tutankhamun as the god Amun, from the Temple of Karnak.*

appears to have been considerable. A large number of statues of the gods, made during the reign of Tutankhamun and with his distinctive features survive (although most have been usurped by later kings).

During Akhenaten's reign, effective Egyptian control over much of Asia had been lost. It would seem that Tutankhamun launched at least one campaign against the Asiatics, although it is not altogether clear if he led it in person. Certainly we know that the army was active and ready for action and that the king's general, Horemheb, was involved, as his own accounts tell us. Horemheb was an experienced and able general and we know of others, such as Nakht-Min, who also rose to high rank in the army at this time.

There are several representations of Tutankhamun in battle, for many objects found in his almost-intact tomb show the young king in his chariot fighting both Asiatics and Nubians. Again, in the absence of any other evidence, it must remain a matter of conjecture if these scenes represent real rather than ritual events.

Inscriptions in the contemporary tomb of the Viceroy of Kush, Huy, in Nubia record that "The chiefs of Retenu … who knew not Egypt since the time of the God [Amenhotep III?] are craving peace from his Majesty." If they are "craving peace" then there must have been a period of war. Other decoration in the same tomb shows the king receiving the tribute from Retenu and from Nubia and includes a scene of a Nubian princess visiting Egypt, drawn in an Egyptian-style chariot but pulled by a pair of bulls rather than horses.

303. The General Nakht-Min.

Tutankhamun may also have been responsible for bringing back to Thebes the royal burials made at the abandoned (and therefore no longer secure) city of Akhetaten. These would have included the burial found in Tomb 55 in the Valley of the Kings, which contained the body of Queen Tiye (Tiye's body was subsequently

304. Tutankhamun in battle. Scene from the side of his painted chest, found in his tomb.

306. A piece of gold foil from the Tomb of Tutankhamun showing the king smiting his enemy.

moved to another tomb) and possibly the body of Akhenaten himself.

With no heir, it would appear that Tutankhamun had named Horemheb as Crown Prince, but on the death of the king after only a short reign, it was the elderly Ay who became pharaoh. We do not know the circumstances surrounding the apparently premature death of the young king. Again there have been many suggestions (most being more fanciful than based on any hard evidence) including a much-vaunted theory

307. Tutankhamun as a sphinx, trampling his enemies underfoot. Scene from one end of his painted chest.

that Tutankhamun was murdered

It is easy to construct a scenario for such a plot, with Ay and Horemheb as the main conspirators. It is also easy to imagine the motive for a plot: Perhaps on reaching maturity Tutankhamun was seeking to assert his independence and his considerable power as pharaoh. Perhaps the King wanted to return to the religion he had been brought up with as a child, that of the Aten. Perhaps Ay and Horemheb were ambitious. All this must, however, remain pure conjecture (at least until any hard evidence surfaces). Those seeking to explain Tutankhamun's supposed premature death often overlook unexplained damage to the chest area of the king's mummy. Perhaps, like Seqenenre before him, Tutankhamun died in battle. We will probably never know.

Tutankhamun appears to have been the last of the Eighteenth Dynasty royal blood line, although there may well have been some minor branch of the family surviving who could rightly claim the throne. We must assume there was a brief power struggle.

308. Relief from the Tomb of Ay at Akhetaten, showing Ay and his wife with the famous Hymn to the Aten above them.

Ay needed to act quickly to secure his position and he did just that, presumably with the support of the army and the priesthood.

Ay is shown as a reigning Pharaoh on the painted walls of Tutankhamun's tomb, performing important rituals at the funeral of the king, so we know the matter was resolved in the seventy days needed from the death of the king to the time of his burial. This scene, which was never intended to be seen after the burial of Tutankhamun, is unique and nothing comparable has survived in either earlier or later royal tombs. Perhaps the scene showing Ay performing the rights for the dead king and before the re-established gods of Egypt was a powerful image that offered magical protection to the *new* pharaoh.

It is from this period that some unique letters survive, discovered in the state archive at Akhetaten and translated in the early years of the last century. A queen of Egypt wrote the letters to Suppiluliumash, King of the Hittites. Exactly *which* queen was the author is unknown (was it Ankhesenamun or Nefertiti?) and remains a matter of great conjecture, depending on which theory needs to be substantiated by the limited number of facts available.

It is generally presumed that the letters were written by Ankhesenamun the widow of Tutankhamun, soon after the king's death. In the first letter the queen explains that the king her

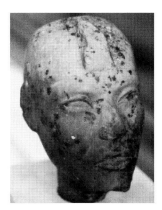

309. Head of a statue, believed to be of Ay.

310. *Tutankhamun and Queen Ankhesenamun, as shown on the Little Golden Shrine from the Tomb of Tutankhamun.*

husband is dead and asks for the Hittite king to send one of his sons to Egypt for her to marry and to make king. She explains that there is no Egyptian candidate for the position.

Considering Amenhotep III's reluctance, not many years before, to allow Egyptian royal women to marry foreigners, the Hittite King was understandably suspicious and wrote back querying the strange request. The queen, who was probably embarrassed enough about having to write the first letter, replied and repeated the request and Shuppiliumash responded by sending his son Zannanzash to Egypt.

Exactly what happened next is not clear, but Zannanzash never reached Egypt. Either he was turned back or, as some would have it, he was murdered by a band of Egyptian conspirators. Ankhesenamun never married her Hittite prince and the meagre evidence surviving implies that she married Ay. A ring survives, bearing their joint cartouches. Whatever the reason for the failed Hittite marriage alliance, it can have done no good whatsoever for Egyptian/Hittite relations and this incident may well have led the Hittites to distrust the Egyptians and have been ultimately responsible for the deterioration in relations in the following years.

Shuppiliumash clearly believed that his son had been murdered and when he heard the news he "… let his anger run away with him and he went to war against Egypt and he attacked Egypt. He smote the foot soldiers and charioteers of the Country of Egypt …"

Later correspondence between the

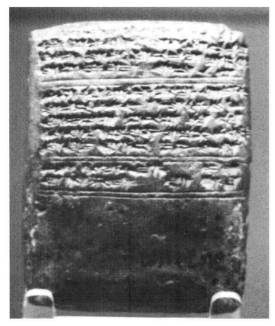

311. *Diplomatic letters on clay tablets, found at Tell el Amarna.*

234

Egyptians and Hittites, possibly from Ay, show that he appealed to the Hittite king for a continuation of the "brotherhood" which had existed before between the Hittites and Egyptians, but this appeal seems to have been ignored.

Little is known for certain about the war that followed. In fact the Hittites appear to have been weakened by an outbreak of plague, which lasted for many years. The lack of any reference in the diplomatic archive of any on-going conflict implies that the two countries settled into a period of uneasy peace, which was confirmed by a treaty between the two countries made at the end of the Eighteenth Dynasty.

Ay's direct role in any military action is unclear. A fragment of inscribed gold leaf found in the Valley of the Kings shows Ay in his chariot, drawing his bow. The traditional enemies of Egypt beg for mercy before the King. Once again it is not certain if this represents any real event, or is the usual royal propaganda.

312. Decoration on a piece of gold leaf found in the Valley of the Kings, showing Ay in his chariot.

Whilst the royal archives may be surprisingly silent on military matters, it would appear from surviving reliefs in the Memphite Tomb of Horemheb at Sakkara, that, as a general of the army, he was active during the reigns of Tutankhamun and Ay.

The reliefs, which may, of course, be propaganda, show Horemheb with his soldiers. Both northern and southern prisoners are led before him securely manacled. Horemheb also received the "gold of valour" from one pharaoh, presumably as a reward for some military success, so perhaps these scenes portray real events, the exact details of which may never be known.

It would appear, therefore, that Horemheb might have spent much of his career outside Egypt on active service, perhaps on routine border patrols, but also dealing with any minor uprisings. Although there may have been no major campaigns, the Egyptian army appears to have been in fine form and able to flex its muscles when needed.

313. Manacled prisoners led by Egyptians. Scene from the Tomb of Horemheb at Sakkara.

Tutankhamun's widow Ankhesenamun seems to disappear from the records soon after this time, and again theories abound about how she was "removed" to allow Ay full control. It is often either forgotten, or overlooked, that the twice-widowed queen, far from being the helpless, young, grief-stricken widow as she is often portrayed, was probably much older than Tutankhamun and her "disappearance" may mean nothing more sinister than her death from natural causes.

While he was King, Ay appointed his son, Nakht Min as Crown Prince, but it was general Horemheb who succeeded to the throne. Perhaps the Crown Prince died before his father and Ay was, like Tutankhamun, left with no direct heir. The arrangements for the succession may have been made during the reign of Ay to ensure a smooth transition of power, unless of course, Horemheb, with the backing of a frustrated army, led a rapid and effective military coup. With no obvious successor and with the Thutmoside dynasty ended, had Horemheb not acted swiftly, or the succession not been established in advance, there could well have been civil war and a disastrous struggle for the throne among distant members of the Thutmoside royal family.

The relationship between Ay and Horemheb is not known: he may have married a daughter of Ay and therefore been related by marriage. Egypt was at a critical period in her history and did not need internal disputes over the succession at this time.

The Reign of Horemheb: 1321-1293

As pharaoh, Horemheb continued the programme of restoration of the temples of Amun. He seems to have relied heavily on the support of the priests of Amun to consolidate his position.

One of his first tasks as pharaoh was to restore some of the royal burials in the Valley of the Kings at Thebes following a series of robberies there, including that of Thutmose IV. The implication was that the Valley had not been well-guarded during earlier reigns.

It was probably during the reign of Horemheb that most of the buildings erected by Akhenaten at Thebes, seen as an affront to Amun, were demolished. Horemheb used many of the blocks as infill for his own building work at these sites – ironically preserving them in the process. Recent discoveries during restoration work on some of Horemheb's buildings have disclosed thousands of decorated blocks from Akhenaten's earlier structures. It has even been possible to determine the exact decorative schemes of Akhenaten's buildings (mostly so far only on paper, but one large wall section has been re-erected in the Luxor Museum).

Within a generation, the city of Akhetaten was almost wiped from the landscape. Any items of value were probably salvaged as people left the city and these included wooden columns and decorated stonework. The site was used as a quarry and, until the last century, all that could be seen of the once great city was a series of mounds and depressions, marking where buildings had once stood. Only in recent years have excavations at the site revealed the foundations and the scant remains of Akhenaten's "lost" buildings.

Throughout Egypt, Horemheb launched an effective campaign to erase the name of Akhenaten, simply referred to as the "Heretic", from the records of Egypt and this work was to continue into the next Dynasty.

Horemheb dated the beginning of *his* reign from the end of the reign of Amenhotep III. The reigns of Akhenaten, Smenkakare, Tutankhamun and Ay were simply forgotten and Horemheb usurped their building works, replacing the cartouches of the earlier monarchs with his own. The removal of Ay's name from the records is, perhaps, surprising, for Horemheb must

314. *Statue of Horemheb as king.*

have worked closely with Ay over a period of many years. As with so many uncertainties that abound during this period we will perhaps never know the real answer.

Luckily for Egyptologists, Horemheb's workmen were not as diligent as he would have liked and some names, albeit in obscure and dark corners of temples and on inaccessible parts of heavy statues, survived.

Scenes on the walls of his buildings at Karnak show Horemheb, no longer as a general, but as pharaoh, receiving tribute from Nubia and presenting Asiatic and Nubian captives to the god Amun. Horemheb had begun the process of consolidating Egypt's boundaries after years of neglect. Although he may not have launched any major campaigns he was able to re-establish

Egyptian control in areas that had been neglected in previous reigns.

Horemheb himself had no heir and it appears that, like Ay, he chose his own successor, selecting a man of similar age to himself who was a friend and fellow general, and who was to become Ramesses I, the founder of the Nineteenth Dynasty.

Ramesses was an ideal choice, as he had a strong adult son, Seti, who himself had a young family. Ramesses and Seti both had military training and perhaps Horemheb realised that Egypt needed a new dynasty of young warrior pharaohs, to, at best, re-establish its Empire, or at worst, to prevent Egypt being invaded by the rising nations in Asia. A scene from the Tomb of Horemheb at Sakkara shows the figure of a man standing behind the chair of Horemheb. Some believe that this may be Ramesses.

Horemheb's splendid tomb at Sakkara was never used by him; instead he was buried in a very different and much larger royal tomb in the Valley of the Kings at Thebes.

The succession of pharaohs such as Ay, Horemheb and Ramesses causes some problems to Egyptologists. Often these men are classed as "commoners" and the presumption is always that they only achieved power by devious methods or because of their control over the priesthood or army. This may be unfair, for, very much like the British aristocracy, these men might well have been able to claim some royal blood. We do not know their family trees, but the court circle was small and the royal family large, so many official posts would have been held by royal sons, and their children. It may well be, therefore, that Ay, Horemheb and Ramesses were actually regarded by the Egyptians as "royal". They may have been related, albeit

316. *Horemheb, as depicted in his tomb in the Valley of the Kings.*

distantly, to the Thutmoside royal line and have been heirs in their own right, rather than the often-claimed usurpers or military men who claimed the throne by might rather than right. It is also wrong perhaps to see each successive dynasty as separate and distinct from the previous one. Even in Great Britain, each royal dynasty, be it Tudor, Stuart or Hanoverian, has a direct link through family members with the others.

The Nineteenth Dynasty: 1293-1187

Ramesses I	1293-1291
Seti I	1291-1278
Ramesses II	1279-1212
Merenptah	1212-1202
Amenmesse	1202-1199
Seti II	1199-1193
Siptah	1193-1187
Twosret	1187-1185

317. Figure, possibly of Ramesses I before he became King, from the Tomb of Horemheb at Sakkara.

The elderly Ramesses I reigned for less than two years and appears to have conducted one military campaign in this time, although it may well have been his son Seti who led the army. As Horemheb and Ramesses had planned, the Dynasty was secure, for Ramesses's son was ready and able to take control as the new pharaoh.

Ramesses's short reign left little in the way of monuments and he was buried in a small, but finely decorated, tomb in the Valley of the Kings. It is located not far from the Tombs of Horemheb, Tutankhamun and of the Amarna cache Tomb KV55, which probably at this time still contained the body of the heretic king

The Reign of Seti I: 1291-1278

When Seti became pharaoh, he immediately launched a series of major campaigns to re-assert and re-establish Egyptian control over its crumbling Empire. He seems to have been immediately comfortable in the role of a general. We know that he had held a high military position during the short reign of his father and possibly during the earlier reign of Horemheb, when he would have gained much practical and valuable experience.

318. Ramesses I. Painting in his tomb in the Valley of the Kings.

Seti even seems to have married into a military family, for his wife, Tuya, was the daughter of a chariot officer. (With the similarity of names, one wonders if Tuya was a descendant of Yuya, Master of Chariots to Amenhotep III, and his wife Thuya).

Still in the early years of a new Dynasty, Seti was keen to show that this was also to be a new beginning in Egypt's history and a time for the revival of the country's fortunes and power. During the reigns of the kings at the end of the Eighteenth Dynasty, military action abroad had been limited to little more than policing interventions in disputes. Whilst the Egyptian Empire still flourished, the level of Egyptian influence over the more remote regions had waned. For the first time, probably, since the reign of Thutmose IV, an Egyptian army, under the personal command of the King, would leave Egypt on an aggressive campaign.

Like Thutmose III before him, Seti realised that his first priority was to regain absolute control of the Phoenician coast. In his first year as king he received reports of a rebellion being plotted against him in Syria and Palestine and he mounted and led a small campaign into southern Palestine. It was clear that the disputes in the area were between neighbouring states and not directed at Egypt, but this presented a potential problem for Egypt, whose overland trade routes and access for any military action in parts of the Empire lay through these states.

The campaign was successful and Seti claimed to have "… extended the boundaries of Egypt as far as the heavens on every side." It meant that Seti was able to re-establish good sea-links and communications for trade, but, most importantly, to know that he had the future military capability to move his army through this area and keep it supplied.

It appears to have been Seti's aim to push the boundaries of the Egyptian Empire back to those established by Thutmose III in the previous dynasty. It was on this first campaign that Seti encountered the Hittites, although he was not able to break their hold over the area, for they had become stronger and more organised than they had been in previous reigns.

Once his coastal base had been established, Seti was then able, like Thutmose III before him, to push into the heart of Syria in a second campaign where he managed to recapture the

319. Seti mounting his chariot. From his battle scenes in the Temple of Karnak.

city of Kadesh, which had been lost during the reign of Tutankhamun. The Hittite defence of the city was minimal and this seems to have been because a major part of the Hittite army was dealing with a border dispute with the Assyrians to the east. Kadesh was only to remain under Egyptian control for a short time and reverted, without any military action, to the Hittites. The Egyptians did not press home any advantage they had gained and the Hittites somehow managed to hold their ground. Sadly no detailed account of this campaign survives. When Kadesh fell to the Hittites, Seti withdrew from the area, allowing the Hittites to extend their sphere of influence closer to Egypt.

On his way back to Egypt, Seti stopped at Tyre where he accepted a token of submission, gifts of cedar wood, from the princes there. On one wall of the Temple of Karnak there is a scene of a fortress in this area, where the ruler is shown breaking his spear across his knee. It is likely that all parties in the disputed area realised that any military action would be counter-productive against the might of the new pharaoh and that hostilities ceased. The trading links had been protected, which was vital not just for the prosperity of Egypt, but also for its near neighbours.

As in previous reigns, Seti launched a campaign southwards into Nubia, to re-impose Egyptian control over the area, or possibly just for propaganda and field training for his troops.

Seti "… joined battle with them, the might of Pharaoh being before them like a blast of fire, trampling the hills." On this campaign, Seti was keen on *removing* any troublemakers, not killing them, and he returned to Egypt with four hundred and twenty captives, fifty being men of military age, who were presumably taken into Seti's army. He established a number of new fortified towns in Nubia, including Akshra and Amara West. This was the start of important new development in the area, which continued in the reign of his son, Ramesses II.

Seti inscribed his battle scenes on the exterior of the northern wall of the Hypostyle Hall in the Temple of Amun at Karnak. Although Ramesses II usually gets the credit for this most impressive part of the temple, it was actually constructed almost entirely in the reign of Seti. Ramesses simply finished the decoration of some of the walls and columns after his father's death.

The battle scenes are well illustrated but the inscriptions are basic and their interpretation is difficult, especially the sequence of the individual campaigns, as there are no dates recorded. The reliefs show the victorious Seti, having subdued Libyans, Syrians, Hittites and Nubians. These scenes are amongst the first large-scale "battle scenes" to survive in Egypt but they have

320. *Captured prisoners, from the battle reliefs of Seti I at Karnak.*

a mainly religious context, situated as they are in the great Temple of Amun. The scenes illustrate the relationship between Seti and his god. The god grants Seti the power and ability to prevail in battle over all nations and the king offers to his god the spoils of victory: the gold, plunder and captives.

The detailed scenes show fortified towns that have surrendered to Seti, whilst the enemy soldiers flee to the safety of nearby towns or to higher ground away from the Egyptians. There is little doubt that Seti led his troops personally in battle, and he is shown returning across the Delta to Egypt, to receive the thanks of his people and to hold a victory celebration where the captured and bound enemies are paraded before him and the assembled court.

In one scene, the victorious Seti is shown with two captives under each arm. From the scale of these figures, it is likely that they represent captured tribal chiefs, subdued by the all-powerful pharaoh.

From this period onwards, the typical bombastic and self-glorifying accounts of the military exploits of the pharaohs were illustrated for all to see and admire. When freshly carved and brightly painted, these scenes, usually on the outside walls of the temples, would be a potent and visible reminder to all of the authority of the king.

Having dealt with problems in the Levant and to the south in Nubia, Seti also had to deal with Libyan invasions along the Western Delta. The Egyptian army was well-blooded by this time and the invaders were quickly and easily driven out of Egypt. The Karnak battle reliefs depict Seti fighting a Libyan who is shown as the same size as the king. Perhaps this indicates that there was a personal encounter with the Libyan leader. Seti has the Libyan secured by the neck, using his bow as a lasso, and is ready to strike him with his raised scimitar.

After his initial sharp, if relatively brief, campaigns, Seti seems to have then concentrated on re-establishing diplomatic and trading links with most of his enemies. He recounts how he secured great lengths of cedar from the Lebanon, for use in building his royal barge and also to make flagpoles for the Temple of Amun. Relationships with the Hittites, however, remained strained, with a period virtually of cold war between the two nations. Neither side was effectively able to press home any military advantage.

Seti enjoyed a long reign and built extensively, something he would not have been able to do had the country's resources been concentrated on foreign campaigns. Tribute flowed into

321. Seti I with his prisoners.

Egypt and Thebes flourished once again. Seti benefited from the wealth of Egypt and the national security that his campaigns had achieved.

At home, Seti managed to increase the gold output from the Eastern Desert at Gebel Zebara. The journey to the mines was long and difficult, with inadequate supplies of water, and mining at the site had, as a consequence, all but ceased. Seti arranged for a new well to be dug, and then for a small temple and a permanent settlement to be erected at the site. With such a

323. *Seti smiting his enemy before the god Amun.*

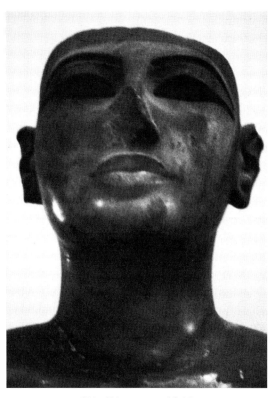
324. Alabaster statue of Seti I.

valuable commodity travelling the route, adequate security was essential and the whole area needed to be well guarded.

Under his patronage, the arts flourished and Seti employed a veritable army of craftsmen in his building works. Some of the finest relief carving surviving in Egypt today comes from the walls of Seti's monuments. Of particular note is his temple at Abydos and his work in the Temple of Amun at Karnak. His tomb in the Valley of the Kings is one of the largest ever excavated there and has some of the finest painted and carved decoration seen in the royal necropolis.

Seti firmly re-established the worship of the ancient gods. At Abydos his temple was dedicated to seven of the main gods of Egypt, and the important rituals were inscribed on the walls, thereby ensuring magically that they would always be observed in the future. Before the reign of Seti the kings stood as *equals* with the gods and looked them in the eye. In Seti's reliefs, he assumes a subservient position, stooping or bowing to the deities, as if to atone for the failure of the rule of Maat in earlier reigns. He was keen to be seen as the one who restored the rule of Maat and to be placating the gods, whose worship had been interrupted during the reign of Akhenaten.

Seti used at least part of his army to help with the moving of some of the larger stones for his monuments, sending a detachment of one thousand men from his army to the quarries at Silsila.

The men were well equipped for this trip. Seti records that they were provided with "… ox flesh, fish and plentiful vegetables without limit. Every man of the army had twenty deben of bread daily, two bundles of vegetables, a roast of flesh and two linen garments monthly. Thus they worked with a loving heart for His Majesty."

For many years the army may well have been relatively inactive, and this new series of expeditions and campaigns meant that the men under Seti's command had the opportunity for action. This would explain their eagerness to follow him, especially on campaigns where the mere presence of the Egyptian army probably occasioned surrender by the enemy, without a long, bloody and dangerous conflict.

The mummy of Seti I, although damaged by tomb robbers, was found in a cache of royal mummies at Deir el Bahri in 1881 AD. His original tomb had been robbed in antiquity and the mummy moved several times before it reached its last resting-place. Although the mummy had been stripped of all its jewellery (apart from one small amulet still hidden beneath layers of resin) and robbers had roughly handled it, Seti has the best-preserved features of any of the surviving royal mummies.

The Reign of Ramesses II: 1279-1212

Seti was succeeded as pharaoh by his son, the twenty-five year old Ramesses, who had taken his name from his grandfather, Ramesses I. Ramesses appears to have been made co-regent with his father towards the end of Seti's reign and is shown with him in many surviving reliefs, including some of the battle reliefs at Karnak, which indicates he received military training from an early age.

Interestingly, in some of Seti's early reliefs, the figure of Ramesses appears to have been added or to have replaced the figure of another prince, who may have pre-deceased him. Perhaps Ramesses was attempting both to re-write history and to strengthen his own position when he was king.

The new dynasty founded by Ramesses I appears to have encountered no Egyptian

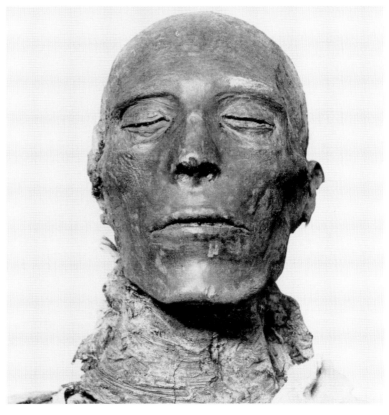

326. The head of the mummy of Seti I.

resistance; Ramesses, and later Seti, were reasonably secure in their rule from the very beginning and in full control of the situation. The start of any new dynasty was always a period of potential unease as possible rival claimants to the throne might appear. Ramesses may have still needed to be cautious.

Like Ramesses I and Seti before him, Ramesses II continued the campaign against the memory of Akhenaten and his immediate successors. This action against earlier and vilified pharaohs served to remind the Egyptians that they were actually better off with the new Ramesside dynasty rather than with the family who had built an Empire only to squander its wealth and cause religious upheaval.

Ramesses II reigned for sixty-seven years and led many campaigns against northern and southern enemies, recording them on the walls of his temples. At his mortuary temple (known today as the Ramesseum) and in the Temple of Abu Simbel in Nubia, Ramesses is shown receiving the emblems of royalty, the crook and flail, from the god Amun, but he also receives a weapon, the new scimitar. From the beginning, Ramesses's reign continued the military campaigns begun by his father.

Ramesses's first military action as pharaoh seems to have been the, by now almost obligatory, journey into Nubia, to re-assert the power of Egypt and that of the new and untested ruler. Nubia was probably familiar to Ramesses, for he may have campaigned there when he was still crown prince.

327. *Statue of Ramesses II, originally from the Ramesseum at Thebes.*

At the Temple of Beit el Wali, in Nubia, Ramesses is shown attacking Nubian fortifications on hills. The success of this campaign is shown by the usual scenes of captured prisoners and tribute being paraded before the victorious pharaoh.

In year four of his reign there was a revolt in the Levant and Ramesses led his first campaign, which secured Palestine and southern Lebanon and prepared the way for further campaigns in the area and beyond.

In year five of his reign, Ramesses began a campaign against the Hittites. Relations with the Hittites had deteriorated badly since the end of the Eighteenth Dynasty and the Hittite Empire had expanded and encroached on Egyptian territory in Syria and Lebanon. The main threat was the disruption to trade and in particular to the supplies of cedar, which came from Lebanon. Seti I had not managed to resolve the problem before his death and the Hittites had continued to advance southwards into Egyptian-controlled areas. Ramesses was the aggressor in this matter and his action actually went against a previous agreement which had established

328. *Painted cast of a scene from the Temple of Beit el Wali, showing Ramesses defeating the Nubians.*

spheres of influence in this area.

The Hittites, led by their king Muwatallis, anticipated an attack by Egypt by raising a strong army and entering into a coalition with neighbouring states. This time there was no other internal or external distraction for the Hittite army, and, unlike in the reign of Seti I, the Hittites were able to turn *all* of their energies against the Egyptians.

The Hittite army was well equipped and manned. The Hittite infantry were equipped with similar weapons to their Egyptian counterpart, although they may have had more iron-bladed weapons. As in Egypt, chariots had an important role to play. The Hittite chariots were designed to carry three men, rather than the Egyptian two; the occupants were the driver, a spear thrower or archer and a shield bearer to protect the other two. Horses and men were protected by bronze scale armour. All this extra weight meant that the Hittite chariots were larger, heavier and slower than those of the Egyptians.

In the summer of year five of his reign, Ramesses led his army of some twenty thousand men against the Hittites. Moving up into the Levant through the Gaza Strip, he followed in the footsteps of Thutmose III, who had made the same journey some two hundred years before. The army was in four divisions, with the king himself leading the first division, named after the god Amun. Sons

329. *Ramesses II attacking a walled town in the Levant. Painted cast of a scene from the Temple of Beit el Wali.*

of Ramesses commanded the other divisions named after the gods Ptah, Ra and Set (although the sons' role as commanders may have been a nominal appointment only as the princes may have been too young to exercise *real* command).

This was a major campaign, which would have taken a lot of detailed planning and organisation in advance, to mobilise troops and the necessary support. At the Temple of Luxor, a relief shows Ramesses receiving and sending reports and making his plans, which must have stretched the efficient Egyptian bureaucracy to its limits.

Ramesses's army was composed mostly of Egyptian troops in the infantry and chariotry, with some Nubian archers and Libyan and Sherden mercenaries.

The ultimate goal for the Egyptian army was the city of Kadesh. As soon as Ramesses had left the Delta he sent a detachment of troops off in advance along the coastal routes. The commander of this unit was instructed to make sure the coastal towns were still loyal to Egypt, secure the ports to maintain good naval links with Egypt, and then to re-join the main army at Kadesh.

In advance of the main section of his army, Ramesses and the Division of Amun made its way into the valley of the river Orontes, where the city of Kadesh blocked the way northwards. They forded the river some twenty kilometres upstream from the city and entered a wooded area, which would have been ideal for an ambush by the enemy. The terrain was heavy-going

331. A Hittite chariot, with the driver, spearman and shield bearer.

332. Ramesses II in his chariot. Relief from the Temple of Karnak.

for the chariots in particular, which had difficulty on the muddy ground and the king himself was forced to proceed on foot for a while.

Ramesses appears to have not been too concerned about his potentially vulnerable situation: the fact that his whole army was extended over a large area and still on the move. Some of his scouts had picked up two local men who had volunteered to act as guides for the Egyptians. They were able to report that the Hittite army was well to the north, nowhere near Kadesh, and that Ramesses's army was safe from attack. Perhaps surprisingly, the Egyptians believed this and made no effort to scout well ahead themselves; had they done so the outcome of the battle that was to follow might have been very different.

By the time the army was close to Kadesh, the four Divisions of the army had become separated still further and it was the Division of Amun that approached the city first, with the other three Divisions still some way behind.

Ramesses decided to make camp close to the city and the advance part of the Division of Amun was soon busy erecting tents and shield walls, and feeding the horses and men. The army probably expected some time to rest and recuperate after their long march. This was not to be.

Closer to the city of Kadesh, two further Hittite agents were captured and they were taken before Ramesses, who "… sat on a throne of gold." Following a beating, they confessed to the true location of the main Hittite force, not in fact many miles away as Ramesses had originally been told, but very close. The Hittite army of some eight thousand infantry plus cavalry was

333. The Egyptian Army: chariots and Infantry.

actually camped just beyond the city of Kadesh and out of sight of the Egyptians. Ramesses realised the danger he was in and immediately sent a warning to the Division of Ra and orders for it to close on the Division of Amun as soon as it could do so. The Division of Ra was, however, still some eight kilometres away and just emerging from the woods. Although it was heading towards the camp of the Division of Amun, it was already too late.

The Hittites sent a large reconnaissance body of chariots, possibly around two thousand five hundred, towards the Egyptian camp, but they kept well to the south of the Egyptians and were hidden by trees. They crossed the river Orontes and when, at speed, they burst clear of the tree line, they immediately found themselves confronted by the Division of Ra, which was still on the march towards Kadesh. The Egyptians were taken completely by surprise, but so were the Hittites, who with the river to their rear and the bulk of their force still crossing it had nowhere to go but forward into the Egyptians. The Hittites crashed through the Egyptian column, causing mayhem and confusion as they did so and scattering the column in all directions.

Once the Hittite chariots were clear of the Division of Ra, they swept northwards towards the camp of the Division of Amun. Some Egyptian chariots had already raced towards the camp to warn Ramesses, but they arrived at almost the same time as the Hittite chariots. The Egyptians had no time to prepare any organised defence. There was great confusion and possibly panic as the Hittite chariots hurtled into them and the first volleys of spears and arrows arrived in their midst. The Division of Amun was on its own – the other divisions of the army were still too far away to help.

The Hittites easily broke through the simple defences of the camp and the Division of Amun, like the already shattered Division of Ra, began to scatter and flee.

Amidst the confusion in the enemy camp, it appears that Ramesses alone kept his head. Saying a prayer to Amun, he was able to rally the charioteers and troops nearest to him and managed to hold his ground. "His Majesty shone like his father Montu when he took the adornments of war. As he seized his coat of mail he was like Baal in his honour. His Majesty charged into the foe … when His Majesty looked behind him he found two thousand five hundred chariots surrounding him."

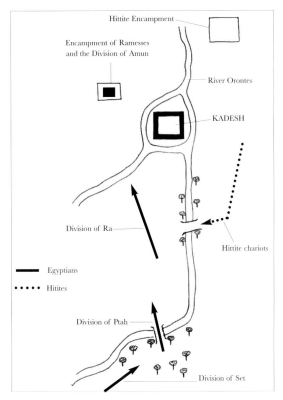

334a. Plan of phase 1 of the Battle of Kadesh.　　　　*334b. Plan of phase 2 of the Battle of Kadesh.*

Although Ramesses claims to have been completely deserted by his troops, in practice he had his personal guard and shield bearer, Menna, with him and probably some of his elite troops and bodyguard, but they needed quick and firm orders. Ramesses rose to the challenge and he drove his own chariot directly towards the Hittites.

The Hittites seem to have been taken aback by this small and unexpected token resistance, in what had previously been a one-sided engagement. It was not long before other Egyptians followed their commander's example and began to rally, whilst the superior and deadly firepower of the Egyptian archers finally began to make some impact on the enemy. The Egyptian chariots, which were faster and lighter than those of the Hittites, also achieved some measure of success. The archers in the chariots were able to get in amongst the Hittite chariots and then move swiftly out of danger. Their tactic was no doubt helped by the fact that the Hittite horses by this time would have been very tired and slowing down.

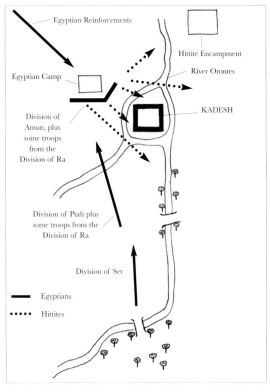

Ramesses's prayer to his god Amun seemed to have been heard, for just as Egyptian discipline had broken down at the battle of Megiddo under Thutmose III, so the Hittite commanders lost control over their troops at a critical stage of the battle. The initial Hittite attack had lost its impetus and many of the Hittites, who had overrun the Egyptian camp meeting little or no resistance, considered the battle already won, stopped fighting and began plunder the site. This gave Ramesses just the breathing space he needed.

334c. Plan of phase 3 of the Battle of Kadesh.

Although Ramesses continued to rally and organise his troops, they were still in a desperate situation. At the critical moment the day was saved when the troops Ramesses had sent along the coastal route fortuitously appeared and quickly came to his rescue. Although still outnumbered, the Egyptian infantry was soon able to stop any further damage by the Hittite chariots and Ramesses's own chariots were able to mount a number of short and sharp charges straight into the enemy ranks.

It is difficult to understand why the Hittites did not use its superior infantry against the Egyptians. For the whole of the time the camp of Amun was being attacked, the Hittite infantry remained inactive in its own camp behind the city of Kadesh. Perhaps the Hittite intelligence was not aware of the other Egyptian force in the area. It is more likely, however, that the Hittites believed their surprise attack by chariots would be more than sufficient to defeat the Egyptians in one fell swoop.

Once the attack had been launched, it would not have been easy to see exactly what was happening as the two sides clashed. In the confusion of battle, and perhaps with the view

335. Ramesses in his chariot, ploughs through the Hittites. Relief from the Temple of Ramesses II at Abu Simbel.

336. Egyptian chariots defeating the Hittites. Relief from the Temple of Ramesses II at Abu Simbel.

blocked by clouds of dust thrown up by the chariot wheels, the fact that the Egyptians had rallied under Ramesses and the timely arrival of reinforcements probably went unnoticed by the Hittite commanders until it was far too late to do anything about it.

With the Hittites on the run, the Egyptians pursued their enemy, who fled towards the city of Kadesh. Ramesses's reliefs in his temples show this stage of the battle, where the reinforced Egyptian army attacks the remains of the Hittite force. The Egyptian chariots are shown in orderly and neat rows, whilst the Hittites are shown in absolute confusion, with upturned chariots, dead and wounded horses. Dead Hittites litter the ground beneath the wheels of the Egyptian chariots.

The Hittites were pushed back towards and then into the river Orontes which surrounded part of the city. The Prince of Aleppo is shown in Ramesses's reliefs being pulled from the river,

337. Ramesses attacking the Hittites.

253

338. *The city of Kadesh, showing the walls surrounded by the river Orontes. Relief on the Pylon of the Temple of Luxor.*

having swallowed a lot of water. His comrades had to turn him upside down, to let the water run out! As the Egyptians gained ground, the Hittites withdrew into the city, where the gates were firmly closed (but before some of the Hittites were able to get back inside – many are shown in reliefs being frantically hauled up over the defensive walls into the city).

With the Hittites inside the walled and easily defended town and the Egyptians outside, the fighting soon ended and the conflict became a stalemate. The Egyptians recovered their wounded and the hands of slain Hittites were cut off for the official record of the battle. The Egyptians were jubilant, but Ramesses was not pleased and rebuked many of his officers for

339. *The Hittites fleeing back into the city of Kadesh. Relief on the pylon of the Temple of Luxor.*

their cowardice and for their failing to support him when he most needed it. The King however, allowed the army to celebrate and the prisoners and the severed hands of the dead were paraded before him. He was described as "the Good God, mighty in valour, great in victory", whose personal action in battle was "like a fierce-eyed lion."

Ramesses had had a lucky escape and faulty intelligence both on the part of the Egyptians and the Hittites meant that neither side had obtained a clear and decisive victory.

The battle fought by Ramesses at Kadesh was not the first, nor the most significant, at this site and the circumstances of the campaign were no different from the campaigns of earlier pharaohs. Even the weapons and tactics used had not changed. It is solely because of the importance given to this battle by Ramesses II himself that it has assumed such significance.

Ramesses had his own account of the battle recorded in a total of ten inscriptions carved on the walls of five Egyptian temples. (There may have actually been more, but most of the temples in the Memphis and Delta areas have not survived.)

Ramesses's account of the battle remains the most detailed. None of the accounts have survived intact, but the number of them means that when there are gaps in one account, they can be filled by surviving portions in other versions. The Temple of Ramesses II at Abydos contained the finest version with superbly illustrated scenes of the whole campaign. Sadly this temple is greatly ruined and much of the account has been lost. The version in the Temple of Amun at Karnak is similarly damaged, with the best surviving accounts now being in the Temple of Luxor, the Ramesseum and the great Temple of Ramesses II at Abu Simbel.

Ramesses's battle reliefs are much more graphic than those of his father Seti I. Within the rigid conventions of Egyptian art, we can actually see the full pell-mell of an ancient battle.

From these inscriptions, we are told that Ramesses achieved a major victory, but whilst it is clear that his own personal bravery was impressive, his survival on the day was due ultimately to Hittite blunder and the chance, albeit timely, arrival of reinforcements.

The Hittites themselves were under the distinct impression that *they* had won the battle. In a surviving Hittite relief we learn that "… at the time that Muwatallis took the field against the king of the land of Egypt and the country of Amurru, and when he then had defeated the king of the land of Egypt and the country of Amurru, he returned to the country Apa …."

Even today military historians still argue over how the battle was fought and who actually did win the battle, or if indeed there actually was an overall victor. This was undoubtedly a major battle, but one where the substantial part of both armies did not actually fight. The entire

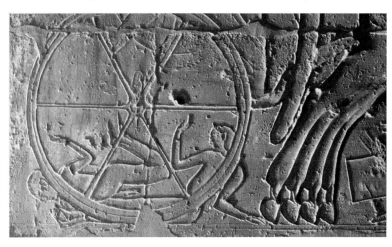

340. The aftermath of the battle, with the Hittite dead and wounded beneath the wheels of Ramesses's chariot. Relief from the Ramesseum at Thebes.

Hittite infantry had been deliberately kept in reserve and at least half of the Egyptian army arrived at the site of the battle too late.

After Ramesses left Kadesh he led his army to the south away from the city. Muwatallis and his army left the safety of Kadesh and shadowed the Egyptian army as it withdrew, accompanying it (at a safe distance) as far south as Damascus. Muwatallis was making absolutely sure that Ramesses and the Egyptian army left the area.

In the following years Ramesses campaigned repeatedly in the area, and although he went into territory beyond Kadesh, he avoided any direct clash with the Hittites. He realised he would not be able to keep up the substantial and sustained military effort that would have been needed to keep them at bay.

It was not until some sixteen years after the battle of Kadesh that the Egyptians and Hittites finally acknowledged the stalemate between them and formally called a halt to continuing hostility between the two nations.

A peace treaty between Ramesses and the new Hittite king, Hattusilis, was agreed. The text still survives and is the oldest for which there is a full record, with both Egyptian and Hittite versions surviving. Ramesses did not sign the treaty in person – this was delegated to Ambassadors. Only recently the Tomb of Netjerwymes, one of Ramesses's Ambassadors who probably signed the treaty, has been discovered by Alain Zivie and a French team working at Sakkara.

The treaty established clear boundaries between the two countries:

> "There shall be no hostilities between them forever. The great chief of Kheta shall not pass over into the land of Egypt forever, to take anything therefrom. Ramesses-Meriamon the great ruler of Egypt shall not pass over into the land of Kheta to take anything from them forever."

341. A list of captured enemy towns, from the Temple of Ramesses II at Abydos.

The treaty included clauses where it was agreed that each country would assist the other in the event of any attack by other enemies and even an extradition clause to prevent political or criminal fugitives from fleeing across the borders to safety.

It finished with a curse against anyone who violated the terms of the treaty:

"As for him who shall not keep them, the thousand gods of the land of Kheta and the thousand gods of the land of Egypt shall desolate his house, his land his subjects." Conversely, there was a special blessing from the gods included, for those who made sure that the terms of the treaty were adhered to. This treaty lasted well and only failed when the Hittite Empire was destroyed by invasion from western Anatolia and the Aegean.

A further thirteen years after the treaty had been agreed, relations between the Egyptian and Hittite Empires were reinforced when Ramesses II, by this time in his fifties, married the eldest daughter of King Hattusilis. Ramesses received his new bride (who was given the Egyptian name of Maathorneferure) in his new Delta city of Per-Ramesse. It would appear from inscriptions that the King of the Hittites actually journeyed to Egypt with his daughter, demonstrating the good relations between the two previously hostile nations. The event was recorded on a stela at Abu Simbel.

Some seven years after this marriage, a second daughter of Hattusilis was sent to Egypt to join her older sister as a wife of Ramesses.

The treaty and the subsequent royal marriages gave great stability to the whole area. Ramesses seems to have been delighted with his new peaceful relationship with the Hittites, although he never seemed to tire of having himself portrayed as the all-conquering military hero, still referring to himself as the conqueror of the Hittites. It is easy to image

342. The King of the Hittites with his daughter.

343. Ramesses II smiting a Libyan. Painted cast of a relief from the Temple of Beit el Wali.

the ageing Pharaoh re-telling the story of the battle of Kadesh, no doubt with the details being embellished each time!

Ramesses also faced problems in the Western Desert, where the Libyans were proving to be a threat. He tried to control, if not stop completely, the gradual invasion of the Delta area and he built a series of forts to the east of the Delta, from what is now Alexandria to the west of el Alamein.

It was thought that some of these forts were just small garrisons, intended as an "early warning system" for any invasion. However, excavations at the site of Zaiwat Um el Rakham have revealed a substantial fort, which possibly held five hundred or more men in the Ramesside Period. Indications are that the garrison grew its own crops of grain and flax and was a thriving working community.

Like many others this fort was located on the coast and seems to have functioned as a trading post for imports from Crete and Cyprus.

Minor disturbances in Nubia seem to have continued, but were overshadowed by the campaigns in the north. The exact sequence of any military activity in Nubia is not clear and many scenes that do survive may be more symbolic than representing actual events.

The prosperity of Egypt and a period of relative peace meant that Ramesses, like other pharaohs before him, was able to devote much of his time and effort to great building works. Ramesses is often called a megalomaniac, because of the sheer number of buildings, chiefly temples, that bear his name. Perhaps the king's near brush with death early in his reign made him keen to honour the god to whom he had turned in his hour of need, for it was Amun who benefitted most from the new building campaign.

344. The Ramesseum, Mortuary Temple of Ramesses II at Thebes.

Ramesses had a long reign and he was able to undertake many major projects, having first completed many that had been started by his father Seti I. Ramesses was also not above usurping the monuments of earlier pharaohs and inscribing his name on the statues and temple walls. However, it is likely that many of the earlier sites may have fallen into disrepair and Ramesses was either re-building or simply re-cycling materials.

The scale of many of his monuments is immense and the organisational skill and manpower needed for many of them would have been phenomenal. Like many pharaohs before him, he may well have used parts of his army, supplemented by large numbers of foreign mercenaries, to help with some of the major works.

Whilst many of Ramesses's buildings in the north of Egypt no longer survive, in the Theban area he added substantially to the Temples of Amun at Luxor and Karnak and built a splendid mortuary temple on the west bank at Thebes.

Ramesses certainly seemed keen to make an impression on the Nubians and erected new temples at a number of sites. The huge rock-cut temples at Abu Simbel were the largest and most impressive. The great temple was dedicated to four gods, whose images still sit in the sanctuary, Amun, Ptah and Ra, the fourth being Ramesses himself. The second, smaller, temple at Abu Simbel was dedicated to Hathor and the Chief Wife of Ramesses, Nefertari. Anyone entering Egypt from the south would have little doubt about the power and influence of the Egyptians in Nubia under their God-King Ramesses, for these temples in the cliffs overlooked the river Nile and all the passing river traffic.

With an Empire that stretched well around the eastern edge of the Mediterranean Sea, Ramesses found that the ancient administrative capital at Memphis was less than ideally placed. Under Ramesses many new cities were established early in his reign to the north of Memphis in the Delta. The site of Avaris, once the capital of the Hyksos before the New Kingdom, assumed a new importance (possibly a process already begun under Seti I) as did a new city named Per Ramesse. These cities had excellent trade and communication routes and were an ideal

345. Statue of Ramesses II in the Temple of Luxor.

346. The great Temple of Ramesses II at Abu Simbel.

place for the bulk of the army to be garrisoned. The Delta provided plenty of space and food for the extensive royal stables.

Ramesses took his sons with him on many campaigns. The Beit el Wali temple reliefs, in Nubia, show two of his sons riding in their own chariots in the Nubian campaign. The younger, Khaemwaset, can have only been five or six years old at the time. The young princes are shown after the battle, presenting the spoils of victory to their father.

347. Sons of Ramesses II, shown with the distinctive "side-lock of youth", in battle.

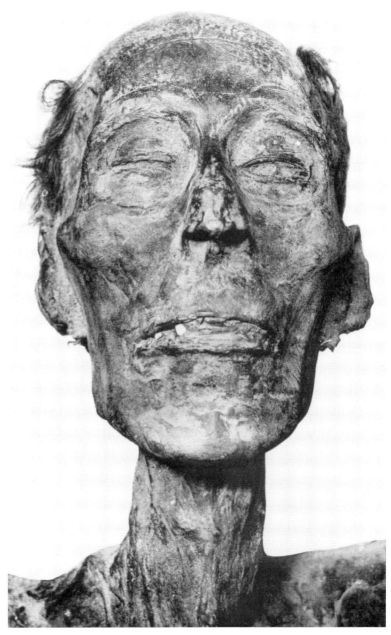

*348. The head of the mummy of
Ramesses II.*

We know that some royal princes were at Kadesh, although they were probably kept well away from any immediate danger. One surviving inscription says "… to tell the royal children … keep yourselves clear of the battle."

Such military training from a very early age was to prove useful for at least one of Ramesses's sons. Outliving many of his children, Ramesses died in his eighties and was succeeded by his thirteenth son, Merenptah. The deceased sons of Ramesses already lay in a huge tomb close to the tomb of Ramesses himself in the Valley of the Kings (Tomb KV5, which has only recently been re-discovered by archaeologists).

The work of clearing this tomb is being led by Egyptologist Kent Weeks. The remains of four bodies have been found so far and are presumed to be of royal princes. One of the skulls shows a fatal injury, perhaps inflicted by a mace or club. Kent Weeks has suggested that this might possibly be the skull of Prince Ramesses, who we know served in the army, and who may have died in battle. More research is needed on the human remains to help date and confirm their possible identity.

The unusual size and importance of Tomb KV5 may perhaps indicate that the princes buried there were far more important than the princes of earlier or later sovereigns. Perhaps in the last years of the long reign of Ramesses, some of his sons played a much more significant role in the affairs of state and religion than usual. We know that the elderly king was probably not in physical good health. He suffered from arthritis and had severe dental problems, which would have caused him great discomfort.

The reign of Merenptah: 1212-1202

Merenptah was himself an elderly man by the time he became pharaoh (he was probably in his sixties) and he inherited a peaceful and prosperous Empire. It was not long, however, before he had to put his practical military experience, gained during the reign of his father, to the test.

The rich and fertile area of the Delta was always attractive to the Libyan tribes whose own habitat was little more than an arid desert. Throughout Egyptian history, successive pharaohs had managed to keep the Libyans at bay, but a major problem occurred during Merenptah's ten-year reign.

349. Statue of Merenptah.

Details of Merenptah's war against the Libyans are recorded in a long inscription in the Temple of Amun at Karnak and also on several stelae. It is clear from these texts that the threat was very real and that Egyptians in the Delta had been driven from their homes by Libyans, who then harvested all their crops.

During the early years of the reign of Ramesses II, and possibly before, a series of defensive forts had been established to try to keep the Libyans out of Egypt. By the time of Merenptah, the defences may have fallen into disrepair or were inadequately garrisoned. One of the main reasons for the success of the Libyans was that, for the first time, under their chief Mauroy, they had allied with several other tribes and also with the "Sea Peoples".

Too late, Merenptah realised the reality of the threat and fortified some of the main Delta sites as well as the great cities of Memphis and Heliopolis. By the time the ageing king set out with his troops, however, the situation had deteriorated and the

Egyptians had been overwhelmed by the number of Libyans who invaded part of the western Delta.

So confident of success was the Libyan leader Mauroy that he took to Egypt his wives and personal possessions; clearly he was anticipating a long stay.

In the fifth year of his reign, Merenptah rallied his forces and marched to meet the enemy head-on in the Delta. In a pitched battle, which commenced at dawn and was to last for six hours, the enemy were completely routed with immense slaughter. Nine

350. A Libyan, as depicted on a cast of a relief from the Temple of Ramesses II at Beit el Wali, in Nubia.

thousand of the enemy were slain and as many taken prisoner. Other plunder included horses, weapons and cattle. The Egyptians (whilst not recording their own casualty figures) carefully counted phalli which were severed from the enemy dead and noting carefully in the process how many were circumcised and how many were not.

Merenptah pursued the fleeing enemy well into the Libyan Desert. Mauroy managed to escape, but his wives and possessions were captured and Merenptah was able to celebrate with a victory parade when the prisoners, plunder and severed phalli were paraded before him. As an example, some of the captives (probably the leaders of the rebellion) were executed by being impaled on stakes. Most of the other captives were allowed to settle in Egypt.

Merenptah notes in one of his accounts of his Libyan and other campaigns, made on a large stela now in the Cairo Museum, that the Egyptians were jubilant that the Libyans had at last been driven from the Delta. We know this stela today as the Israel Stela, because in the last section of the text the name

351. The Israel Stela of Merenptah.

352. Detail of the Israel Stela, showing the reference to Israel.

353 A captive secured by wooden manacles.

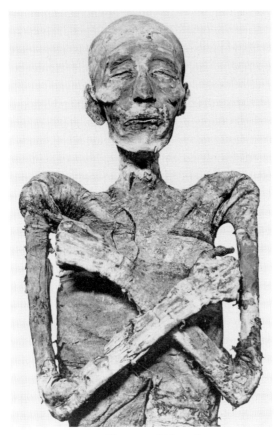

354. The mummy of Merenptah.

Israel appears. It is the earliest known reference to Israel.

It is clear from the inscription on the stela that Israel and the surrounding area had been invaded and plundered by Merenptah, probably around year three of his reign, although we do not have more specific details. It was at this time that the Egyptians may have made the first direct contact with the "Sea Peoples", who were gradually moving through the Levant towards Egypt.

Relations with the Hittites remained on good terms following the peace established under Ramesses II.

During the reign of Merenptah, the Hittites actually asked Egypt for help under the terms of the peace treaty. The northern borders of the Hittite Empire were under attack and the country had suffered a poor harvest. Merenptah did not send the military aid he was asked for, but did send supplies of Egyptian grain, thereby fulfilling the detailed terms and spirit of the treaty.

Merenptah was also able to continue the building work left unfinished by his father, but in his own relatively short reign he completed few buildings of his own. He did, however, restore a number of earlier buildings in the huge temple complex of Amun at Thebes, adding his name to these monuments.

Merenptah left Egypt in a stable position on his death. The Hittites were still friendly and the Libyan threat of invasion had been removed, at least for the time being.

Merenptah's successors appear to have been in conflict with one another and there is evidence that the throne, on occasion, passed by usurpation rather than descent. In such a situation, the winner is the most powerful candidate and power usually means the ability to control the army. If the army was used at all, it was within Egypt, although there is no evidence of a full-scale civil war, more a jockeying of position amongst the large family of the great Ramesses II.

It is likely that most of Merenptah's children were themselves elderly and this may explain the instability of the end of the Nineteenth Dynasty, which was marked by a number of pharaohs, each only ruling for a short period.

Merenptah was succeeded as pharaoh by Amenmesse, whose relationship to Merenptah is not clear. We know that the crown prince of Merenptah was called Seti and he finally became king as Seti II *after* Amenmesse's short reign.

Seti II ruled for only a short time and his son, Siptah, was still a minor at his accession. Seti's Queen, Twosret, acted as Regent for the young prince, but when Siptah died (possibly from poliomyelitis) after a reign of only six years, Twosret declared herself to be pharaoh in her own right, taking on the full pharaonic titles as Hatshepsut had done some three hundred years before.

355. Seti II, in a relief from his tomb in the Valley of the Kings.

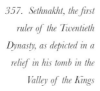

357. Sethnakht, the first ruler of the Twentieth Dynasty, as depicted in a relief in his tomb in the Valley of the Kings

Twosret was the last ruler of the Nineteenth Dynasty. We do not know the circumstances of her death or how the throne passed to her successor, Sethnakht, and the founder of the next Dynasty.

The Harris Papyrus, written some years later, gives some indication of this period of disorder and shows it was a time when central authority had broken down. "The land of Egypt is in the hands of chiefs and of the rulers of towns – one slew his neighbour, great and small. They made gods like men and no offerings were presented in the temples."

356. The mummy of Siptah.

The Twentieth Dynasty: 1185-1070

Sethnakht	1185-1182
Ramesses III	1182-1151
Ramesses IV	1151-1145
Ramesses V	1145-1141
Ramesses VI	1141-1133
Ramesses IX	1126-1108
Ramesses XI	1098-1070
Herihor	1080-1072

The Dynastic troubles at the end of the Nineteenth Dynasty were resolved when Sethnakht, who may have been a distant relative of the earlier kings, took control of the country, supported by the civil authorities. Sethnakht may have been a military man, which would mean he had the all-important support of the army in his coup. After only a short reign, Sethnakht's son became pharaoh as Ramesses III. The Tomb of Sethnakht was built in the Valley of the Kings and was also the Tomb of Twosret, for there are two burial chambers. Sethnakht appears to have usurped the tomb, but it is possible that there may have been a direct relationship between the last ruler of the Nineteenth Dynasty and the first of the Twentieth.

358. Statue of Ramesses III.

The Reign of Ramesses III: 1182-1151

The reign of Ramesses III is well documented, chiefly from the inscriptions and reliefs which decorate his huge Mortuary Temple at Medinet Habu, which is one of the best-preserved of the New Kingdom temples in Egypt.

In a long reign, Ramesses built extensively, emulating (but not surpassing) the works of his namesake, Ramesses II. (There was probably no *direct* family relationship between Ramesses II and III). Sandstone for much of his building work was quarried at Silsila and an inscription from year five of his reign records that he sent two thousand troops to work with four hundred quarrymen. The troops were used to move the blocks after the quarrymen had cut them from the bedrock.

The numerous military inscriptions of Ramesses at Medinet Habu are difficult to

359. The Mortuary Temple of Ramesses III at Medinet Habu.

interpret as there is often no obvious order to the narrative and the text is written in a flowery and poetic style, rather than simply being descriptive.

It is clear that one of the first problems Ramesses had to face was a Libyan invasion. The circumstances were almost identical to the invasion years earlier during the reign of Merenptah. The Libyans, allied with other states, had again invaded the Delta with the clear intention of staying there. Many towns in the eastern Delta had been plundered and Ramesses was forced to take action.

Marching against the Libyans and meeting them in battle, like Merenptah before him, Ramesses was victorious and ruthless. A total of twelve thousand, five hundred and thirty five enemy were killed, with one thousand taken prisoner. The spoils and captives were paraded before the king in a victory celebration.

The valour of the king is emphasised in the inscriptions, which are similar to those used by his earlier namesake, "… he is like a bull standing in the field, his eye and his two horns ready and prepared to attack the rear with his head … a valiant warrior … he is like the lion … whose terror is feared from afar."

360. Ramesses III in battle. Relief from the Mortuary Temple of Medinet Habu.

361. Relief from a door jam at the Mortuary Temple of Medinet Habu, showing lines of captured prisoners and Ramesses III offering to the gods.

The inscriptions tell us that the Libyans had been assisted in their unsuccessful invasion by tribes from the southern coast of Asia Minor and that the maritime people of the Aegean had supplied ships. The latter is the first direct reference to the so-called "Sea Peoples" who were a collection of tribes who were trying to settle in Egypt. This was a major land-borne movement of people who had become sufficiently powerful to stand up against the Hittites. Their army was accompanied by the soldiers' families and possessions and at sea their fleet followed their advance along the coastal region of the Eastern Mediterranean. The Sea Peoples proved a threat to international trade both on land and sea.

Ramesses took the offensive and met the enemy both on land and at sea and in both areas he was successful. The Egyptians effectively stopped any further trouble from this source for the rest of his reign.

362. Egyptian soldiers about to board an enemy ship. Drawing of a relief at the Mortuary Temple of Medinet Habu.

Ramesses's naval action is one of the first major battles on water to be recorded. Fighting with ships had occurred before, but on a smaller scale, on the river Nile within Egypt or on the southern borders in Nubia.

The battle is often presumed to have taken place in the open sea, but the exact location is not known. The texts describe the "Great Green" which had previously been thought to mean the Mediterranean Sea, but is now believed to have actually been the huge fertile and green area of the Nile Delta. If this is the case, the threat to Egypt was much closer to home and far more dangerous than had previously been thought. Most ancient shipping avoided the open water as much as possible, preferring to remain in the safer coastal waters.

We know that some of the fighting was close to the shore, as Ramesses had detachments of archers based on the land, firing volleys of arrows against the enemy ships, causing considerable casualties. Ramesses may even have lured the enemy ships into the shallows and straight into a well-prepared ambush.

The defeat of the enemy was absolute and Ramesses describes them being "… dragged, overturned and laid low upon the beach. Slain and made heaps from stern to bow of their galleys, while all their things were cast upon the water."

The northern external wall of the Mortuary Temple of Medinet Habu is decorated with scenes of the battle. The ships were essentially used as fighting platforms. Soldiers on the ships fired arrows into the enemy and used grappling hooks to secure the enemy vessels before boarding them and fighting at close quarters.

The Sea Peoples' vessels appear to have been smaller than the Egyptians and are decorated at the bows and sterns with birds heads. The men on the enemy boats seem to have acted as both rowers and soldiers.

In the larger Egyptian ships, the rowers were protected by the high sides of the ships and the soldiers on board were able to fight. This meant that the oarsmen, protected from missiles

363. An Egyptian warship.

364. An Egyptian warship with some captured enemy on board.

could still manoeuvre the ship, giving the Egyptians a distinct advantage. The Egyptian ships are also equipped with the earliest recorded "crows nests"; a fighting platform at the top of the mast which was both an ideal vantage point, but also enabled archers to fire down on the enemy below.

365. An enemy warship, showing the disordered and routed crew. The men wear distinctive helmets decorated with feathers.

366. Relief from the Mortuary Temple of Medinet Habu showing Ramesses III smiting his enemy, with his pet lion beside him.

In the reliefs depicting the battle the Egyptian ships appear orderly, fully manned and undamaged, whilst the enemy ships are shown capsized and with the water around them full of enemy dead. As is usual in such scenes, any Egyptian casualties (and there must have been some) are not shown.

Although the reliefs do not show it, one reference in the inscriptions implies that the Egyptians used fire arrows against the enemy. Fire on board any wooden ship was greatly feared and would have distracted the enemy sufficiently to force them to stop fighting and make them vulnerable to attack.

The Libyans and the Sea Peoples had been soundly defeated, but after only a short period of peace, by year eleven of Ramesses's reign the Libyan threat appeared again. The Libyans had themselves been invaded in the west by a tribe called the Meshwesh, and it was they who forced the Libyans to join them in an attack on Egypt. Ramesses began a second Libyan war, the outcome of which was the same as before, with two thousand one hundred and seventy-five Libyans and Meshwesh killed and over two thousand taken prisoner. Ramesses drove the fleeing enemy back for over eleven miles to the west.

Once again Ramesses had successfully repulsed another full-scale invasion, but it was to be only a temporary interruption to the steady stream of immigrants who were moving across the western desert into Egypt.

From reliefs at Medinet Habu, it is clear that Ramesses also conducted a campaign in Syria, as the king is shown storming five fortified cities, two of which are clearly defended by Hittites. One of these cities, which bears no name, might be Kadesh. Ramesses's campaigns in this area made no permanent conquests, although he was able to return to Egypt with much plunder and tales of victory. In the battle scenes, Ramesses is shown in his chariot with his pet lion running beside it (another attempt to emulate Ramesses II, who had similar scenes shown on his temples).

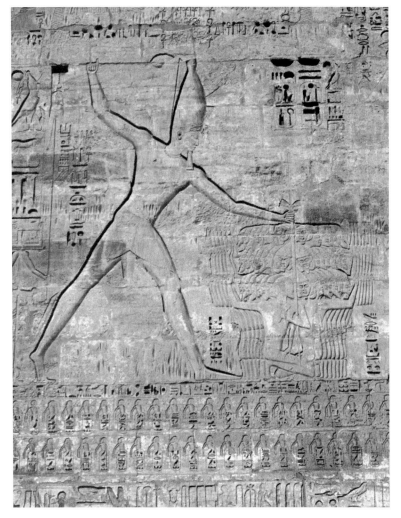

367. Ramesses III smiting his enemy, with the names of all the captured towns detailed below him. Relief from the pylon of the Mortuary Temple of Medinet Habu.

Other scenes show action in Nubia, although by this time Nubia had become so Egyptianised that any trouble in the area must have been minor – possibly only on the extreme southern borders or against tribes to the east of Nubia. Such scenes, however, may just be the obligatory symbolic "smiting the enemy". They may also be used to illustrate the epithet Ramesses used of "slaying the chiefs of all countries."

In addition to the Medinet Habu reliefs, Ramesses's long reign is also documented in the Harris Papyrus, the largest document to survive from Egypt, with a total length of one hundred and thirty-three feet. The papyrus is dated to the day of the death of Ramesses III and we thus know that his reign was exactly thirty-one years and forty-one days long. The text is chiefly a list of the actions of Ramesses in favouring the gods and his good deeds, all intended to assist his journey in the afterlife. The papyrus gives some fascinating facts about the wealth of the temples and the land ownership of the country. Much of the wealth (of temples and of the King) came from plunder from the various military campaigns and the increased wealth and power of the priesthood was to cause considerable difficulties for Egypt in the next Dynasty (as indeed it had done in the Eighteenth Dynasty).

Another interesting document survives from towards the end of the reign of Ramesses III and tells of a major conspiracy within the palace.

A Queen of Ramesses, called Tiy, planned to depose the king (presumably by having him killed, although this is not clear) and then place her son, prince Pentawere on the throne. The Queen was assisted by a number of minor officials, most of whom worked in the royal harem. As their scheme developed, many others were involved and when the plot was discovered (and we do not know how) the conspirators and their assistants were brought to trial.

Ramesses established a court, which included two senior army men, and gave it full discretion as to any verdict or punishment deemed fit. His only instruction was that none but the guilty should be punished.

At least some of the minor conspirators were clearly not under close arrest, for a number of the ladies under suspicion sought to influence four of the all-male court. The men were caught in a somewhat compromising position with the women, and found themselves facing a court for their indiscretion.

In four sessions, the court dealt with the conspirators. In the first session twenty-two individuals were tried and found guilty. Their sentence is not recorded, but is presumed to have been death.

In the second session, a further six people were found guilty, including an officer of the army. They were sentenced to death but were permitted to commit suicide without leaving the court. The third session saw another four conspirators found guilty, including prince Pentawere. Again, all were allowed to take their own lives (the method of death chosen is not recorded).

The final session of the court tried the judges who had misbehaved and they were condemned to have their noses and ears cut off. One of the condemned men committed suicide before the sentence could be carried out.

The record of this conspiracy is a rare survival of a trial document and an insight into the intrigue of the period. It also gives us a glimpse into the Egyptian legal system and the punishment of convicted criminals.

The fate of the Queen is not known for the record of her trial has not survived. The reason for the plot may have been the large size of the royal family, causing various senior members of the family to jockey for position, status and power.

During the reign of Ramesses III, there was also an early indication of civil unrest, caused mainly through a lack of communication between the King and parts of the administration. The craftsmen who cut and decorated the royal tombs in the Valley of the Kings, and who lived in the village of Deir el Medina, refused to work, as they had not received the supplies they were owed. They staged the world's first-recorded (and ultimately successful) strike. It would appear that local officials were either withholding or diverting (possibly both!) the supplies intended for the village. It was only following an appeal made directly to the King that the matter was resolved.

It is often assumed that Ramesses III finally met his death as a result of another palace conspiracy, but there is no real evidence to prove this and certainly his mummy has not revealed any obvious foul play (although of course poison would leave no visible trace).

Ramesses was able to pass on to his successor a stable and secure Egypt, but, as had happened so many times before, the stability was short-lived and many of the problems he faced were to reappear in future generations.

The Reigns of the Later Ramesside Kings

The exact relationship between Ramesses III and his successors is unclear. Ramesses IV, V, VI and VIII appear to have been his sons and Ramesses VII was probably the son of Ramesses VI. Their short reigns produced few monuments and reliefs and information on this period is scanty.

Ramesses IV (1151-1145) recorded details on two stelae at Wadi Hammamat concerning a huge expedition to quarry stone, which he claimed was the second largest such expedition ever mounted (the largest being that of Mentuhotep IV over five hundred years before). Ramesses recorded that some five thousand soldiers, plus quarry men and numerous others took part in the expedition and that they were all well-provisioned, being supplied with "… bread, meat and cakes without number."

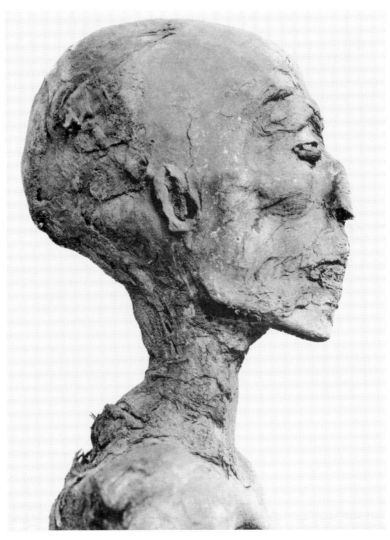

369. The head of the mummy of Ramesses IV.

370. Drawing on an ostracon showing
Ramesses VI.

Exactly why Ramesses IV should want or need to mount such a large expedition is uncertain. He is not known as one of the most prolific of the builder-Pharaohs, although he did complete the rear part of the Temple of Khons at Karnak, started by Ramesses III. Perhaps Ramesses IV thought it was a good idea to keep the army occupied.

Successive reigns, most of fairly short duration, saw continued internal disputes, power shifts and struggles. The iconography still showed the image of the all-conquering king triumphing over the enemies of Egypt, although the reality may have been different. An unusual statue in the Egyptian Museum in Cairo shows Ramesses VI holding an enemy captive by the hair and an ostracon, also in the Museum, shows him in a smiting pose.

By the reign of Ramesses IX the High Priests of Karnak had become increasingly powerful and influential. Reliefs in the temple show the priests and the king, unusually, the same size, the

371. *Statue of Ramesses VI, holding the hair of a captive enemy.*

372 The High Priest of Amun, Amenhotep, before Ramesses IX. Relief in the Temple of Karnak.

implication being that the priests considered themselves equal in status to the king. The result was that this period was marked by internal disorder and violence.

It was during the reign of Ramesses IX that a number of tombs in the Valley of the Kings were robbed, and written accounts survive of the tomb inspections and trials of some of the robbers. The exact location of the tombs in the Valley, certainly those after the Nineteenth Dynasty, was not necessarily secret. Their security relied exclusively on a strong guard in the area. A papyrus records a severe breakdown of local law and order. Many senior local officials seem to have been implicated in the robberies, although most avoided conviction.

The last Ramesses, Ramesses XI, was a ruler in name only, for in his reign, the High Priest of Thebes, Herihor, effectively ruled the south of Egypt and Smendes ruled the Delta from Tanis. Evidence of a continued decline in the status of Egypt abroad is contained in the account of an official called Wenamun, who was sent by Herihor to the Lebanon to obtain new cedar to build a barque for the Theban god Amun.

Wenamun's journey was full of problems. He was robbed and the rulers of the countries through which he passed did little to assist him. These were countries which had in the past been

ruled by, and who had worked closely with, Egypt, to their mutual benefit, but when an important Egyptian official on State business needed help, he was treated with little short of contempt.

373. Statue of a bound, captive, enemy of Egypt, dating to the late Ramesside Period.

THE THIRD INTERMEDIATE PERIOD: 1069-525

The Twenty-First Dynasty: 1069-945

Smendes	1069-1063
Psusennes I	1059-1033
Amenemope	1033-981
At Thebes:	
Herihor	1080-1074
Pinedjem	1074-1070

With the death of Ramesses XI the Twentieth Dynasty effectively ended and the country was split between two sets of rulers. A dynasty of kings, based at Tanis, ruled the north of the country, whilst the priests of Thebes ruled the south of the country and adopted the titles and duties of the king. The two royal houses appear not to have been in open conflict, indeed there were many royal marriages made between them, but it would seem that the kings of Tanis were the more powerful and influential.

The history of this period is very difficult to unravel and interpret and it is not clear if some of the Dynasties and reigns were consecutive or concurrent. Because of this the exact sequence of events is a matter of great debate, and the accurate fixing of dates is even more so – all of which must remain outside the scope of this volume.

It was during the reign of Smendes that the northern capital was moved from Per Ramesse to Tanis. Per Ramesse was built on a branch of the river Nile, but this had silted up since the city was created, making access to the city difficult. The old city was largely dismantled and many buildings were re-erected at the new location, whilst new buildings included much re-used material from other abandoned Delta sites, some dating back to the Middle Kingdom.

374. View of the Royal Tombs at Tanis.

Consequently Tanis is full of monuments of Ramesses II, including colossal statues and a number of obelisks, and even includes some Middle Kingdom sphinxes, dating to the reign of Amenemhat III. Great temples were erected in the new city and, even in their ruinous state today are still impressive. Most of the town site is yet to be excavated.

With the administration of the country split in half, there was no clear and organised national policy. This period was prosperous as we can tell from the scale of building work undertaken in the Delta and the wealth of the northern kings in particular. When their intact burials were found at Tanis, a considerable amount of gold and silver was found, including silver coffins and a number of gold masks. Interestingly, many of the precious objects found in the Tanis tombs were actually re-cycled from earlier tombs, including those in the Valley of the Kings, which we know had seen a series of robberies by this time.

Whilst much of the surviving wealth of this period may have arisen from the simple re-cycling of earlier wealth, it is clear that all the main trade routes to both the north and south of the country must have remained open. There appear to have been no major difficulties in international relations, but in the Levant, the Egyptian hold and control over many of the states was gradually being eroded.

375. The gold mask of Psusennes, from his tomb at Tanis.

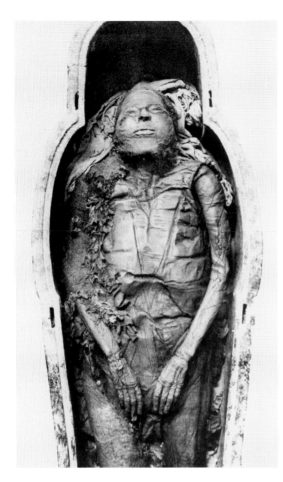

This was still a time when officers in the army could attain high status. Masaharta, a Libyan, was a general in the army and also became High Priest of Amun at Karnak. He was given an elaborate burial and was laid alongside the bodies of contemporary kings and queens, in the Royal Cache at Deir el Bahri. That he lived well is evidenced by the fact he was quite corpulent when he died.

The Twenty Second Dynasty: 945-712

Shoshenk I	945-924
Osorkon I	924-889
Shoshenk II	890
Osorkon II	874-850
Takelot II	850-825
Shoshenk III	825-773

The Twenty-Second Dynasty is often referred to as the Libyan or Bubastite Period, as the kings came from the Bubastis area in the Eastern Delta and their ancestors were originally from Libya.

Despite the efforts of earlier pharaohs such as Merenptah and Ramesses III, Libyans still continued to move into the Delta and became a major part of the population. In addition to those who had migrated to Egypt, a large number of Libyans had been kept in Egypt as prisoners after the great battles. Several generations later they were still there, but in increased numbers and firmly "Egyptianised".

It is ironic that it was the organised Libyan Egyptians who were the ones to save Egypt from the state of chaos into which the country had fallen.

Shoshenk was a senior military commander, and as such, had the backing of the army when he seized power. The army at this time contained large numbers of Libyan mercenaries and prisoners who had been pressed into service for the Egyptians.

By his actions Shoshenk was able to re-unite the two ruling Dynasties of Tanis and Thebes, and only when that had been done did he turn his attention to the old Egyptian possessions in the Levant. There had been little Egyptian interest or action in these areas for several reigns and Shoshenk had no alternative but to take direct and swift action. He recorded on the walls of the Temple of Karnak his successful campaign into Palestine, giving the names of all the captured towns and cities. In reality his "campaign" may have been more of an elaborate trading expedition to re-establish good relations in the area. Typically the Egyptian accounts imply conquest and the receipt of "tribute" rather than trade.

Shoshenk (usually identified with Shishak in the Biblical account) surrounded the city of Jerusalem, but he did not enter it. He was effectively bought-off by a huge bribe – the treasures of Solomon. As the Bible tells us "… the treasures of the House of the Lord and the treasures of the king's house, he took away all; and he took all the shields of gold which Solomon had made …"(1 Kings 14:25). The famous Ark of the Covenant appears to have remained in the temple at Jerusalem.

Shoshenk drove his army northwards as far as Megiddo where he set up a stela to commemorate his victories, just as Thutmose III had done at the site five hundred years earlier.

The campaigns and the Egyptian presence in Palestine put the Egyptians in direct conflict with a new and rapidly emerging power, that of Assyria, but neither Shoshenk nor his immediate successors were able to meet the threat head-on and check its progress.

By the Twenty-Third Dynasty (c. 818) Egypt had again fragmented into a number of separate kingdoms and principalities. In the south, the Nubian state which had existed side by side with Egypt, for much of the time overshadowed and subdued by its more powerful neighbour, now increased its influence as the control of the pharaohs in the north gradually waned.

The Nubians, under the influence and control of Egypt for generations, had adopted the Egyptian life-style and religious beliefs. Their enthusiasm for the religion, particularly for the worship of the god Amun, was such that when the Egyptians themselves seem to lose their religious zeal, the Nubians regarded it as *their* duty to ensure that the worship of Amun continued. To do this they actually invaded Egypt in the name of Amun, restoring and adding to the great temples.

The Twenty-Fifth Dynasty: 712-656

Piye	753-713
Shabaka	713-698
Taharka	690-664

Piye the ruler of Nubia gradually expanded the territories under his control northwards, into most of Egypt apart from the north and the Delta. At this time, a northern ruler called Tefnakhte was also expanding his influence and was extending his area of control southwards.

Piye made the first move and launched an attack on Tefnakhte, defeating him on water and on land. Tefnakhte's army escaped and fled northwards pursued by Piye. On his way into the Delta, Piye captured the city of Hermopolis after a siege of some five months. When Piye entered the city he plundered all its wealth and reported in his campaign accounts that he was distressed to find that the horses had not been properly looked after during the siege. No doubt he soon ensured that the horses were placed in his own stables and adequately fed.

Once Hermopolis fell, other cities soon capitulated to Piye without a fight. His last obstacle was Memphis and the city was besieged and finally taken. He pursued Tefnakhte further north and finally defeated the remnants of his army. After making offerings to the gods in their various temples he took as much booty as his ships could carry and returned south to his capital Napata, where he celebrated his triumph and erected a great stela, detailing his conquests.

Piye left a detailed account of this action (parts of which have already been mentioned in the chapter on Siege Warfare). Some of Piye's exploits were recorded on a large stela, the

wording of which echoes that of Thutmose III of the Eighteenth Dynasty. Piye clearly though that his exploits equalled those of his illustrious predecessor.

Piye, a Nubian and, therefore, one of the "enemies" of Egypt, now found himself in control of the country. He seems to have regarded his conquest not as an invasion of a foreign country, but more a crusade to restore the old status quo and the supremacy of the god Amun.

The success of the Nubian King Piye meant that his immediate successors effectively ruled a united country, although the always rebellious Thebans seem to have been given a degree of independence and were effectively ruled by a princess who took the title of "God's Wife of Amun". The God's Wife Shepenwepet II was the daughter of Piye. The God's Wives were unmarried women, each of whom, during her lifetime, adopted a younger female relative to succeed her. The younger women were usually members of the family and took the title of "Divine Votress of Amun". Shepenwepet chose as her successor Amenirdis.

Tomb Chapels for these important women were built at Medinet Habu, within the mud brick enclosure walls of the Mortuary Temple of Ramesses III.

The God's Wives were in charge of spiritual affairs and the rulers of the Twenty-fifth and Twenty-sixth Dynasties ensured that their daughters occupied the position. Secular control over the Theban area was exercised by powerful local dignitaries, who called themselves mayors or chiefs. Montuemhat, who may have been related to the Nubian royal family, was one such mayor and also the Fourth Prophet of Amun. His status was such

378. *Alabaster statue of The God's Wife of Amun, Amenirdis.*

282

379. One of the Chapels of the God's Wives of Amun at Medinet Habu.

380. The mud brick entrance pylon of the Tomb of Montuemhat at Deir el Bahri.

that he constructed a huge tomb for himself at Deir el Bahri (which is one of the largest in Egypt ever built for a private individual). Interestingly the tombs of the God's Wives are modest in comparison. Perhaps the God's Wives were figureheads whilst the real power and wealth rested with their officials.

Piye was buried in Nubia under a small pyramid, with eight of his favourite horses buried nearby. He was succeeded by his brother, Shabaka, in whose reign the Assyrians first invaded the north of Egypt, reaching as far south as Memphis. The Assyrians' hold on Egypt was, however, weak. They were distracted by periodic rebellions elsewhere in their new Empire, which had to be dealt with, and the north of Egypt reverted to Egyptian control.

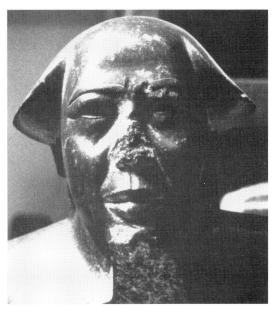

381. Statue of Montuemhat.

383. *The column of Taharka in the Temple of Karnak.*

382. *Statue of Taharka.*

It was in the reign of the next pharaoh, Taharka, that relations with the Assyrians deteriorated still further. The Assyrians, like the Egyptians, needed good timber for their building works and the cedars of Lebanon were the most prized. They tried to control its supply and actually issued orders that no timber be supplied to Egypt. It would appear that Taharka had allied himself with the Phoenicians against Assyrian aggression.

Taharka added substantially to the Temple of Amun at Karnak. Part of his entrance colonnade to the temple still stands today (now in the first court of the temple). It is believed this impressive colonnade may have had a timber roof, hence Taharka's eagerness to secure the supplies of cedar from the Lebanon.

Around 674, the Assyrians under their king Esarhaddon tried to push their frontier further to the south and met the Egyptians in battle at Ashkelon, on the borders of Egypt and Palestine. Taharka was the victor, but when the Assyrians again pushed southwards into Egypt, they were more successful and he was unable to stop their progress. Memphis fell after a siege, which only lasted half a day, the Assyrians having used "… mines, breaches and assault ladders." The city was burnt and ransacked and much booty carried off to Assyria. The Assyrians appointed local kings to rule Egypt for them.

Taharka himself seems to have taken an active role in this campaign and even appears to have been wounded. The Assyrian King Esarhaddon reported that he "… fought very bloody battles against Taharka king of Egypt and Kush, the one accursed by all the great gods. Five

384. Assyrians attacking an Egyptian town.

times I hit him with the point of [my] arrows [inflicting] wounds [from which he should not] recover …"

The royal palace was plundered and whilst Taharka himself escaped, his wife and children were captured and taken to Assyria. The Assyrians were keen to remove all trace of the Nubian rule of Egypt. The Nubian officials were dismissed (many being taken to Assyria) and Assyrian officials appointed in their place. Curiously, Egyptian officials were allowed to retain their positions.

We have no scenes surviving from Egypt showing any of the battles where they were defeated, but Assyrian reliefs, from the Palace of Nimrud, do survive, showing their side of the

385. Assyrians mining the walls of an Egyptian town.

events and what was obviously (Assyrian propaganda notwithstanding) a bloody victory. The scenes are graphic and portray the full extent of siege warfare, employing techniques against Egyptian towns that the Egyptians had been using against their enemies for centuries. Soldiers raise scaling ladders against walls, whilst others try to undermine the walls, having first built protective barriers to allow them to work without being fired on from above.

Many of the defenders appear to be Nubians and part of the scene shows a detachment of Nubian soldiers being marched from the captured Egyptian town. An Assyrian raises two severed Nubian heads in triumph as they pass.

The Assyrians seemed largely content to rule Egypt from afar, having once set up their own bureaucracy. Most of the cities were left under the control of the Egyptian authorities, but they must have been left in little doubt as to who controlled the country, for the Assyrians were fairly brutal in their treatment of those officials and leaders who opposed them.

387. Assyrians marching captured Nubian soldiers from a conquered town.

Three years later, Taharka briefly regained control over the whole country, and replaced the Assyrian officials, but his success did not last for long, for after the death of the Assyrian king, the new ruler, Assurbanipal, re-asserted Assyrian control over Egypt, once again taking more plunder and prisoners back to the Assyrian capital, Nineveh.

Taharka's successor, Tanutamen, briefly recaptured Memphis, before it fell again to the Assyrians, who pushed southwards into Egypt as far as Aswan, taking Thebes on their way and permanently driving the Nubian rulers of Egypt back into their homeland. Stopping on the southern borders of Egypt, the Assyrians returned to Thebes where the city was effectively plundered, although the buildings seem to have been left otherwise intact. The Assyrians were not above destroying everything they could and it would seem that they may have struck a bargain with the local rulers which enabled full scale plundering without the usual wholesale destruction and loss of life that was experienced by other captured towns and cities.

During the period of the Assyrian control of Egypt, the military history of the country became complicated as various local vassal rulers vied for supremacy over one another. The Egyptians had adopted the policy in the past of playing off the princes of the Levant against each other, and the Assyrians now did the same to their Egyptian rulers. With many local disputes, any concerted and united effort against the Assyrians was doomed to failure.

The Twenty-Sixth Dynasty: 664-525

Psamtik I	664-610
Necho	610-595
Psamtik III	526-525

The princes of the Delta based in Sais became vassal kings under the Assyrians and prevented the return of the Nubian rulers. It was a Saite King, Psamtik I, who was briefly to re-unite Egypt, when Assyria herself went into a period of decline.

By the end of his reign he had built up a substantial army, with a large number of foreign mercenaries in its ranks, and also established treaties with neighbouring countries against the Assyrians. Psamtik was able to restore the flow of trade into and out of Egypt and launched a renaissance in the art of the period, adopting styles and ideas which looked back to Egypt's glorious past in the Middle and Old Kingdoms. The re-emergence of Egypt as a world power was, however, all too brief and was totally eclipsed by the conquest of Egypt by the Persians.

This period of Egyptian history, known to us as the Saite Period, is of great importance and is often underestimated. The rulers managed to preserve many of the stories and myths and revive building and artistic skills that had almost been lost, by copying the style of surviving earlier works of art.

Effectively this period preserved the culture of Egypt, at a time when it was in serious danger of being swamped by outside influences. Perhaps this interest in the past helped to encourage some "nationalism" amongst the Egyptians and pride in their heritage, all good fuel to add to the defence of the country at a time of danger.

The Saite rulers were keen to expand trade with neighbouring states, and as such the culture of Egypt was exposed to many new countries around the Mediterranean, in particular to the Greek states. The influence of Egypt on the culture of Greece has probably been significantly understated, thanks to the work of many early scholars. With their rigid Classical training, they regarded the civilisation of Greece as the first and finest in the world, and would not acknowledge that the earlier civilisations could possibly have been influential. Without the Saite rulers of Egypt, Egyptian culture could so easily have been lost; as it is we can see a direct link between Egypt, the Classical world and our modern civilisation.

It was Psamtik III who had to face the next emerging power in the Middle East, the Persians, who, like the Assyrians, were looking to take Egypt and advanced on the country in 525. Cambyses, the Persian king, first took control of Phoenicia, and with the captured Phoenician fleet planned his assault on Egypt from both land and sea. Psamtik met the advancing Persian army to the east of the Delta at Pelusium.

THE LATE PERIOD: 525-332

The Twenty-Seventh Dynasty: 525-404

Cambyses	525-522
Darius I	521-486
Xerxes	485-465
Darius II	424-405

The Persians, led by Cambyses, had been guided across the Sinai desert by Bedouin, on the advice of a defecting Egyptian mercenary general called Phanes. Before the battle for Egypt, as the armies lined up to face each other, the Egyptians paraded the two sons of Phanes before the armies and, in view of the enemy and of their father, their throats were cut. If the Persians lacked motivation, this extreme and provoking act by the Egyptians provided just the incentive they needed and the Egyptian army suffered the consequences. The Egyptian army under Psamtik was crushingly defeated. The King fled back to Memphis, but the Persians followed, taking the city and capturing Psamtik who was taken to the Persian capital, Susa.

The Persians were quick to secure Egypt and met little further resistance. A large detachment of troops was sent southwards, but it seems to have been badly equipped and organised. It ran out of food on its journey and the soldiers limped back with tales of cannibalism. Despite its obviously weak state, the Persian army encountered no opposition at all, which indicates perhaps that the Egyptians lacked strong leadership at the time.

Another large detachment of troops (possibly equally ill-provisioned) was sent westwards towards the Siwa Oasis. Probably leaving from the Theban area, the soldiers made their way from oasis to oasis until they reached Bahariya, the last resting place before Siwa. They set off on a thirty-day march across the Western Desert, with the prospect of no water and no shade.

The army never arrived at Siwa. Exactly what happened to it is still a mystery and has been a matter of conjecture for centuries. The inhabitants of Siwa were later to report that a great sandstorm blew up, which probably buried the whole army. Only recently have reports been made of spears and arrowheads emerging from the sands, along with pieces of textile and human bones. Perhaps the "lost" army has been found. If this is so, it promises to be one of the most remarkable finds to come from Egypt, for never before will a large fully-equipped army have been found intact. The sand will have preserved absolutely everything, so the finds could be a revelation to military historians of all ancient periods and cultures, for we know the Persians employed mercenary soldiers in their ranks.

Cambyses was succeeded by his son, Darius I, who took a closer interest in Egypt than his father had done. Egypt functioned well and was prosperous, the local administration in the towns and cities of the country worked as smoothly as it had always done, but the wealth of Egypt, and in particular much of the agricultural produce, was taken by the Persians. Darius, however, commissioned several construction projects in Egypt during his thirty-five year rule. Egypt was the richest of all Persian provinces and despite the Persian drain on the resources, during the reign of Darius the country prospered.

Egypt formed the western boundary of the Persian Empire and it was in the far west where two new temples were built, at Qasr Gueida and Hibis, both being dedicated to Amun and intended to protect the frontier. The Hibis temple was probably built on the site of an earlier shrine, but the new building was constructed in the Egyptian style and of the finest materials and workmanship.

The Persians seem to have appreciated Egyptian architecture and the ground plan of Darius's palace at Persopolis is almost identical to that of the Hibis temple. Egyptian features appear in

389. *The Persian King, Darius.*

the detail of the Persian buildings too, such as winged sun discs and floral column capitals.

There was a brief flare of revolt against the Persians, which occurred when the Persians were occupied on their northern borders with wars with the Greeks. By this time Darius was dead and his successor, Xerxes, quickly suppressed the revolt, executed its leaders and restored order. A second revolt in Egypt after Xerxes had been assassinated, was also quickly suppressed by Darius II.

A succession of vassal kings in Egypt, each ruling a part of the country, meant that there was constant conflict and many small revolts, which were all put down by the Persians.

In the Twenty-Eighth Dynasty, a prince from Sais briefly re-established some Egyptian supremacy and many Greeks were employed as mercenaries. However, this period too was not to last long and a second period of Persian control followed in 343. The Persians showed a disinclination to change the way Egypt was ruled and left much of the bureaucracy intact. It would appear that more than a few Egyptians accepted the Persian control.

The Egyptians were faced with a repetitive cycle of conquest and pillage and the country was split into vassal states, subject to the new Empires that had arisen. The role of Egypt as a major power had ended and its military capabilities were reduced to an insignificant level.

THE GRAECO-ROMAN PERIOD: 332-AD 323

Alexander the Great	332-323
Ptolemy I	323-282
Ptolemy II	285-247/6
Cleopatra VII	51-30
Ptolemy Caesarion	36-30

The Persian Empire had for many years been at war with the Greeks, led by Philip of Macedon. When Philip was assassinated in 336, his twenty-year-old son, Alexander, took up the campaign. After a series of battles, Alexander advanced southwards and finally defeated Darius III at the battle of Issus in 333, then marched on to Egypt, arriving in the country in 332. He

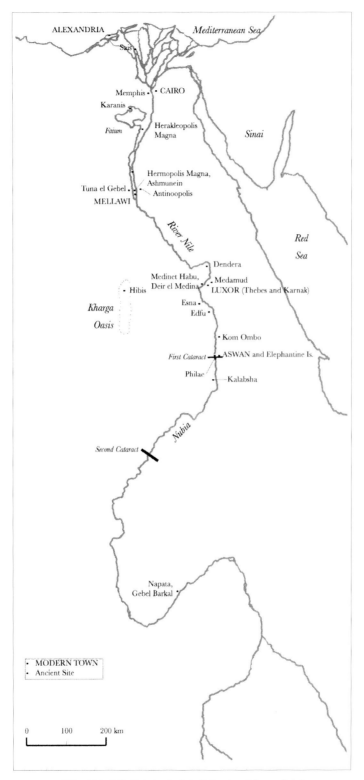

ALEXANDRIA
Mediterranean Sea
Sais
Memphis
CAIRO
Karanis
Herakleopolis
Magna
Fauum
Sinai
Hermopolis Magna,
Ashmunein
Tuna el Gebel
Antinoopolis
MELLAWI
River Nile
Red
Sea
Dendera
Medinet Habu,
Medamud
Deir el Medina
LUXOR (Thebes and Karnak)
Hibis
Esna
Edfu
Kharga
Oasis
Kom Ombo
First Cataract
ASWAN and Elephantine Is.
Philae
Kalabsha
Nubia
Second Cataract
Napata,
Gebel Barkal
• MODERN TOWN
• Ancient Site
0   100   200 km

391. Map of Egypt during the Late, Ptolemaic and Roman Periods.

went directly to the remote Siwa Oasis to see the famous Oracle of Ammon, who recognised Alexander as the son of the god and, therefore, the rightful ruler of Egypt. The Egyptians themselves had anticipated this and had already hailed Alexander as a liberator. The young Macedonian appeared to be a preferable alternative to the Persians, whose rule over Egypt, after the death of Darius I in 486, had been oppressive and had drained Egypt's resources.

Alexander founded a new city, which was named after him, Alexandria. He founded many other cities that bore his name, but the Egyptian city was by far the largest and the only one to survive the centuries. Situated in the west side of the Delta, Alexandria has an excellent natural harbour, which was better placed for communications with the Classical world. In a short space of time, it was to become one of the most important cities of antiquity and was regarded as a centre of learning and culture.

During the following period of Greek rule, many more Greeks moved into Egypt, particularly into Alexandria.

Alexander was also a prolific builder elsewhere in Egypt and he rebuilt parts of many of the ancient temples, which had fallen into disrepair or been neglected. At Luxor, for example, he rebuilt the most sacred part of the temple, the sanctuary of the god Amun.

Alexander was in Egypt for less than one year, leaving in 331 to continue the expansion of his Empire to the east. Egypt was left under the control of a viceroy.

When Alexander died suddenly in 323 there was no obvious and capable successor. His Empire was ruled only briefly by his brother and then his son. One of his generals,

393. *Alexander shown as an Egyptian Pharaoh. Relief on the sanctuary of Amun in the Temple of Luxor.*

Ptolemy, who had effectively been ruling Egypt jointly with the viceroy of Egypt, moved quickly to secure his own position.

The body of Alexander was to be taken back to Macedonia for burial, but Ptolemy intercepted the funeral procession en route and took the body back to Egypt. Ptolemy explained that Alexander had told him that his body was to be buried in Siwa, where Alexander had visited the Oracle when he first conquered Egypt. Ptolemy must have been accompanied by a military presence, but the funeral escort was probably not expecting the body to be stolen from them.

Once back in Egypt, Ptolemy took Alexander's body to Memphis, where it lay for a while, whilst a tomb was prepared for it, not at Siwa, but in Alexander's own city of Alexandria. Ptolemy realised the power that the possession of Alexander's remains could give him and no one resisted his actions.

By 305 Alexander's successors had themselves died and his huge Empire was divided amongst his other generals. Ptolemy's swift action had secured his own position and he became the sole and absolute ruler of Egypt and founder of a new Dynasty. Ptolemy crowned himself King Ptolemy I, Soter (Saviour) of Egypt.

The Egyptians seem to have welcomed, or perhaps been indifferent to, their new rulers. Greeks ... Persians … they were used to changes at the top, but at least the Ptolemies lived in Egypt and the wealth of the country was no longer being drained away to foreign Empires.

Ptolemy established many more cities, mostly inhabited by Greeks. In the Faium the production of food was increased to cope with the growing population of the new cities. Most of the Greek settlements were in the north of the country, but recent studies have also revealed

394. Greek period tomb in Alexandria.

a substantial Greek population present in the Theban area. In these cities the Greek inhabitants adopted and adapted many Ancient Egyptian ideas. Their bodies were embalmed and many tombs have survived with coffins and decorations showing the deceased worshipping the ancient Egyptian gods.

Ptolemy passed new laws to protect Egypt's maritime rights and introduced the first coinage seen in the country.

Ptolemy and his successors continued Alexander's policy of building work in Egypt and they seem to have worked closely with the local centres of administration. Perhaps their interest in local affairs kept the population happy; it certainly would have generated considerable employment opportunities for the areas concerned. The building works of the Ptolemies were impressive in scale and some of the largest and best preserved of Egyptian temples date from this period. They include Esna, Edfu, Kom Ombo, Dendera, and Philae, which were substantially extended or rebuilt at this time.

These temples were built in a traditional Egyptian style, but in other parts of Egypt, notably in the Delta cities, most, if not all of the building was in the Greek style. After a period of time, the two styles became mixed, probably to the detriment of both traditions. Remarkably few of the Classical buildings have survived.

395. The Temple of Isis at Philae.

On the walls of the temples, the Ptolemies inscribed reliefs showing them in the classic smiting of the enemy scenes. Ptolemy XI is shown this way on the great pylon of the Temple of Horus at Edfu.

The priests and scribes of Egypt were supported and encouraged by the Ptolemies, and they were the main source of the knowledge of the Egyptian culture and history.

Greeks continued to settle throughout Egypt. Towns were given Greek names and Greek became the main language, which means that many of the local administrators would have needed to have been bilingual. Greek bureaucracy built on the established Egyptian system. Much correspondence and documentation survives from this period, in particular at a personal level, including letters, accounts and even party invitations.

At Alexandria, work began on the lighthouse, the Pharos (one of the Seven Wonders of the Ancient World) marking the harbour entrance, and the great Library was established.

Ptolemy I was succeeded by his son, Ptolemy II who extended his rule into Syria, Asia Minor and parts of the Aegean, using political marriages to align himself with the neighbouring countries. His sister, Arsinoe, was married to a Macedonian, Lysimachos, who had been in the

bodyguard of Alexander the Great. On Alexander's death, Lysimachos had been given land in Thrace and the North Aegean and when he died in 281, Arsinoe immediately took control of it.

Arsinoe then convinced her brother Ptolemy II that his wife was conspiring to kill him. The probably innocent wife was arrested and exiled and Ptolemy married Arsinoe soon after. With their combined land, Egypt once again became one of the most powerful kingdoms in the Middle East.

It was Arsinoe who first invited official Roman envoys to visit Alexandria, which was the start of a long and ultimately fatal link between the two countries. In the new Egyptian kingdom there appears to be have been much military activity, most probably outside Egypt. Arsinoe granted her military veterans land in the area of the Faium, and the impact there was so great the area became known as the Arsinoite nome.

In Egypt, Ptolemy II and Arsinoe continued a programme of building, not just in Alexandria but in the rest of Egypt too. It was at this time that the Pharos at Alexandria was completed.

The work of consolidating Egyptian control over the countries around the Eastern Mediterranean, begun under Ptolemy II, was continued by Ptolemy III, although this work was to be soon undone in successive reigns as Egyptian control in these areas was, once again, lost.

In the later period of the Ptolemaic Dynasty, Egypt was frequently at war with her neighbours, which caused financial pressures on the Egyptian economy, and there were many internal revolts. The army was used to quell internal disturbances but was also used

397. *Ptolemy XII.*

295

to help neighbouring countries, when allied to Egypt, in their disputes. Whilst there would have been many Egyptians in the army, a large number of the men were mercenaries from other countries.

Many of the tombs from this period in Alexandria are of military men. Stelae and drawings on funerary urns show soldiers in uniform with their swords and shields (Greek in design) and also many mounted troops. The implication is that a large proportion of the army was equipped like a Greek army.

The latter half of the Dynasty was plagued by family quarrels as members of the family vied for position and power. Kings were deposed, reinstated and deposed again by close members of their own royal family. (Sons and daughters opposed fathers and each other!) This was the beginning of the end, for some of the deposed rulers looked outside Egypt for support to enable them to regain their thrones. This was when Egypt fell under the increasing influence of the newest, and perhaps most formidable, of powers, that of Rome.

When Cleopatra VII (married to her fifteen-year-old brother Ptolemy XIII) discovered a plot to kill her and give sole rule to Ptolemy, she fled to Syria, where she met the Roman general Julius Caesar. Caesar decided to support the young Queen in her struggle against her brother, no doubt seeing some benefit for Rome in the process. The Roman army, commanded by Caesar, with its experienced and disciplined troops, found no match in the Egyptian army, and Ptolemy was defeated. The king fled, but never escaped, for his body was found later in an irrigation ditch where he appears to have drowned.

398. Cleopatra VII and her son by Julius Caesar, Caesarion. Relief on the rear wall of the Temple of Hathor at Dendera.

Cleopatra then married her younger brother, another Ptolemy (XIV), and they ruled together. Cleopatra took her role seriously and it was not long before she saw the benefits of sole rule. Her brother was removed following another apparent plot.

Rome's influence on Egypt was initially minimal. The Roman general Pompey had been made a guardian to the young Cleopatra and Rome began to exert its influence. Egypt was rich and fertile, and Rome, in need of wealth and increased supplies of food, was waiting for an opportunity to make a move.

Pompey, who was involved in a dispute with Rome, was killed by the Egyptians in 48 BC and from that moment on the fate of Egypt became inextricably intertwined, with that of Rome through the relationship between Cleopatra VII and Julius Caesar.

Cleopatra's liaison with Caesar is legendary and she spent some time in Rome with him. It says much for the stability of the Ptolemaic court that the ruler could be confident enough to leave Egypt. Cleopatra bore Caesar a son, Caesarion. The exterior of the temple of Hathor at Dendera, decorated by Cleopatra VII, shows a large relief of the Queen and her son.

When Julius Caesar was assassinated in 44 BC, Cleopatra returned alone to Egypt.

399. Julius Caesar.

The Roman generals Mark Antony and Octavian moved swiftly to defeat the army of the assassins whose stated aim was to restore the Roman Republic. Once this had been achieved, a dispute arose between the two generals and Cleopatra allied herself with Mark Antony, gaining in the process his legions. Cleopatra saw Antony as an ideal ally, who shared her own ambitions. Each, however, needed the support of the other to achieve their aims.

The quarrel between Octavian and Mark Antony escalated and the Roman Empire was effectively divided in two with Octavian ruling the west and Antony the east; both wanted to be the sole ruler. The relationship between Antony and Octavian deteriorated when Antony ignored Octavian and divided his part of the Roman Empire between Cleopatra and her children, an act which nominally restored to Egypt much of the territories over which she had an ancient claim. This act caused uproar in Rome and gave Octavian the excuse he needed to launch an attack on Antony, in furtherance of his own aim to be the sole ruler of the Roman Empire, of which Egypt was considered an essential part. The armies gathered for battle. In the event, the fate of Egypt was decided in a major sea battle fought at Actium, where the forces of Antony and Cleopatra were defeated. The soldiers of Antony's army, who had watched the

400. Octavian, later known as Augustus Caesar.

battle from the land, swiftly defected and joined Octavian.

Antony and Cleopatra fled back to Egypt, but with their navy destroyed and with only remnants of a shattered and demoralised army, they could do little but wait for Octavian's forces to land in Egypt.

Octavian took his time, but finally entered Egypt virtually unopposed, when both Antony and then Cleopatra famously committed suicide rather than be taken as captives to Rome to appear in any triumphal procession.

Egypt submitted easily to Roman rule and became a province of the Roman Empire. Once again her wealth and her produce were used for the benefit of a foreign power. Although the country was to enjoy an almost unprecedented period of peace under the protection of Rome, the natural resources were ruthlessly exploited by the new rulers.

Octavian declared himself to be the King of the Two Lands, although he had no plans to keep court in Egypt and returned to Rome as soon as he could manage to celebrate his Triumph as a victorious general and conqueror. He seemed to regard Egypt as his personal property, forbidding Roman Senators and even members of his own family to visit the country without his permission. Perhaps he was afraid that someone else would realise the wealth and lure of Egypt and would try to restore its independence from Rome.

The Roman Emperors: 30 BC-AD 323

Octavian (Augustus)	30 BC-AD 14
Tiberius	14-37
Claudius	41-54
Titus	79-81
Trajan	98-117

The Romans found in Egypt a well ordered and efficient administration and bureaucracy. Like the Persians before, they changed little, simply benefiting from the wealth of Egypt now at their disposal.

Grain and wine were shipped from Egypt to Rome in huge quantities. Most exports left from the city of Alexandria around June each year and would take up to two months to travel by sea to Rome. Minerals were exploited, mainly the hard stones such as granite from Aswan. A newly discovered purple stone, porphyry, which the Romans particularly favoured, was quarried at Mons Porphyrites.

Gold too was mined for the Romans, and as in pharaonic times, this commodity was particularly precious and warranted detachments of troops to protect the movement of the metal. This time it was soldiers in the Roman army who had to suffer the hardships of the mining areas in the deserts. The Romans employed soldiers from many nations, and it would not have been surprising if many Egyptians saw the life in the army as a better alternative to life in the towns or the country.

More Romans moved into Egypt, and many new Roman towns were established in the north of the country. As had happened with the Greeks, the Romans soon settled and adopted Egyptian ideas.

Some Romans moved southwards and recent excavations at Thebes have revealed a large and prosperous Roman population in the area. The burials discovered are much simpler than those found in the north, but nevertheless indicate a good life style. Many of the burials were made in the Egyptian manner, with the embalmed bodies being provided with elaborate coffins decorated with images of the Egyptian gods.

401. Tomb at Kom es Shugafa in Alexandria, from the First/Second century. AD.

402. Anubis, dressed as a Roman soldier, from a tomb in Alexandria.

The Roman Emperors added their names to the ancient temples, extending and repairing them, and in some cases building new temples to the ancient gods.

The walls of the new temples were decorated with scenes that would have been familiar to the pharaohs of the New Kingdom and before. Roman rulers were shown as the all-conquering

403. The Roman Emperor Titus smiting the enemies of Egypt before the God Khnum, from the Temple of Khnum at Esna.

pharaoh, smiting the enemies of Egypt. The Emperors Titus and Trajan were even shown with tame lions running by their side, copying the earlier reliefs of Ramesses II and III.

Egypt remained a Roman Province until the fall of the Roman Empire, which was then divided into two, with the Western Empire ruled from Rome and the Eastern Empire ruled from Constantinople (Byzantium). This division followed almost the same boundaries as arranged

404. Relief in the Temple of Kom Ombo, showing a lion running beside the figure of Trajan, in a "smiting of the enemy" scene.

405. *The Kiosk of Trajan at Philae.*

406. *Scene of the King smiting his enemies, shown on a kilt worn by Trajan. Relief in the Temple of Hathor at Dendera.*

between Octavian and Mark Antony over three hundred years before. Egypt then became a province of the Byzantine Empire, until the Arab invasion and conquest in 642 AD.

407. View of the Temple of Isis at Philae, the last temple in Egypt where the Ancient Egyptian gods were worshipped.

The common perception of Ancient Egypt is as a land of plenty, with an ever-abundant supply of water and food: the workers toiling contentedly in the fields and the wealthier enjoying a life of relaxed luxury.

It is all too easy to overlook the fact that Egypt as a country and civilisation was built on the strength of her military prowess and control. The king was a dictator, ultimately responsible for the prosperity of the country and preserving the rule of Maat. This concept and ethic meant that the rulers of Egypt without exception did not run the country for their own benefit or siphon away its wealth – if the king prospered so did the country. All the population from the nobility to the workers in the fields owed their position and livelihood to the king.

The king could elevate people to high status and wealth with gifts of land and other commodities or luxuries, but because there was no monetary system, it was difficult for individual wealth or status to be passed on to future generations. The status of an individual was based on personal merit, and wealth, if passed on to new generations, was diluted as estates were divided between the heirs. Perhaps this factor encouraged competition: to succeed and prosper by catching the eye of the king depended upon an individual's abilities, rather than upon the exploits of ancestors.

In a bureaucratic state, there was plenty of opportunity to stand out, be it as a local administrator, scribe or soldier.

Egypt was unified by the strength and ambitions of the early kings and the country only prospered when there was a strong king and when the country was united. At such times, Egypt could look beyond her own frontiers, initially for trade, to the south and north of the country.

408. The enemies of Egypt under the hooves of Seti I's horses.

The importance of the trade was so great that military activity was often needed to protect the trade routes. Egypt began to face problems when countries on her borders became more organised, with their own agenda to follow. From the New Kingdom onwards, these neighbours became more troublesome and aggressive and Egypt had to expend considerable energies to expand her sphere of influence, and then, when the Empire was in decline, to try to keep the enemy out.

As a country based on the unification of many local administrative centres, the nomes, Egypt ran surprisingly well, whether or not there was strong central control. For most Egyptians it probably did not matter who was on the throne, or which neighbouring states were causing unrest many hundreds of miles away. Each local community could survive alone, even in isolation from its nearest neighbour if necessary.

When central control was weak, the crops still grew, the people were fed, they paid their local taxes and worshipped their gods, but this was the time when international affairs went unnoticed and when neighbouring states could infiltrate into areas of Egyptian influence and even into Egypt itself. Re-establishing central control was often a long and bloody business, and Egypt seems to have been locked into a repetitive cycle of strong central control followed by times of disorder and dissent.

For much of Egyptian history, there were, therefore, periods of conflict, either within Egypt or when the army was on campaign abroad. This military activity must have caused severe disruption to the whole community in one way or another, not just to those directly involved with the army.

Communities must have suffered by losing many or most of their young men to the army. Many recruits to the army would have left and never returned, others would have returned

409. Battle relief of Seti I from the Temple of Karnak.

wounded and disabled, their lives and those of their families changed forever. Such problems are still, sadly, familiar to communities all over the world today.

When there was conflict within Egypt, whole communities could suffer directly and life was dangerous for civilian and soldier alike. Armies needed to be fed and billeted as they moved around the country. (Even in times of peace this must have caused much disruption.) If there was an invading foreign army to face, then the consequences could be much more dangerous, with the likelihood of major pillaging, destruction and stealing of property, or worse.

410. The classic "smiting scene" from the Narmer Palette.

The army was essential to the survival of Egypt as a nation state and was a major factor in the longevity of the civilisation. All this activity and the success it produced was not achieved without a real human cost in terms of fatalities, casualties, shattered lives and bereaved relatives. This is the aspect of history which is not directly apparent from the records and surviving images, but which was the reality.

The outcome of any campaign or battle may have been in the hands of the gods, but it mainly depended on the training, discipline, equipment, motivation and willingness to fight of the individual soldiers. In all of these areas, the Egyptian army, its commanders and its soldiers excelled.

Some two thousand years after the end of the Dynastic Period of Egyptian history, another famous general, Napoleon, said "In war, three quarters turns on personal character and relations [i.e. morale]. The balance of manpower and materials counts for only the remaining quarter." He could well have been talking about the ancient Egyptian army, for the problems faced by armies and individual soldiers changed little from century to century and many are still faced today.

None of the great achievements of the Ancient Egyptians would have been possible without the military machine. The discipline and organisation that was needed to maintain Egypt's position as a major ancient power was ultimately responsible for the security and prosperity of the country for some three thousand years. The blood, sweat and tears of the Egyptian soldier and the sweat and toil of the farmers and builders, raised pyramids, temples to the gods and the many surviving wonders we see and are still inspired by today.

Egypt's direct contact with so many of the world's emerging cultures around the Mediterranean, and her influence on them, means that there is an almost-unbroken link from the ancient world, through the Classical world and right up to the present day. The history of Egypt, far from being the history of a remote and mysterious land is truly part of everyone's past.

BIBLIOGRAPHY

ADAMS, Barbara.   *Predynastic Egypt.* Shire Egyptology. 1988.

ALDRED, Cyril.   *Egypt to the end of the Old Kingdom.* Thames and Hudson. 1965.

ALDRED, Cyril.   *The Egyptians.* Thames and Hudson. 1961.

ALDRED, Cyril.   *Akhenaten, King of Egypt.* Thames and Hudson. 1988.

ARNOLD, Dorothea.   *The Royal Women of Amarna.* The Metropolitan Museum of Art. 1996.

BAINES, J.R. and   *Atlas of Ancient Egypt.* Phaidon. 1980.
 MALEK, J.

BLACKMAN, A.M.   *The Rock Tombs of Meir*, Volumes I-VI. Egypt Exploration Society, 1914-1953.

BLUNDEN, Victor.   *Assyrian Warfare in the British Museum.* B.A. Thesis. 1992.

BOWMAN, Alan K.   *Egypt After the Pharaohs.* British Museum Press. 1986.

BREASTEAD, J.H.   *Ancient Records of Egypt.* 5 Vols. Chicago, 1906.

BRYAN, Betsy M.   *The Reign of Thutmose IV.* John Hopkins University Press. 1991.

CAIGER, Nesta.   *Amarna Royals, or, Who was Nefertiti.* Threeways. 1996

CAMINOS, Ricardo A.   *The New Kingdom Temples of Buhen.* The Egypt Exploration Society. 1974.

CARTER, Howard and   *The Tomb of Thoutmosis IV.* Cairo Museum. 1904.
 NEWBERRY, Percy E.

CARTER, Howard and   *The Tomb of Tutankhamen* (three volumes). Cassell and Co. 1923.
 Mace A.C.

CLAYTON, Peter A.   *Chronicle of the Pharaohs.* Thames and Hudson. 1994.

COTTRELL, Leonard.   *Warrior Pharaohs*. London, 1968.

DAVIES, W.V. (Editor).   *Egypt and Africa. Nubia from Prehistory to Islam.*
  British Museum Press. 1991.

DAVIES, W.V and   *Egypt*. British Museum Press. 1998.
  FRIEDMAN, Renee.

DAVIS, Nina M.   *Tutankhamun's Painted Box*. Griffith Institute. 1962.

DAVIS, Theodore M.   *The Tomb of Thoutmosis IV*. Archibald Constable. 1904.

DAVIS, Theodore M.   *The Tomb of Ioyiya and Touiyou*. Archibald Constable. 1907.

DAVIS, Theodore M.   *The Tombs of Harmhabi and Toutankhamanou.*
  Archibald Constable. 1912.

DAWSON, Warren R.   *Who was Who in Egyptology*. Egypt Exploration Society. 1972.
  and UPHILL, Eric P.

DODSON, Aidan.   *Monarchs of the Nile*. Rubicon Press. 1995.

DODSON, Aidan.   *After the Pyramids*. Rubicon Press. 2000.

EMERY, W.B.   *Archaic Egypt*. Penguin Books. 1961.

EMERY, W.B.   *Egypt in Nubia*. London, 1965.

EMERY, Walter B.,   *The Fortress of Buhen: The Archaeological Report.*
  SMITH, H.S. and   The Egypt Exploration Society. 1979.
  MILLARD, A.

ERMAN, Adolf.   *Life in Ancient Egypt*. Dover Publications. 1971.

FILER, Joyce.   *Disease*. British Museum Press. 1995.

FLAMARION, Edith.   *Cleopatra, From History to Legend*. Thames and Hudson. 1997.

FLETCHER, Joann.   *Egypt's Sun King: Amenhotep III*. Duncan Baird. 2000.

FOX, Penelope.   *Tutankhamun's Treasure*. Oxford University Press. 1951.

FREED, Rita.   *Rameses the Great*. The Brooklyn Museum. 1973.

FREED, Rita.(and others). *Pharaohs of the Sun*. Thames and Hudson. 1999.

FREIDMAN, Renee.   *Nubians at Hierakonpolis. Excavations in the Nubian Cemeteries*. Sudan & Nubia 5: 29-38.

GAHLIN, Lucia.   *Egypt: Gods, Myths and Religion*. Lorenz Books. 2001.

GARDINER, A.H.   *Egypt of the Pharaohs*. Oxford, 1961.

GARDINER, A.H.   *The Kadesh Inscriptions of Ramesses II*. Oxford, 1975.

GRIFFITHS, W.B.   *The Hand-Thrown Stone*. Arbeia Journal I. 1992.

GRIFFITHS, W.B.   *The Sling and its place in the Roman Army*. Proceedings of the Fifth Roman Military Equipment Conference. 1989.

GRIFFITHS, W.B. and CARRICK, P.   *Reconstructing Roman Slings*. Arbeia Journal III. 1994.

HANSEN, Kathy.   *The Chariot in Egypt's Age of Chivalry*. KMT Magazine. Spring 1994.

HARPUR, Yvonne.   *Decoration in Egyptian Tombs of the Old Kingdom*. KPI. 1987.

HART, George.   *A Dictionary of Egyptian Gods and Goddesses*. Routledge and Kegan Paul. 1986.

411. The enemies of Egypt. Relief from the Temple of Ramesses II at Abu Simbel.

HEALY, Mark.   *Qadesh 1300 BC*. Osprey Publishing. 1993.

HEALY, Mark and   *New Kingdom Egypt*. Osprey Publishing. 1992.
  McBRIDE, Angus.

HOFFMAN, Michael.   *Egypt Before the Pharaohs*. Routledge and Kegan Paul. 1980.

JAMES, T.G.H.   *Egypt: The Living Past*. British Museum Press. 1992.

JONES, Dilwyn.   *Boats. Egyptian Bookshelf*. British Museum. 1995.

JONES, Dilwyn.   *Model Boats from the Tomb of Tutankhamun*. Griffith
                        Institute, Oxford. 1990.

KEMP, Barry J.   *Ancient Egypt: Anatomy of a Civilisation*. Routledge. 1989.

KITCHEN, K.A.   *Pharaoh Triumphant: The Life and Times of Ramesses II*. Aris
                        and Phillips. 1982.

KITCHEN. K.A.   *Further thoughts on Punt and its neighbours. From Studies on Ancient
                        Egypt in honour of H.S. Smith*. Egypt Exploration Society. 1999.

KOZLOFF, Arielle and   *Egypt's Dazzling Sun: Amenhotep III and his World*.
  BRYAN, Betsy.   Cleveland Museum of Art. 1992.

LANDSTRÖM, Björn.   *Ships of the Pharaohs*. George Allen and Unwin. 1970.

LEPSIUS, Karl Richard.   *Denkmaler aus Aegypten und Aethopien*. 1849.

LITTAUER, M.A. and   *Chariots and related equipment from the Tomb of Tutankhamun*.
  CROWEL, J.H.   Griffith Institute. 1985.

LUCAS, A.   *Ancient Egyptian Materials and Industries*. Edward Arnold
                        and Co. 1926.

McLEOD, W.   *Composite Bows from the Tomb of Tutankhamun*.
                        Griffith Institute. 1970.

McLEOD, W.   *Self Bows and other Archery Tackle from the Tomb of Tutankhamun*.
                        Griffith Institute. 1982.

MANLEY, Bill.   *The Penguin Historical Atlas of Ancient Egypt*. Penguin Books. 1996.

MASPERO, Gaston.   *The Struggle of the Nations*. SPCK. 1896.

MASPERO, Gaston.   *Ancient Egypt and Assyria*. London, 1892.

MONTET, Pierre.   *Everyday Life in Ancient Egypt*. Edward Arnold. 1958.

MORKOT, Robert.G.   *The Black Pharaohs: Egypt's Nubian Rulers*. Rubicon Press. 2000.

MORLEY, Jacqueline.   *Egypt in the time of Ramesses II*. Simon and Shuster. 1993.

MURNANE, William J.   *The Penguin Guide to Ancient Egypt*. Penguin Books, 1983.

MURNANE, William J.   *The Road to Kadesh - A Historical Interpretation of the battle reliefs of King Seti I at Karnak*.
                          The Oriental Institute of the University of Chicago. 1985.

NEWBERRY, P.H.   *Warrior Pharaohs*. Book Club Associates. 1980.

NIBBI, Alessandra.   *The Sea Peoples - A re-examination of the Egyptian Sources*. Oxford. 1972.

PARKINSON, R.B.   *Voices from Ancient Egypt*. British Museum Press. 1991.

PARTRIDGE, Robert B.   *Faces of Pharaohs: Royal Mummies and Coffins from Ancient Thebes*. The Rubicon Press. 1994.

PARTRIDGE, Robert B.   *Transport in Ancient Egypt*. The Rubicon Press. 1996.

PETRIE, W.M.F.   *Palace of Apries - Memphis II*, British School of Archaeology. 1909.

PETRIE, W.M.F.   *Tools and Weapons*. Egypt Research Account. 1916.

PETRIE, W.M.F.   *Deshasheh*. Egypt Exploration Fund. 1898.

PETRIE, W.M.F.   *A History of Egypt*. Methuen and Co. 1904.

POSENER, Georges.   *A Dictionary of Egyptian Civilisation*. Methuen and Co. 1959.

PRISSE D'AVENNES, E.   *Atlas of Egyptian Art*. American University in Cairo. 1997.

PRITCHARD, J.B.   *Ancient Near Eastern Texts*. Princeton, 1965.

QUIBELL, J.E.   *The Tomb of Yuaa and Thuiu*. Cairo Museum. 1908.

QUIRKE, Stephen.   *Who were the Pharaohs*. British Museum Press. 1990.

QUIRKE, Stephen.   *The Cult of Ra.* Thames and Hudson. 2001.

REDFORD, Donald B.   *Akhenaten, the Heretic King.* Princetown University Press. 1984.

REDFORD, Donald B.   *The Oxford Encyclopedia of Ancient Egypt.*
  (Editor).   Oxford University Press. 2000.

REEVES, Carole.   *Egyptian Medicine.* Shire Egyptology. 1992.

REEVES, Nicholas.   *The Complete Tutankhamun.* Thames and Hudson. 1990.

REEVES, Nicholas.   *Ancient Egypt: The Great Discoveries.* Thames and Hudson. 2000.

REEVES, Nicholas.   *Akhenaten: Egypt's False Prophet.* Thames and Hudson. 2001.

REISNER, George.   *Models of Ships and Boats.* Cairo Museum. 1913.

ROBERTS, David.   *Sketches in Egypt and Nubia.* Colophon. 1995.

ROSE, John.   *The Sons of Re.* JRT. 1985.

SALEH, Mohamed and   *The Egyptian Museum Cairo.*
  SOUROUZIAN, Hourig.   Organisation of Egyptian Antiquities. 1987.

SCHEEL, Bernd.   *Egyptian Metalworking and Tools.* Shire Egyptology. 1989.

SHAW, Ian.   *Egyptian Warfare and Weapons.* Shire Egyptology. 1991.

SHAW, Ian. (Editor).   *The Oxford History of Ancient Egypt.* Oxford University
                             Press. 2000.

SHAW, Ian and   *British Museum Dictionary of Ancient Egypt.* British
  NICHOLSON, Paul   Museum Press. 1995.
  (Editors).

STROUHAL, Eugene.   *Life in Ancient Egypt.* Cambridge University Press. 1992.

THOMAS, Angela P.   *Egyptian Gods and Myths.* Shire Egyptology. 1986.

TOOLEY, Angela M.   *Egyptian Models and Scenes.* Shire Egyptology. 1995.

TYLDESLEY, Joyce.   *Hatchepsut, the Female Pharaoh.* Viking Books. 1996.

TYLDESLEY, Joyce.   *Nefertiti, Egypt's Sun Queen.* Viking Books. 1998.

TYLDESLEY, Joyce.   *Ramesses, Egypt's Greatest Pharaoh*. Viking Books. 2000.

TYLDESLEY, Joyce.   *Judgement of the Pharaoh*. Viking Books. 2000.

UPHILL, Eric P.   *Egyptian Towns and Cities*. Shire Egyptology. 1988.

VINSON, Steve.   *Egyptian Ships and Boats*. Shire Egyptology. 1994.

VOGELSANG-
   EASTWOOD, Gillian.   *Tutankhamun's Wardrobe*. Rotterdam. 1999.

412. Statue of Ramesses II in the Temple of Luxor, showing the King's kilt and dagger.

WALKER, Susan and
HIGGS, Peter (Editors).
Cleopatra of Egypt. British Museum Press. 2001.

WATTERSON, Barbara. *Amarna: Ancient Egypt's Age of Revolution*. Tempus, 1999.

WEEKS, Kent. *The Lost Tomb*. Weidenfeld and Nicholson. 1998.

WESTERN A.C. *A Wheel Hub from the Tomb of Amenophis III*. Journal of Egyptian Archaeology Vol. 59, 1973.

WILKINSON,
Richard H.
Reading Egyptian Art. Thames and Hudson. 1992.

WILKINSON,
Richard H.
Symbol and Magic in Egyptian Art. Thames and Hudson. 1994.

WILKINSON,
Richard H.
The Complete Temples of Ancient Egypt. Thames and Hudson. 2000.

WILSON, Hilary. *Egyptian Food and Drink*. Shire Egyptology. 1988.

WINLOCK, H.E. *The Slain Soldiers of Nebhetepre-Mentuhotep*. Metropolitan Museum of Art Egyptian Expedition, Vol. XVI. 1945.

WISE, Terence. *Ancient Armies of the Middle East*. Osprey. 1981.

WEB SITES:

There are a huge number of sites on the World Wide Web that feature Ancient Egypt. Many are excellent, whilst many have information of a less than reliable nature.

Web sites come and go, but the following sites are recommended and they provide links to other good sites which are regularly updated.

The Egypt Exploration Society: http://www.ees.ac.uk/

The Friends of Nekhen: http://www.hierakonpolis.org

The Griffith Institute, Oxford: http://ashmol.ox.ac.uk/griffith.html

The Manchester Ancient Egypt Society   http://maes.org.uk/

LIST OF ILLUSTRATIONS

Unless otherwise stated all the drawings and maps are by the author and all photographs are from "The Ancient Egypt Picture Library" and have been taken by the author.
Every effort has been made to trace the holders of any copyright material included in this book. However, if there are any omissions we will be happy to rectify them in future editions.

Cover:	Design and Artwork by David Soper.
Front cover:	Pharaoh in battle.
Back cover:	Narmer smiting his enemy.
Photograph of the Author:	David Montford.
Frontispiece:	Narmer smiting his enemy.

1.   Map of Egypt showing the principal sites. Drawn by Peter Phillips.
2.   Image of Narmer smiting his enemy. Scene from the Narmer Palette.
3.   Drawing from the Painted Tomb at Hierakonpolis. After Barry Kemp. 1989.
4.   The bound enemies of Egypt on the base of a statue of Ramesses III in his Mortuary Temple at Medinet Habu.
5.   Gilded and inlaid wooden footstool from the Tomb of Tutankhamun, showing the enemies of Egypt. Egyptian Museum Cairo.
6.   One of Tutankhamun's sandals, showing the enemies of Egypt depicted on the sole. Egyptian Museum Cairo.
7.   Soles of Graeco-Roman sandals depicting the enemies of Egypt. Egyptian Museum, Turin.
8.   A footstool from the Tomb of Tutankhamun depicting the "Nine Bows", nine images of the enemies of Egypt. Egyptian Museum Cairo.
9.   The "Nine Bows" shown on the base of a statue of a king of the Middle Kingdom, in the Temple of Montu at Medamud.
10.   Map of the Eastern Mediterranean. Drawn by Peter Phillips.
11.   Image of a Nubian, from a glazed tile from the Mortuary Temple of Ramesses III at Medinet Habu. Egyptian Museum, Cairo.
12.   Eighteenth Dynasty painting of Nubians presenting tribute. British Museum.
13.   Ramesses III in the act of killing a Libyan. Relief on the southern wall of his Mortuary Temple at Medinet Habu.
14.   An Asiatic family arriving in Egypt. Scene from the Middle Kingdom Tomb of Khnumhotep at Beni Hassan. From Prisse D'Avennes.
15.   Image of an Asiatic from a glazed tile from the Mortuary Temple of Ramesses III at Medinet Habu. Egyptian Museum, Cairo.
16.   An Assyrian archer and spearman. Relief from Nimrud. British Museum.
17.   Persian soldiers. Glazed brick relief from the palace of Susa. Bode Museum, Berlin.
18.   A Minoan bearing tribute. Drawing of a scene from the Eighteenth Dynasty Tomb of Rekhmire at Thebes.
19.   Marble portrait bust of Alexander the Great. British Museum.
20.   The great Temple of Horus at Edfu, built during the reign of the Ptolemies.
21.   The fertile fields of Egypt as shown in a harvesting scene from the Tomb of Sennedjem at Deir el Medina.
22.   The Roman Emperor Trajan, depicted as an Egyptian Pharaoh on a column from the Temple of Kom Ombo.
23.   Ramesses II in battle, using a bow and arrow. Relief from the Temple of Luxor.

24. Copper and flint axe heads from the early Dynastic Period. British Museum.
25. Flint knives with serrated edges from the Fifth Millennium BC. British Museum.
26. The smelting of copper. Metal workers of the Old Kingdom from a relief in the Tomb of the "Two Brothers" at Sakkara.
27. Late Period bronze statue of Osiris. City of Plymouth Museum and Art Gallery.
28. The iron-bladed dagger from the Tomb of Tutankhamun. Egyptian Museum Cairo.
29. The gold-bladed dagger from the Tomb of Tutankhamun. Egyptian Museum Cairo.
30. Detail of the chariot of Yuya, showing the leather panels and tyres. Egyptian Museum Cairo.
31. Women weaving linen into cloth. Model from the Tomb of Meketre. Egyptian Museum Cairo.
32. Example of rope from the Old Kingdom, found with the boat of King Khufu at Giza. Boat Museum at Giza.
33. Huge planks of imported timber as used in a wooden coffin from Deir el-Bersha, which dates to the Middle Kingdom. Egyptian Museum Cairo.
34. Selection of woodworking tools, including drills and a saw. British Museum.
35. A flail from the Tomb of Tutankhamun, made of gold and lapis lazuli. Egyptian Museum Cairo.
36. Soldiers shown in a relief from the Mortuary Temple of Queen Hatshepsut,one of whom carries a flail.
37. Drawing of an early mace-head (now lost) found in Nubia. After Firth 1927.
38. A flat disc-shaped mace head. British Museum.
39. Pointed mace heads. British Museum.
40. Pear-shaped mace head of limestone. British Museum.
41. Pear-shaped mace head of red Breccia. British Museum.
42. Larger pear-shaped mace head with projections and a simple carved design. British Museum.
43. Detail of a life-sized statue of Tutankhamun, found in his tomb, carrying a mace. Egyptian Museum Cairo.
44. The mace head of the "Scorpion King" in the Ashmolean Museum, Oxford.
45. Man using a sling, from a tomb at Beni Hassan. After Gardner Wilkinson *The Ancient Egyptians* 1853.
46. Hunting in the Marshes. A New Kingdom painting from the tomb of Nebamun. British Museum.
47. Collection of throwsticks found in the Tomb of Tutankhamun. Egyptian Museum Cairo.
48. Hatshepsut's soldiers armed with throw-sticks. From a relief in the Mortuary Temple of Hatshepsut at Deir el Bahri.
49. Spearmen: Model from the Tomb of Mesehti. Egyptian Museum Cairo.
50. Spearhead made of silver. British Museum.
51. Spearhead made of bronze. British Museum.
52. Two bows. British Museum.
53. An archer carrying spare arrows in his hand, from a tomb at Thebes. After Gardner Wilkinson *The Ancient Egyptians* 1853.
54. Group of bow staves from the Tomb of Tutankhamun. Egyptian Museum Cairo.
55. Archers stringing their bows. Scenes from tombs at Beni Hassan and Thebes. After Gardner Wilkinson *The Ancient Egyptians* 1853.
56. The tips of a Middle Kingdom bow, with some of the gut bowstring still in place. From the tomb of the soldiers of Mentuhotep at Deir el Bahri. Photo from *The Slain Soldiers of Nebhetepre Mentuhotep*. Metropolitan Museum, of Art, 1945.
57. Collection of reed arrows tipped with ivory or bone heads. Early Dynastic Period. Egyptian Museum Cairo.
58. Arrows with bronze heads, found in the Tomb of Tutankhamun. Egyptian Museum Cairo.
59. Flight feathers from arrows of the Second Intermediate Period found at Hierakonpolis, Tomb B5. Photo courtesy of the Hierakonpolis Expedition.
60. An arrow maker checking the straightness of his arrow. From an unknown tomb at Sakkara. After G.T. Martin 1991.
61. Composite bows from the Tomb of Tutankhamun. Egyptian Museum Cairo.
62. Detail of the decoration on a bow case found in the Tomb of Tutankhamun. Egyptian Museum Cairo.
63. Middle Kingdom model from the Tomb of Meshti at Assuit depicting Nubian archers. Egyptian Museum Cairo.
64. The head of the mummy of the Nubian soldier, Maiherpri Egyptian Museum Cairo. From Daressy, *Fouilles de la Vallee des Rois*. 1902.
65. Arrows and leather quivers from the Tomb of Maiherpri. Egyptian Museum Cairo.

66. The decorated leather wrist-guard of Maiherpri. Egyptian Museum Cairo.
67. A simple leather archer's wrist guard of Middle Kingdom date. Photo. from *The Slain Soldiers of Nebhetepre Mentuhotep*. Metropolitan Museum, of Art, 1945.
68. The left hand of the body of a Middle Kingdom archer, with his leather wrist guard still in place. Photo. from *The Slain Soldiers of Nebhetepre Mentuhotep*.Metropolitan Museum, of Art, 1945.
69. An archer wearing a wrist guard, from a tomb at Thebes. After Gardner Wilkinson *The Ancient Egyptians* 1853.
70. Drawing of the head of a New Kingdom axe, showing how it was secured in place by leather thongs. British Museum.
71. Bronze axe blade of the New Kingdom. British Museum.
72. New Kingdom battle axe, showing the distinctive shape of the haft. British Museum.
73. Poleaxe made of silver. British Museum.
74. Poleaxes made of bronze. Egyptian Museum Cairo.
75. Flint-bladed dagger with a gilded wooden handle. Middle Kingdom. British Museum.
76. Flint-bladed dagger with a wooden handle and the remains of its scabbard. British Museum.
77. A selection of New Kingdom daggers. British Museum.
78. A New Kingdom dagger with a gilded handle. British Museum.
79. A bronze kepesh or scimitar. British Museum.
80. Tutankhamun's kepesh. Egyptian Museum Cairo.
81. The mace/kepesh as wielded by Ramesses II, from a relief in the Temple of Abu Simbel.
82. Middle Kingdom tomb model of a hide covered shield and matching quiver. Metropolitan Museum of Art, New York.
83. Painting showing a soldier with a large shield, from the Tomb of Djehutihotpe. Twelfth Dynasty. British Museum.
84. A leopard-skin covered shield from the Tomb of Tutankhamun. Egyptian Museum Cairo.
85. An open work, gilded shield from the Tomb of Tutankhamun. Egyptian Museum Cairo.
86. Middle Kingdom model from the Tomb of Mesehti of Egyptian spearmen with cowhide shields. Egyptian Museum Cairo.
87. Guards at the entrance to a military camp with a shield wall, from a tomb at Thebes. After Gardner Wilkinson *The Ancient Egyptians* 1853.
88. A suit of protective armour made of overlapping bronze scales. From the Mortuary Temple of Ramesses III at Medinet Habu. After Gardner Wilkinson *The Ancient Egyptians* 1853.
89. Pieces of bronze scale armour. British Museum.
90. Tutankhamun's leather armour as found in a box in his tomb. Photo Harry Burton, The Griffith Institute, Ashmolean Museum, Oxford.
91. The corslet or armour of Tutankhamun. Egyptian Museum Cairo.
92. Bronze helmet from Thebes. Manchester Museum, University of Manchester.
93. The head of a Middle Kingdom soldier, showing his curled and greased hair. Photo. from *The Slain Soldiers of Nebhetepre Mentuhotep*. Metropolitan Museum of Art, 1945.
94. The Blue Crown, as worn by Tutankhamun, from a relief in the Temple of Luxor.
95. Gloves from the Tomb of Tutankhamun. Egyptian Museum Cairo.
96. Ay showing off his new gloves. After Davies, *The Rock tombs of el Amarna*. 1908.
97. A horse. After a painting from the Tomb of Thanuny at Thebes.
98. A skewbald horse, shown in a painting from the Tomb of Menna at Thebes.
99. Hieroglyph of a horse in the titles of Ramose. Relief from his tomb at Thebes.
100. Relief from the New Kingdom Tomb of Horemheb at Sakkara, showing a man astride a horse in the so-called "donkey seat".
101. Man on a horse, from the battle reliefs of Ramesses II in the Temple of Luxor.
102. Userhet, an officer from the reign of Amenhotep II, in his chariot. Painting from his tomb at Thebes.
103. Diagram showing the component parts of a chariot wheel. After Dimitri Tonkil & Hansen. *KMT* Vol 5, no 1.
104. Diagram showing the construction of the spokes of a chariot wheel. After Dimitri Tonkil & Hansen. *KMT* Vol 5, no 1.
105. Chariots and horses. Painting from the Tomb of Nebamun. British Museum.

106. Ramesses II's horses, equipped with coloured cloths and ostrich feathers. A painted cast of a scene from the Temple of Beit el Wali in Nubia. British Museum.
107. Detail of the decoration on the chariot body of Thutmose IV, showing captured Asiatic prisoners. Egyptian Museum Cairo (Carter and Newberry. *Tomb of Thoutmosis IV*).
108. Drawing by Howard Carter of the decoration of the exterior of the right side of the body of the chariot of Thutmose IV. (Carter and Newberry. *Tomb of Thoutmosis IV*).
109. Drawing by Howard Carter of the decoration of the interior of the left side of the body of the chariot of Thutmose IV. (Carter and Newberry. *Tomb of Thoutmosis IV*).
110. The mummy of Yuya, Master of Chariots to Amenhotep III. From Elliot Smith, *The Royal Mummies*. 1909.
111. Chariot found in the Tomb of Yuya and Thuya. Quibell, *The tomb of Yuaa and Thuiu*.
112. Rear view of the chariot found in the Tomb of Yuya and Thuya. Quibell, *The tomb of Yuaa and Thuiu*.
113. One of Tutankhamun's state chariots Egyptian Museum Cairo. Photo. Burton: The Griffith Institute, Ashmolean Museum, Oxford.
114. Detail of the decoration of the body of one of Tutankhamun's state chariots, showing the god Bes. Egyptian Museum Cairo.
115. Tutankhamun's courtiers in their chariots. Detail from the painted chest of Tutankhamun. Egyptian Museum Cairo.
116. The god Amun. Relief from the Mortuary Temple of Ramesses III at Medinet Habu.
117. The god Amun presenting Ramesses with weapons. Scene from the Temple of Ramesses II at Abu Simbel.
118. The god Anhur. Drawing of a bronze figure in the Egyptian Museum Cairo.
119. The traditional appearance of Bes as a dwarf, in the Louvre, Paris.
120. Bes as a war god, shown carrying a sword and shield in the British Museum.
121. The falcon headed god Montu, from the Temple of Tod. Relief now in the Open Air Museum at Karnak.
122. Gilded wooden figure of the god Ptah from the Tomb of Tutankhamun. Egyptian Museum Cairo.
123. The sun god Ra-Horakhty, from the Temple of Ramesses II at Abu Simbel.
124. The sun god Aten, spreading his rays on Akhenaten and Nefertiti. Egyptian Museum Cairo.
125. Statue of the goddess Sekhmet, originally from the Temple of Mut at Karnak. British Museum.
126. The God Set, detail from a statue of the god with Ramesses III and Horus. Egyptian Museum Cairo.
127. Scene from the New Kingdom Tomb of Nebamun, showing a man herding cattle. British Museum.
128. New recruits as shown in the Tomb of Userhet at Thebes.
129. New recruits receiving their military haircut. Scene from the Tomb of Userhet at Thebes.
130. Man exercising using bags of sand as weights. From a tomb in Beni Hassan. After Gardner Wilkinson *The Ancient Egyptians* 1853.
131. Men wrestling. From a tomb at Beni Hassan. After Gardner Wilkinson *The Ancient Egyptians* 1853.
132. Men wrestling. New Kingdom drawing on an ostracon. Egyptian Museum Cairo.
133. Men throwing knives at a wooden target. From a tomb at Beni Hassan. After Gardner Wilkinson *The Ancient Egyptians* 1853.
134. Men fighting with single sticks and arm-guards. From a tomb at Thebes. After Gardner Wilkinson *The Ancient Egyptians* 1853.
135. The hieroglyphic determinative, showing a man being executed by being impaled on a stake. After Joyce Tyldesley *The Judgement of Pharaoh.*
136. Sherden mercenaries. Scene from the Temple of Ramesses II at Abydos.
137. A Syrian mercenary drinking beer. Relief found at Tell el Amarna. Bode Museum, Berlin.
138. Scribes at work, from the Memphite Tomb of Horemheb at Sakkara.
139. A nome standard as seen on a statue of Menkaure of the Old Kingdom. Egyptian Museum, Cairo.
140. Examples of Egyptian military standards.
141. Military standards being carried by soldiers of Hatshepsut. Relief from the Mortuary Temple of Queen Hatshepsut at Deir el Bahri.
142. Gilded figure of a hawk on a pole, similar to military or nome standards. From the Tomb of Tutankhamun. Egyptian Museum Cairo.
143. Loincloth from the Tomb of Tutankhamun. Egyptian Museum Cairo.
144. Leather kilts worn by Nubian archers. Middle Kingdom tomb model. Egyptian Museum Cairo.

145. Nubian mercenaries, wearing distinctive leather skins over their kilts and carrying a military standard depicting men wrestling. From the New Kingdom Tomb of Thanuny at Thebes.
146. Example of a gazelle skin kilt. British Museum.
147. Ranks of soldiers. Scene from Hatshepsut's Mortuary Temple at Deir el Bahri.
148. The so-called "way-station" above the Valley of the Kings.
149. Harvesting scene showing soldiers, from the Tomb of Menna at Thebes.
150. New Kingdom boat, of the type used to transport goods and passengers on the Nile. After Landstrom *Ships of the Pharaohs*.
151. Boat with a sail. Middle Kingdom tomb model, now in the British Museum.
152. Boat with oars. Middle Kingdom tomb model, now in the British Museum.
153. Shields on the cabin of one of Meketre's boats. Metropolitan Museum of Art, New York.
154. Map of the principal desert routes in Egypt. Peter Robinson.
155. Donkey and driver. From the tomb of Panehsy at Thebes.
156. Ox and a baggage cart. From the Kadesh scenes of Ramesses II. After Lepsius. *Denkmaler aus Aegypten und Aethopien.*
157. Old Kingdom model of a porter, from the Tomb of Niankh-Pepi at Meir. Egyptian Museum Cairo.
158. The Egyptian army in camp. Scene from the battle reliefs of Ramesses II. After Gardner Wilkinson *The Ancient Egyptians* 1853.
159. The canopy and furniture of Queen Hetepheres. Egyptian Museum Cairo.
160. The portable canopy from the Tomb of Tutankhamun. Egyptian Museum Cairo.
161. One of the trumpets of Tutankhamun. Egyptian Museum Cairo.
162. Detail of the decoration on the bell of the silver trumpet of Tutankhamun. Egyptian Museum Cairo.
163. Drummer and trumpeter. From Thebes. After Gardner Wilkinson *The Ancient Egyptians* 1853.
164. A rare surviving example of a drum. The Louvre, Paris.
165. A copper or Bronze drum, possibly of 18th Dynasty in date. The Egyptian Museum Cairo.
166. Military musicians at the Festival of Opet in the Temple of Luxor.
167. Pharaoh in battle. Seti I in his chariot ploughs through his enemy. Relief from the north wall of the Hypostyle Hall at Karnak.
168. The chaos of battle. Dead and wounded enemy as shown in a battle relief of Ramesses II from his temple at Abydos.
169. Captured prisoners. Relief from the Mortuary Temple of Ramesses III at Medinet Habu.
170. The gold flies of valour of Queen Ahotep. Egyptian Museum Cairo.
171. Horemheb being presented with gold collars. Relief from his tomb at Sakkara, now in the National Museum of Antiquities in Leiden.
172. Shebyu collar found in the royal tombs at Tanis. Egyptian Museum Cairo.
173. Manacled prisoners being led in triumph. Scene from the Tomb of Horemheb at Sakkara now in the National Museum of Antiquities in Leiden.
174. Egyptian Bread. Egyptian Museum Cairo.
175. A basket of fruit. Egyptian Museum Cairo.
176. Skull, showing evidence of a mace wound injury. Elephantine Museum, Aswan.
177. The head of one of Mentuhotep's soldiers from the tomb at Deir el Bahri, showing a fatal wound. Photo. from *The Slain Soldiers of Nebhetepre Mentuhotep*. Metropolitan Museum, of Art, 1945.
178. An arrow still protruding from the back of one of Mentuhotep's soldiers. Photo. from *The Slain Soldiers of Nebhetepre Mentuhotep*. Metropolitan Museum, of Art, 1945.
179. Skull of one of Mentuhotep's soldiers, showing severe injury to the nasal area. Photo. from *The Slain Soldiers of Nebhetepre Mentuhotep*. Metropolitan Museum, of Art, 1945.
180. Skull of one of Mentuhotep's soldiers, showing severe injury to the side of the head, possibly caused by a heavy club or mace. Photo. from *The Slain Soldiers of Nebhetepre Mentuhotep*. Metropolitan Museum, of Art, 1945.
181. Hieroglyphs for fortifications. From Shaw, *Egyptian Warfare and Weapons*. 1991.
182. The Mud brick walls of "The Fort" at Hierakonpolis. Authors Photo, used with the kind permission of the Hierakonpolis Expedition.
183. The great mud brick walls at Elkab.
184. View of the First Cataract at Aswan looking north from the High Dam.

272. Statue of Thutmose III. Egyptian Museum, Cairo.
273. Thutmose III as a victorious Pharaoh smiting his enemy. Relief from his pylon in the Temple of Karnak.
274. List of the names of the towns and cities captures by Thutmose III on his campaigns, on his pylon in the Temple of Karnak.
275. Tribute from Asia. Wall painting. British Museum.
276. The Gebel Barkal stela of Thutmose III. Museum of Fine Art, Boston.
277. The festival Hall of Thutmose III in the Temple of Amun at Karnak, showing the unusual tent-pole columns.
278. Details from one of the botanical scenes in the buildings of Thutmose III at Karnak.
279. The head of the mummy of Thutmose III. From Elliot Smith, *The Royal Mummies*. 1909.
280. Amenhotep II firing his arrows at a copper target. Scene on a granite block from Karnak. Luxor Museum.
281. Statue of Amenhotep II from the Temple of Karnak, now in the Luxor Museum.
282. The stern of a model boat found in the Tomb of Amenhotep II, showing the god Montu killing the enemies of Egypt. Egyptian Museum Cairo.
283. The head of the mummy of Amenhotep II. From *Annales du Service III*, Plate 1.
284. The mummy of Thutmose IV. From Elliot Smith, *The Royal Mummies*. 1909.
285. Drawing by Howard Carter of the left side of the chariot body of Thutmose IV, showing the King defeating his Asiatic enemies.(Carter and Newberry. *Tomb of Thoutmosis IV*).
286. The Sphinx of Khafra and the "Dream Stela" of Thutmose IV at Giza.
287. Detail of the Dream Stela, showing Thutmose IV offering to the Sphinx.
288. Amenhotep III smiting his enemies. Detail from a stela near Aswan. After Morgan, 1894.
289. Queen Tiye. Egyptian Museum Cairo.
290. The funeral mask of Yuya. Egyptian Museum Cairo.
291. The funeral mask of Thuya. Egyptian Museum Cairo.
292. Foreigners paying tribute to Pharaoh. From the Tomb of Ramose at Thebes.
293. Statue of Amenhotep III, found in a cache in the Temple of Luxor. Luxor Museum.
294. Akhenaten beneath the rays of the Aten. Stela in the Egyptian Museum Cairo.
295. Amenhotep IV/Akhenaten smiting the enemies of Egypt. Scene from a recently restored wall in the Open Air Museum in the Temple of Karnak.
296. Image of Nefertiti smiting the enemy, shown on the kiosk of a boat, from a block from Hermopolis, now in the Museum of Fine Art in Boston.
297. Statue of Akhenaten. Louvre, Paris.
298. Akhenaten and Nefertiti escorted by the army in a scene from the Tomb of Merere at Akhetaten.
299. Soldiers from the time of Akhenaten, from a block in the Fitzwilliam Museum, Cambridge.
300. Nefertiti, painted bust from Amarna. Egyptian Museum, Charlottenburg, Berlin.
301. Nefertiti/Smenkhkare? Image from the Tomb of Tutankhamun. Egyptian Museum, Cairo.
302. Statue of Tutankhamun as the god Amun, in the Temple of Karnak.
303. The general Nakht-Min. Statue in the Egyptian Museum Cairo.
304. Tutankhamun fighting the Retenu. Scene from one side of his painted chest. Egyptian Museum Cairo.
305. A visiting Nubian Princess, drawn in a chariot pulled by a pair of oxen. Painting by E. Prisse d'Avennes from the original in the Tomb of Huy.
306. Piece of gold foil from the Tomb of Tutankhamun showing the King in the traditional smiting position. After C. Desroches Noblecourt.
307. Tutankhamun as a sphinx trampling his enemies underfoot. Scene from his painted chest. Egyptian Museum Cairo.
308. Relief from the Tomb of Ay at Akhetaten showing Ay and his wife with the famous Hymn to the Aten above them.
309. Head of a statue, believed to be that of Ay. Egyptian Museum Cairo.
310. Tutankhamun and Queen Ankhesenamun as shown on the Little Golden Shrine from the Tomb of Tutankhamun. Egyptian Museum Cairo.
311. Diplomatic letter on a clay tablet, found at Tell el Amarna. British Museum.
312. Decoration on a piece of gold leaf found in the Valley of Kings, showing Ay in his chariot. From: Davis. *The tombs of Harmhabi and Toutankhamanou*. 1912.

413. Smiting scene of Ramesses II.

414. Cartouche of Sneferu.

415. Cartouche of Senuseret I (Kheperkara).

416. Cartouche of Thutmose I.

417. Cartouche of Ramesses II (Usermaatra Setepenra).

418. Cartouches of Ramesses III (Usermaatra Meryamun).